TREADING
LIGHTLY

THE JOY OF CONSERVATION, MODERATION, AND SIMPLE LIVING

David A. Anderson, Ph.D. with
Elizabeth L. Anderson, M.F.A.
Robert T. Anderson, Ph.D.

PENSIVE
PRESS

Printed on 100% Recycled Paper
in the United States of America

Copyright © 2009 by David A. Anderson

Editor: Kimberly S. Browning
Printing and Binding: Thomson-Shore

Photographs are by the author
unless otherwise noted.

Published by Pensive Press, LLC
205 Bluffwood Drive
Danville, Kentucky 40422
www.PensivePress.com

ISBN: 978-0-9709057-2-7

Library of Congress
Control Number: 2008928742

To the generations of today and tomorrow

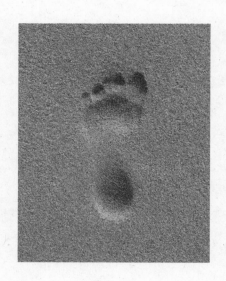

About the Authors

David A. Anderson is a native of East Lansing, Michigan. He received a B.A. in economics from the University of Michigan and an M.A. and Ph.D. in economics from Duke University. He currently serves as the Paul G. Blazer Professor of Economics at Centre College in Kentucky. His other books include *Environmental Economics and Natural Resource Management, Economics by Example, Dispute Resolution: Bridging the Settlement Gap,* and *Sometimes I Get So Angry! Anger Management for Everyone.* His research addresses environmental policy, the valuation of natural resources, law, crime, social insurance, marriage, and child birth. For recreation he enjoys triathlons and running with his wife and two children.

Elizabeth L. Anderson grew up in Plainville, Connecticut. She received a B.A. in home economics from Boston University after transferring from Syracuse University. She earned an M.F.A. in art history from Michigan State University and taught in that field for 20 years at Lansing Community College. Her other publications include an article on African art and culture, "The Levels of Meaning of an Ashanti Akua'ba." Now retired, she takes pleasure in dancing, singing in the church choir, visiting the elderly, sewing, cooking, attending concerts and plays with her husband Robert, and frolicking with her "children's children."

Robert T. Anderson was raised in Syracuse, New York. He received a B.A. in philosophy from Syracuse University and a seminary degree and Ph.D. in biblical literature from Boston University. He taught philosophy at the American University in Cairo, Egypt, studied in India on a Fulbright research grant, and taught in the Department of Religious Studies at Michigan State University for more than forty years. His most recent books are *A Tradition Kept* and *The Keepers: An Introduction to the History and Culture of the Samaritans,* both co-authored by Terry Giles. With Elizabeth, he likes to bike, jog, ballroom dance, and serve as a member of a local church and Neighborhood Association.

Table of Contents

Chapter 1   My Mother Darns Socks   1

Chapter 2   Simple Pleasures and Insatiable Greed   9

Chapter 3   Ode to Moderation   17

Chapter 4   In My Mother's Words   25
Treading Lightly: Sometimes Cheap, Always Valuable

Chapter 5   In My Father's Words   57
The Ethics and Religion of Materialism

Chapter 6   The Thin Foundation of Truth   85

Chapter 7   Our Plastic Lives   101

Chapter 8   The Real Problem with Wal-Mart   115

Chapter 9   Morality Matters   127

Chapter 10   What Goes Around Comes Around   143

Chapter 11   Money, Success, and Happiness   149

Chapter 12   Better Sources of Excitement   159

Chapter 13   A Player's Manual for the Game of Life   169

Chapter 14   Actions Speak Louder   179

Chapter 15   Utopia Isn't So Bad   189

Chapter 16   About Energy   195

Chapter 17   Dealing with Uncertainty   213

Chapter 18   Thinking Globally   231

Preface

Each generation brings different lessons to share at the table. Those with open minds in the 1960s were compelled by the consciousness-raising events, literature, and personalities of that era. Rachel Carson's *Silent Spring* revealed the health and environmental dangers of common pesticides and Michael Harrington's *The Other America* drew public attention to the painful poverty that accompanied rapid economic growth. President John F. Kennedy asked Americans to make sacrifices for their communities and for their country. Dr. Martin Luther King, Jr., demonstrated the strength of peaceful protest. And the Vietnam War proved that fighting is a lose-lose proposition. These influences heightened awareness and moral fortitude among the masses. Then came path-breaking social and political action that ended U.S. participation in the war and launched Earth Day, the Environmental Protection Agency, the Freedom of Information Act, the Occupational Safety and Health Act, the Clean Air Act, and the Endangered Species Act. I began life wrapped in the moral fabric of that period. It was in our town that scientists documented the loss of songbirds discussed in *Silent Spring*. My father went to divinity school with Dr. King and I remember marching in a candlelight vigil after his assassination. I attended Vietnam War protests with my older sister and celebrated Earth Day with my peers. The ethos of those times is parked within my soul.

My parents were born during the Great Depression and their values were similarly defined by the predominant lessons of their formative years. Their families were deliberate in conservation efforts and treated every resource as limited. That value system, ingrained into my parents' generation by economic necessity, is the only solution for the world community on this finite planet where sustainable lifestyles must ultimately come to light lest we perish. I honor my parents and their generation with this writing and my father and mother have each contributed an evocative chapter to this book.

My own two children see life through yet another lens. They have not known environmental disaster or economic depression. They are growing up in the shadow of leaders who say we should spend more time studying environmental threats before we take action. They see policy decisions justified by claims that we help the poor by giving more to the rich, from whom money will "trickle down." Advertising is omnipresent in their lives and increasingly effective as it beckons for more and more consumption that is needed less and less. My children see relatively little exaltation of frugality. In their world, prestige is granted almost exclusively to those who waste the most resources on material possessions and earn the most money at the expense of Kennedy-style community involvement and volunteerism.

Those with open minds in the 21st century need to hear a distinct second message, to hearken to the lessons of the past, and to receive specific information that refutes the well-orchestrated campaigns of people who place monetary gain above societal welfare. This book is for those who relish a focus on loftier goals. It is dedicated to the new generations of the 21st century and written for everyone who must confront the seemingly insurmountable tactics of the greedy Goliaths. My name is David.

Acknowledgments

This project pays tribute to wise elders who foster appreciation for simple pleasures and unselfish goals, and to my parents, Robert and Elizabeth, the focal representatives of that group in my life.

My wife Donna, a frugal devotee to composting, recycling, and the great outdoors, is the chief guardian of natural resources in our household. Her keen instincts also made her a guardian of clarity in the manuscript. I thank her for excellence in both roles.

For valuable comments on drafts of this book, I am indebted to My Vo, Holly Jones, James Chasey, Skeeter Makepeace, Sarah Vahlkamp, Christine Missik, and Eric Mount.

The editing insights of Kimberly Browning were indispensable. In another commendable effort, she guided school fundraisers in her area away from the sale of knickknacks and into the sale of Fair Trade certified food and beverages. Endeavors like hers could make that switch a national trend.

Thanks also to every reader who shares our indulgence in short-term pleasures with long-term benefits. May conservation, moderation, and simple living bring you delight during the day and help you sleep well at night.

Three ground rules:

(1) No preaching. This book is not written to say "you must." It is about information, ideas, inspiration, and saying "you can."

(2) No calls to visit painful extremes. The message here is that pleasure can accompany progress, and that indulgences are appropriate if the true benefits exceed the true costs.

(3) No feigned superiority. Personally, I do plenty of things wrong and some things right. I cherish information on how to do things better, but have no delusions that I do things best or that I am doing all that I can. You see, ...

CHAPTER 1

My Mother Darns Socks

M y mother irrigates the garden with rinse water from the
washing machine. She makes rugs out of old pantyhose.
As the recipient of a holiday card, she cuts off the
artwork to send out as a postcard. She saves hair clippings
to fill pincushions and is rumored to hoard used dental floss.
Plastic storage bags are washed out and re-
used. Uneaten food is frozen and re-served.
My mother's primary mode of transportation
is a decades-old Schwinn and her sewing
machine is a half-century-old Singer. And yes,
my mother darns socks. She is also one of the
happiest people I know.

> **She is also one
> of the happiest
> people I know.**

My mother's conservationist ways are not motivated by
financial need. She thrives on the deep satisfaction of doing
the right thing and caring for humanity. This benevolent fount
of contentment happens to be cheap, sustainable, and available
to all. Inspiration from those cheerfully immersed in simple
pleasures promotes a broader rediscovery of value systems that
place satisfaction and conservation in concert.

The Depression-era generation conquered resource limitations
long before the "Me Generation" cried out for its first round

of plastic action figures. Before manufactured goods tumbled down chain store conveyor belts like the April rains, my parents cherished the superior charm of a handmade doll, a nature walk, and a meal cooked slowly. Author and former news anchorman Tom Brokaw asserts that as the "greatest generation," depression-era progeny set the bar for today's youth.

Perhaps you, your parents, or your grandparents are like my parents. Their sources of motivation and genuine satisfaction are shared by many wise elders, but are largely lost on the baby boomers and younger generations. We, the inheritors of the Earth, exhibit an insatiable appetite for more, bigger, and newer material possessions. In contrast, the children of the Great Depression saw both poverty and prosperity firsthand. Riding the economic roller coaster of the past century, they sampled new-fangled manufactured goods and, with little choice, practiced the art of treading lightly on the planet. They know from experience that the best things in life are not delivered on trucks.

My mother wears clothing until holes appear, mends it, and wears it some more. Her attire represents the authentic, hip, comfortable look people feign with artificially "distressed" and faded products. Popular new jeans come with factory-made rips and holes. My mother asks why people don't just keep wearing their old jeans to accomplish the same end. When her clothes become useless, she stitches them into blankets, crochets them into rugs, or uses them as rags. She makes sturdy, oval doormats out of plastic grocery bags. She carefully folds used wrapping paper and stashes it away until the next holiday.

My mother showed no shame when I became a manager for Macy's after college, but she never spent a dime there either. At best, money serves as an indirect route to happiness; many people get lost along the way. We tend to overlook pleasures that cost only a song. My parents make beautiful music together, literally, with percussion instruments and penny whistles. It's hard to reach them in the evenings because they're so often out ballroom dancing. My mother also enjoys modern dance and teaches improvisational dance at the local community center. Like others who grasp the virtues of simple living, my parents camp, create art, volunteer at nursing homes and shelters, teach, learn, read, write, garden, cook, go to church, run, swim, bike, travel, engage in activism, and share affection. Some of their most relaxing and pleasurable time is spent sitting on their porch conversing with friends. One cannot buy such joys.

Today's younger generations are tempted away from their porches and friends by shopping malls, television shows, computer games, and other aggressively promoted commercial alternatives. If those pastimes lead some people to true bliss, so be it. If those activities prevent some people from discovering life's simple pleasures, it's a shame. Here's hoping for a revival in porch appreciation. *The American Porch: An Informal History of an Informal Place* by Michael Dolan and *Swinging in Place: Porch Life in Southern Culture* by Jocelyn Hazelwood Donlon document the good times to be had on porches and offer optimism for renewed awareness of simple, genuine sources of happiness.

My parents have never owned a microwave oven. There was a dishwashing machine in the house when we moved in 40 years ago. They tore out the machine and use its space to store recycling bins. My mother composts or recycles nearly everything—cardboard, aluminum, steel, and various types of paper and plastic. Usable items such as toys and cookie tins are not discarded, but placed out by the curb with a hand-painted sign that says "free." We joke that my father stays in good shape because if my mother outlives him, he is bound to be set out by the curb to be recycled.

Holiday Mirth and Materialism

Once while visiting my parents' home in East Lansing, Michigan, for the winter holidays I noticed that someone armed with a saw had absconded with the top section of the pine tree in their front yard. I entered their house uttering, "I can't believe someone stole the centerpiece of your yard to save twenty bucks on a Christmas

3

tree!" I then saw their decorated tree and said, "You have a nice tree, where did you get it?" It was a naïve question. I should have known: my father had removed the top of his own tree to bring indoors for Christmas. He was doing his part to protect the forests with a bit of severe pruning in the yard. It was the tree's second tour of holiday duty—it had arrived potted a decade earlier and was planted in the yard after serving time under tinsel in the house. It is now routine for my father to saw off the top of one or another evergreen from his modest quarter-acre lot to erect in the living room for the holidays. I found this shocking at first, but the trees grow back quickly and with improved density. As symbols of conservation, these trees have special meaning and give my parents that "warm glow" associated with both environmentalism and the holiday season.

Do you remember what you received on the last holiday? I remember few, if any, of my gifts. I enjoy the anticipation of receiving gifts, the opening of gifts, and the giving of gifts. But with drawers and shelves and closets and attics already brimming with useless doodads, anything more can only compound the storage nightmare I share with so many Americans. What I do remember about last Christmas is that my two young children ripped open their presents as if racing to defuse bombs held inside. They received hoards of the biggest, fastest, newest toys from family far and near. Honestly, five minutes after the defusion frenzy, they called out, "Chase us daddy!" Hundreds of dollars worth of manufactured goods were quickly trumped by a simple game with no batteries or assembly required. The best things in life are indeed free, and we spend too much time chasing material goods instead of chasing each other in games of tag.

Economist Joel Waldfogel estimates that the net loss from Christmas, due to expenditures on gifts that are not what people really want, is between $6 billion and $18 billion each year.[1] As my father describes it, the commercial build-up of Christmas makes us imagine that with the right combination of plastic toys, jewelry, silk ties, and cookbooks, we will reach nirvana— an ideal state of harmony and joy. After the gifts are open and nirvana is nowhere in sight, the whole event becomes a letdown. The remedy is to de-emphasize the material aspect of the holidays. Of course, that's the message of Dr. Seuss' *How the Grinch Stole Christmas* and other heartwarming family shows in which poverty, theft, or mishap removes gifts from the picture and the victimized families end up having the best holiday ever. Why? Because they focus on each other and remember the reason for the season, which isn't commercialism. We watch those shows with understanding in our hearts, and then, strangely enough, proceed to the stores and shop as usual. Perhaps it has something to do with the multi-billion-dollar advertising blitz designed to assure us that this year nirvana will be wrapped up under a dying tree.

According to a 2005 poll conducted by Widmeyer Research and Polling for the Center for a New American Dream, 79 percent of American adults believe it is unnecessary to spend large sums of money to have a fulfilling and enjoyable holiday, 87 percent feel that the holidays should be more about family bonding and caring for others than about gifts, 74 percent feel that the exchange of gifts is overemphasized during the holidays, and 76 percent say that the holidays worsen an existing problem with materialistic youth.[2] Books such as *Simplify Your Christmas* by Elaine St. James and *Hundred Dollar Holiday* by Bill McKibben are rich with environmentally conscious holiday twists that might just turn us toward the "true meaning" of the holidays that most Americans are seeking.

If you're worried that relief from materialism would hurt the economy, note that we can spend as much as we want to create good jobs in the service sector and in industries that save more

---

1   These figures have been adjusted for inflation. See "The Deadweight Loss of Christmas," *The American Economic Review* 83, no. 5 (Dec., 1993): 1328-1336.
2   See www.newdream.org/holiday/poll05.php.

resources than they eliminate. Let's seek growth in education, alternative energy, cancer research, public transportation, national trail systems, healthcare, entertainment, child care, environmental clean-ups, computer software, and so on, as discussed later in the book.

Adventures in Conservation

For life as for the holidays, eco adventurers explore for us the boundaries of pleasurable conservation. My father does not fly and seldom drives. He traveled to work on leg power for his entire career. While globe-trotting to study world religions as a university professor, he crossed the oceans on cargo ships that were going to his destinations anyway. I remember complaining as a child that we should drive to a restaurant several miles away because I felt the distance was too far to travel on my small, single-speed bicycle. He traded bikes with me and disproved my argument, traveling both ways on my simple little bike. The point was well taken—the barriers to more efficient modes of transportation are mostly in our minds. In fact, bicycles are the most efficient way to go, using less energy per passenger kilometer than any other form of transportation. No, they are not good for transporting pianos, but for unbelievable pictures of what bikes can carry, see http://aistigave.hit.bg/Logistics/. The impressive biking culture of Amsterdam is on display at www.ski-epic.com/amsterdam_bicycles/ (as are a lot of unsafe riding practices). Read Marcia Lowe's book, *Bicycle: Vehicle for a Small Planet,* for more on the virtues of bikes. Enjoy the exercise, and do wear a helmet.

My father eschews machines. When I was a child I didn't believe my father's story that during his youth, milk was delivered to his home by horse and buggy. I should have taken the fact that he rarely uses any sort of motor to this day as a hint of the veracity of this low-tech feat. He mows the lawn with a human-powered reel mower. He clips shrubs with giant scissors. He paints by hand, clears away leaves with a rake, and removes the snows of Michigan from his sidewalk with a shovel. His house has no air conditioner. His boat is a blow-up kayak that inflates with a foot pump. When a power blackout hit the eastern U.S. in 2003, my parents noticed the problem as darkness fell and lights didn't work. Early the next morning when the power returned, the house next door caught on fire. Apparently some of the owner's appliances didn't handle the energy jolt well. Living simply has more than a few virtues. That's not to say we should give up our most beloved modern conveniences, but perhaps we could practice moderation and use more elbow grease.

My father's voluntary adventures with conservation typify those characterized in Thomas Stanley and William Danko's illuminating book *The Millionaire Next Door*. He became financially secure on a professor's salary. He is stiflingly (my mother says "charmingly") frugal and as moral as Jimmy Carter. His credibility rests upon a refusal to say anything unless he's sure about it—very sure. Once I asked him about the starting time of a concert we planned to attend. He replied, "I *think* it starts at 8:00 p.m." When I inquired about the basis for that thought, he said, "That's what it says on the ticket." He wouldn't be sure until the curtain rose. In the face of uncertainty he errs on the side of safety. At the other extreme are those who resist actions to reduce global warming, for example, stating that the evidence of potential harm is not yet convincing. Better safe …

Like most environmental role models, my father puts on his pants one leg at a time and owns one car at a time. Like Jay Leno, he could afford to drive virtually any car made. My father has driven a long line of compact station wagons, keeping each one for almost a decade. In that sense he might be called the antithesis of Jay Leno, who owns more than 150 automobiles and motorcycles, or Jerry Seinfeld, with his stable of 47 Porsches, except that all three are satisfied, intelligent, kind, and gracious men. I feel confident that neither Jay, nor Jerry, nor Bill Gates for that matter, is happier than my father. I wonder if Jerry has any porches.

Looking Forward

Some sources of happiness are innate. Our enjoyment of food, water, and affection are essential to our survival and procreation. Other preferences are learned and malleable. As different as political stances, religions, and tastes may be, most people play by their parents' rule books. In terms of patriotism, people defend what they know. In terms of religion, children tend to follow in their parents' traditions, even when they become adults. When it comes to materialism or conservation, our parents, peers, education, and culture largely determine our goals. Given the certain failure of unsustainable practices, it becomes important for us as parents, peers, educators, neighbors, and friends to know and share the joys of treading lightly.

The message is not that we must all darn socks and ambush bushes at holiday time. We cannot all be environmental saints. I certainly do not qualify as one, although I am inspired by the saints to be less of a sinner. Seasoned conservationists can help us find contentment without the trappings of trying to own everything, or even the latest thing. Those who tread lightly fortify themselves with righteousness and focus on the true joys of life—friends, family, music, art, spirituality, dance, food, nature, and the 100 activities listed in Chapter 12, to name a few. Most of these treats are enjoyed in the poorest pockets of the Amazon basin as well as in money-soaked Beverly Hills, which makes the ownership of considerable wealth trivial in the recipe for a good life. If you have chosen a career you enjoy and take time for simple pleasures, you have played your cards right regardless of your income.

The fleeting excitement of consumerism is preceded by environmentally destructive resource extraction and manufacturing processes and followed by buyer's remorse, storage problems, debt, and distraction from the sources of genuine satisfaction. We can look to the children of the Depression era to put the "need" for material goods in perspective and discover the real meaning and virtues of moderation. Each of us could take a step toward better stewardship of the planet. For some, that will require a new outlook. For most, responsible practices will foster lifelong fulfillment and leave a legacy of natural resources for tomorrow's children, who will reap what we sow in the soil and breathe what we leave in the air. For those who seek the joy of treading lightly, I hope this book can provide a beacon along the way.

To spread the inspiration from my parents' generation throughout this book, I close each chapter with a sentence about their lifestyle.

My parents grow their own tomatoes.

CHAPTER 2

Simple Pleasures,
Insatiable Greed

In my town not long ago a 79-year-old man living in an affluent neighborhood shot his 63-year-old neighbor to death while the neighbor mowed his lawn. The shooter claimed he was hunting skunks. The two had reportedly been wrangling over property lines for years.

The slum of Dharavi, a part of Mumbai (formerly Bombay), India, is home to 600,000 people who own no land at all. They have no air conditioning, televisions, or cars. The street is both their toilet and their scrubbing board for washing clothes. They live for a year on what many Americans spend in a week. Shacks with scrap-wood walls and sheet-metal roofs are erected each against the next. Paths between the shelters are narrower than the hallways in my home.

Alone, knowing no one, speaking none of their language, I walked into Dharavi in the summer of 2004. The layout resembled a corn maze—winding, disorienting, random—with many dead ends and no clear way out. A group of boys came up behind me and began to follow. I was armed with no more than a large camera.

My hope was that in a country of one billion citizens and a city of 10 million people of Hindu, Muslim, and assorted

other faiths, only a respectful attitude of live and let live could persist. Indeed, the boys brandished only smiles. They laughed as I clumsily meandered about. They made "Xs" with their arms to forewarn of dead ends. They patiently tried to help and understand me in ways that made the contrasting brand of "whoopass"[1] international policy look barbaric.

I entered the heart of the slum on a quest to discover the dwellers' greatest needs. What was most wrong and what could Westerners do to help? With my newfound entourage in tow, I passed doorways without doors. The boys introduced me to residents as the "camera man" and explained that I was apparently wandering aimlessly in search of nothing in particular.

On this trek I indeed discovered the crying needs of a culture—not theirs, but our own. In this place devoid of wealth and basic services, I found great warmth and happiness. The people were surrounded by friends and family. They ate simple, home-cooked meals together. They shared affection. They had no option to

---

1 This term refers to hawkish physical aggression. See www.urbandictionary.com/ define.php?term=a+can+of+whoopass.

be distracted by materialism. They worked terribly hard in the recycling industry that prevents Mumbai from choking on its own waste. With no locks or weapons, they held the highest standards of trust, ethics, and spirituality. When Mumbai's Slum Redevelopment Authority took steps toward razing Dharavi in 2007 by offering to transplant residents into free apartments with kitchens and bathrooms, many of the slum dwellers turned down the apartments.[2] Dharavi was seen as a superior choice, a mother lode of the important things affluent society has forgotten.

I do not mean to perpetuate the myth that poor people are fine without our help. Slums may showcase a precious social fabric that upscale suburbs lack, but poor residents often endure painful diseases resulting from malnutrition and pollution. Those who are financially secure could only benefit from sharing the appreciation of simple pleasures exhibited in developing nations. Everyone would benefit if prosperity were shared with the underprivileged to put an end to hunger, disease, overpopulation, and illiteracy.

2   See www.csmonitor.com/2007/0321/p01s04-wosc.html.

Calls for Simplicity

It should be no secret that a simple life is a good life. Hints of this abound. On his public radio program, *A Prairie Home Companion*, Garrison Keillor listed the best things in life as music, sweet corn, spirituality, sex, and learning, "not necessarily in that order." In their own way, the people of Dharavi have these things. Their wealth in simple pleasures surpasses our own and it shows on their faces.

The documentary film *Wild Horses of Mongolia with Julia Roberts* follows Hollywood's highest-paid actress on an extended stay with a nomadic family of modest means. Roberts reveled in the lifestyle of Mongolia, where people own only as much as they can carry with them on an endless journey. Roberts seemed sincerely moved by the simple pleasures of the nomads' existence—children, horses, conversation, food and drink, and natural beauty.

Calls for simplicity are nothing new. In the 19th century, American author Henry David Thoreau prescribed "simplicity, simplicity, simplicity!" and wrote that "a man is rich in proportion to the number of things he can afford to let alone."[3] In *Principles of Political Economy* published in 1848, English philosopher John Stuart Mill advocated a simpler lifestyle in which the quality of life was measured in terms of intellectual climate rather than personal possessions. French theologian John Calvin modeled the joys of moderation and simple living during the 16th century. And appeals for simplicity and frugality appeared in myriad early religious writings as quoted in the next section.

Famous intellectuals, celebrities, and religious figures do not stand alone in their recognition of simplicity's virtues. Nor do the Buddhists, Mennonites, and Amish, among other groups that seek simplicity as a way of life. I suspect that virtually everyone has moments of realization that life would be better with fewer possessions, smaller egos, more free time, and more cooperation.

Sixty-four million people live in rural America, where life can be relatively simple. Amazon.com lists close to 1000 books related to simple living. But simplicity isn't as simple as it should be, due in part to the $150 billion spent annually on advertising

---

3   See www.blupete.com/Literature/Biographies/Literary/Thoreau.htm.

in the United States alone.[4] The ubiquitous ad campaigns implore us to buy more, which means we must work more or borrow more, and thereby encumber our lives with more stuff, less free time, and greater responsibilities. The temptation toward complications and overconsumption also comes from natural instincts to take risks, stimulate our minds, compete with our neighbors, and fall prey to greed.

Greed Rears its Ugly Head

I would argue that there is no food better than simple food. It's hard to beat fresh tomatoes from the garden or homemade jam on toasted wheat bread. Will the Nintendo generation discover the incomparable pleasures of slow food and backyard gardening? Slow and simple fly in the face of greed, and consumers have fallen into the trap of seeking salvation via conspicuous consumption. Merchandise advertising campaigns overshadow sage advice, reason, and religious teachings that renounce greed. Our culture is so entrenched in consumerism that alternative paths are almost unimaginable.

There are other paths. Chinese philosopher Lao-Tzu, the founder of Taoism and presumed author of the Tao Te Ching, wrote, "Seek not happiness too greedily" around 600 BCE. In the Qur'an, the holy book of Islam, it is written that "whoever is saved from the greediness of his soul, these it is that are the successful."[5] The Bible quotes Jesus as saying, "If you want to be perfect, go, sell your possessions and give to the poor, and you will have treasure in heaven," and "It is easier for a camel to go through the eye of a needle than for a rich man to enter the kingdom of God."[6] Nonetheless, out of zeal for more money, lives become painfully complex, politicians who could otherwise help the poor are sidelined, and there is little time for making the music or enjoying the learning, spirituality, and sweet corn that Garrison Keillor prescribed.

During his commencement address at the University of California-Berkeley's School of Business Administration in 1985, infamous securities arbitrageur Ivan Boesky stated, "Greed

---

4   See www.tns-mi.com/news/03132007.htm.
5   The Mutual Deceit, 64.16, *The Holy Qur'an*, translated by M. H. Shakir, New York: Tahrike Tarsile Qur'an, Inc., 1983.
6   Matthew 19:21 and 19:24, *New International Version*, Colorado Springs, CO: International Bible Society, 1984.

is all right, by the way. I think greed is healthy. You can be greedy and still feel good about yourself." The following year the Securities and Exchange Commission found him guilty of insider trading, barred him from trading securities ever again, fined him $100 million, and sent him to prison. Donald Trump says, "You can't be too greedy."[7] Perhaps Boesky should share his hard-learned lesson with Trump: greed is addicting and has a tragic way of backfiring.

There is a common perception that prosperity is around the corner. The status quo is never enough, but we believe we'd be happy if we could earn just a little more money. The fact that the richest of the rich, all the way up to the billionaire corporate leaders, keep fighting tooth and nail for more dollars is evidence that there is no winning that game. The satiation point is always over the next mountain of cash. Former Federal Reserve chairman Alan Greenspan blamed "infectious greed" for causing wealthy corporate executives to exaggerate profits and inflate stock prices—dishonesty that helped trigger the recession of the early 2000s.[8] If the millionaires and billionaires still find themselves wanting more and more, the message is clear: quests for contentment via acquisitions have no end. Or as the Roman philosopher Seneca wrote in the first century C.E., "For greed all nature is too little."

> **"For greed all nature is too little."**

Adam Smith's Invisible Hand

Eighteenth century political scientist Adam Smith, the father of modern economics, is thought by some to have issued a license for greed. Smith popularized a model in which an individual acting in his own self-interest would bring efficiency and welfare to society as if "led by an invisible hand to promote an end which was no part of his intention."[9] To Smith, competition among businesses was the great enforcer that held greed at bay. Should one business charge too much, another business would hasten to provide the same product at a lower price. Acting selfishly to steal profits from one another, competing businesses would serve the public interest by keeping prices in check.

7   See www.donald-trump.info/#quotes.
8   See www.federalreserve.gov/boarddocs/hh/2002/july/testimony.htm.
9   See www.econlib.org/LIBRARY/Smith/smWN.html, book IV, Ch. 2, paragraph IV.2.9.

The notion of free markets rendering socially desirable outcomes has captured the fancy of generations of laissez-faire advocates who summon Smith's work to support avarice. The rub is that Smith was a moral philosopher, and his theories assumed a foundation of righteousness and human decency. His premise was that markets compel ethical behavior. Smith abhorred monopolies and rested his case on perfectly competitive markets that are unlike most that have ever existed. The "invisible hand" only works its magic when goods are standardized, buyers and sellers are plentiful, competitors can enter and leave the market costlessly, all costs associated with goods are paid by the producer or consumer, and everyone involved in the market has full information about what is available from whom at what price.

In light of the unrealistic assumptions that underlie Smith's model of perfect competition, economists Richard Lipsey and Kelvin Lancaster advanced the General Theory of Second-Best to show that when one of the conditions for perfect competition is not met, remedial intervention may well lead to a better outcome than a hands-off approach, even if every other condition is met.[10] If free markets cultivate either dominant businesses, misinformation, or costs such as pollution not borne by market participants, then antitrust legislation and environmental regulations may be warranted to rein in greed and better serve society.

Adam Smith wrote that we should be ruled neither by big government nor by big business, and that we should exhibit behavior that would earn the approval of a panel of impartial observers. I often wonder what Smith's hypothetical panel of observers would think about such things as big-box retailers, disposable tableware, the state of the environment, the level of the minimum wage, fur coats, and gas guzzlers. If given the opportunity, perhaps the progenitor of modern economic policy would revoke the license for unbridled greed that has become his unfortunate legacy.

Sing and Dance

Sometimes it takes an act of nature to help us find the true sources of happiness. In September of 2004 I sat in an Orlando hotel with my wife and two young children as Hurricane Jeanne's 75 mph

10 See "The General Theory of Second Best," *The Review of Economic Studies* 24, no. 1 (1956 - 1957): 11-32.

winds stole our electricity and confined us to one simple room. We had few provisions, but we were together, focused on each other, and forced to rediscover the pleasures of life. We sang, danced, played charades, and listened to each other tell stories. When the winds permitted, we met our neighbors on the common porch in front of our room, which gave us a glimpse of the days before air conditioning when verandas were a common place for pleasant summertime congregation and interaction. Amid three days of visits to opulent theme parks, the day the hurricane closed every park was my daughter's favorite. Mine too.

No, it is not necessary to pull the plug on moderate elements of materialism, but we should take an occasional breather from the acquisition race to ponder what really makes us happy. In the classic 1971 movie *Harold and Maude*, 79-year-old Maude asks rich-but-despondent young Harold, "Do you sing and dance?" "No." Harold replies. "I didn't think so," says Maude.

> My parents
> sing and
> dance.

CHAPTER 3

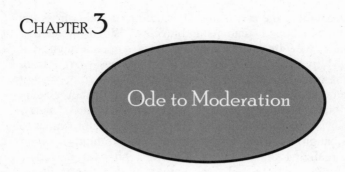

Ode to Moderation

E verything in moderation, right? That standard is seldom upheld in this age of excess. Going to extremes can make things interesting, and occasionally proper, but there is undeniable sensibility to temperance. Aristotle taught that moral virtue is the mean between two vices, just as courage falls between cowardice and rashness, and modesty moderates arrogance and low self-esteem. Any alert viewer of the conservative Fox News programs and the liberal Michael Moore documentaries knows the truth is probably somewhere in the middle.

In *The Wisdom of Crowds,* James Surowiecki explains the superior veracity of the average viewpoint in a crowd. When estimating the number of jelly beans in a jar, for example, the average of all the guesses is far closer to the truth than the vast majority of individual guesses. Yet we so often stray, in our own stubborn way, from the virtues of middle ground. Extreme stances stifle compromise on such topics as immigration, litigation reform, outsourcing, the national debt, abortion, and environmental policy.

Radical mentalities lead to unfortunate misperceptions. When I mentioned in a newspaper column that bicycles can be fun, someone apparently took that to mean that everyone had to bike everywhere, and wrote me to say, "It's hard to travel [across the Midwest] with a hockey team using bicycles." When I wrote that people could live with fewer kitchen gadgets, someone suggested that I must live in a mud hut and wear clothes woven from native grasses. Clearly some people struggle with the concept of moderation. Consider what it means when Britney Spears shows a "little" skin or Donald Trump puts on a "little" party. The danger is that the chronically extreme, from Ralph Nader to Rush Limbaugh, reinforce extreme-constrained thinking without everyone realizing that those people are a bit over the edge. Granted, radicals can be right, but how often does the truth not lie between two extremes? And how often do the best conclusions not come from an objective consideration of both sides?

Here are some talking points to share with extreme-minded individuals:

- Not having *everything* does not mean having *nothing*. Not having too much helps others have enough.

- Not driving *everywhere* does not mean driving *nowhere*. Drive when alternatives are difficult.

- Moderation is not about forgoing prized machines and gadgets, it is about passing on redundancy, impulsiveness, and excess.

- Gun control does not prevent gun ownership, it prescribes extra precautions to save the lives of innocent children and adults.

- To embrace energy conservation is not to live in the dark, it is to turn the lights out when we are out.

- The moderate use of force has nothing to do with allowing the enemy to enslave us and everything to do with waiting until there is credible evidence of a threat before taking preemptive action.

- A moderate level of manufacturing does not require that we live in caves, it requires that we protect natural resources critical to our quality of life.

- To live sustainably is not to suffer, it is to subscribe to thoughtful resource selection and moderated materialism.

Simply put, moderation is essential to long-term success on a planet with limited resources. Extreme thinking can be dangerous and falsely reassuring. To decide that everything associated with one extreme is correct is to be comforted by narrow-mindedness. Political extremists seem to believe they are doing the right thing whenever they follow the hard line of their doctrine. Extreme thinking in the realms of war, peace, religion, business, and the environment can lead to similar ignorance and short-lived bliss. Moderation in thought and action requires scrutiny, creativity, honesty, and frequent decision making, all of which are well worth the effort.

Progress is Easy

> Take the easy steps and make a valuable difference.

Society would like to make advances on the environmental front, the social justice front, the education front, and the health front, among others, but radical changes can necessitate painful trade-offs. Mercifully, the burden of progress starts small. Following the formula of moderation, anyone can take the easy steps and make a valuable difference. In most cases it would be difficult for a full-time employee to become a full-time volunteer, but relatively easy for a worker to carve an hour of volunteer work from the least-valued activities in a week. It would be a better world if everyone recycled the materials that are the easiest to recycle, skipped the car rides that could most easily become bike rides, programmed the thermostat to reach a moderate temperature when no one is home, and donated a moderate amount of the least valuable attic clutter to charity.

As discussed in greater detail in Chapter 7, the health and environmental problems with overconsumption are real, yet the solution of moderation is simple. Few people could make a bigger difference than those who are inactive because they think their actions don't matter. Former Vice President Al Gore emphasizes similar points in *An Inconvenient Truth*[1] and suggests modest steps to stave off global warming, such as replacing incandescent light bulbs with compact fluorescent light bulbs, moderating home temperatures by two degrees, and replacing filters on heating and cooling systems on a regular basis.

1   See www.climatecrisis.net/takeaction/whatyoucando/.

In response to suggestions that people should be more respectful of living things, I've seen extreme-minded thinkers react as if they were ordered to sweep in front of their feet so as not to step on any bugs. That is the practice of the Jains,[2] who believe that every living thing has a worthy soul, but there are not many Jains in the United States. When our peers advocate respect for life, the message is typically that we should use the most violent alternatives such as war and capital punishment sparingly, moderate the use of toxic pesticides that harm a wide range of living things, and discourage the inhumane treatment of animals—such as the debeaking of chickens[3] or the inclusion of life-shortening, mastitis-causing hormones in cattle feed.[4]

Do you know someone who would react to the last sentence by thinking, "What are we supposed to do, outlaw bug spray and ban fried chicken and milk?" Another symptom of extreme thinking is that one hears every suggestion as a call for new legislation. Fortunately, as the result of business owners' desires to encourage spending, markets respond to consumer preferences. That is, business owners want to sell what consumers want to buy. Thus, moderation in consumer behavior can bring about more responsible corporate behavior without new laws. As consumers seek more free-range chickens and hormone-free milk, health food cooperatives[5] and Earth-friendly grocery chains such as Whole Foods[6] spring up to sell them, and the organics sections in traditional grocery stores keep getting bigger and bigger.

The Need for Speed

The moderation of consumption is easier discussed than done. At times we all fight the urge to go shopping for frivolous extras. The items may be unnecessary, hardly affordable, and made with scarce resources, but they briefly conciliate the undeniable force of boredom that motivates us all, for better or worse.

Rather than seeking thrills from new outfits, fast cars, gadgets, junk food, or artificial stimulants, let's pack our carabiners and go climb a mountain. Just for fun, consider camping or skating or biking. Let the green power of gravity propel you down

---

2   See http://en.wikipedia.org/wiki/Jainism.
3   See www.upc-online.org/fall2000/mcdonalds.html.
4   See www.preventcancer.com/consumers/general/milk.htm.
5   For examples in your state see www.organicconsumers.org/foodcoops.htm.
6   See www.wholefoods.com/.

rapids or ski slopes. You may agree that it is more thrilling to be in the great outdoors than in the mall, these activities are safer than doing drugs, and participants earn that warm feeling one receives from respecting the planet and its inhabitants.

Looking for something a bit less ambitious? Enjoy the excitement of the service industries by catching a live show, a sporting event, a good movie, or a massage. Go swim in a lake or make pizza from scratch. Study a book on edible plants and sample something new, design a rock garden, climb a tree,

Photo by Donna Anderson (2008)

or make a snowman. You get the idea. The opportunities are endless for creative fun that will be more memorable than a shopping spree and safer than any sort of consumption binge.

Exploring the Limits

A friend of mine gave away everything she owned and went to South America to work with the poor. She described the freedom from possessions as a joyous release. I might feel uncomfortable with nothing, but I also feel uncomfortable with too much. The more one has, the more one has to worry about, lose, organize, clean, insure, pay for, fight over, protect, and store. Indeed, what you own owns you. Moderation is the solution.

Moderation is the answer to most questions about excesses that tempt us, be they material goods, polluting cars, energy uses, or ice cream sundaes, but moderation is not *always* the answer. When the moderate consumption of something could lead to subsequent consumption at dangerous levels, abstinence can be a better solution. Abstinence is an appropriate strategy for recovering alcoholics, drug abusers, and sex offenders. Moderate oil drilling in the Arctic National Wildlife Refuge (ANWR) or in Antarctica might not be wise, for it would open the door for environmental devastation in the last pristine expanses on Earth and tempt executives overeager to provide short-term profits for stockholders without appropriate attention to the costs. Drilling is banned in both places as of this writing, but there have been several attempts to lift the ban in ANWR, and there are fears that high oil prices will motivate a lifting of the ban in Antarctica, which will be lifted in 2048 anyway. Russia already has an "experimental" drill ready to break ground in Antarctica.[7]

I eat a moderate amount of meat, but an eloquent lecture by vegan Leslie Dodd convinced me that it would be better to avoid eating animal flesh.[8] Among the compelling arguments for a plant-based diet are these:

- Heart disease is the leading cause of death in the United States.[9]

- There is a remarkable efficiency loss when we eat animals that eat plants rather than eating plants directly. With a plant-based diet, the same calories can be acquired from a fraction (some estimates are in the 5-10 percent range or less) of the amount of land and energy, with correspondingly less water, pesticides, and manure problems.[10]

- Animals in factory farms are often confined to such a small space that they cannot even turn around.[11]

---

7   See www.csmonitor.com/2006/0803/p05s01-woap.html.
8   This was presented at the Unitarian Universalist Church of Lexington, Kentucky on July 30, 2006.
9   See www.cdc.gov/nchs/fastats/lcod.htm.
10 See, for example, http://geosci.uchicago.edu/~gidon/papers/nutri/nutriEI.pdf and www.ivu.org/oxveg/Publications/Oven/Editorials/2002-04.html.
11 See www.goveg.com/factoryFarming_pigs_farms.asp and www.animalfreedom.

A truckload of factory farmed, compacted, (mostly) living chickens on the way to slaughter. Meat makes for a resource-intensive meal.

- It takes roughly 100,000 liters of water to produce one kilogram of beef, compared to 500 liters per kilogram of potatoes.[12]

- Methane from livestock digestion and waste is a problematic contributor to global climate change.[13]

As with materialism, the important first step of de-emphasizing meat is easy. Who needs sausage and bacon for breakfast? The Kellogg brothers invented cornflakes in their efforts to provide satisfying, healthy, meatless breakfast foods.[14] According to the organization called People for the Ethical Treatment of Animals, if consumers in the United States decreased their meat consumption by 10 percent, the reduction in livestock would free-up enough grain to feed the 60 million people who starve to death each year.[15] For those who choose to practice

org/english/information/abuses.html.

12 See www.news.cornell.edu/releases/Aug97/livestock.hrs.html.

13 See http://earthsave.org/globalwarming.htm.

14 See www.buyandhold.com/bh/en/education/history/2006/kelloggs.html.

15 See http://veggie.org/veggie/peta-articles/facts/veg/veggie-eat-for-life-peta.
    shtml. It should be pointed out that starvation is often related to transportation and

abstinence from meat there are clearly even greater gains. The roughly six million adult vegetarians in America serve as inspirational role models and tread lightly in a particularly healthy and meaningful way.[16]

Centrist views are not always best, and diversity should never be diluted, but when we are purchasing, partying, parenting, penalizing, preserving, prohibiting, polluting, or making policy, we must not be blind to the virtues of moderation.

> My parents
> buy books
> but not
> bric-a-brac.

distribution problems with food, rather than quantity problems.

16 See estimates of the number of vegetarians see www.vrg.org/journal/vj2003issue3/vj2003issue3poll.htm.

CHAPTER 4

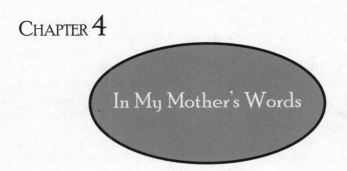

In My Mother's Words

Treading Lightly:
Sometimes Cheap, Always Valuable

An invitation from our son to write about my homemaking, for the sake of sharing my ideas with ecologically minded people, was an invitation I could not refuse. The confessions and recommendations I collect here from my 56 years of married life are mostly applications of the 1930s depression necessities I learned from my parents, the World War II conservation mindset of the early 1940s, and the careful and scientific philosophy of my 1950s Home Economics education at universities in Syracuse and Boston. Exposure to the humanities, including art, history, ethics, literature, and religion, makes us all sensitive to the feelings and intuition we call upon to make decisions, helps us develop critical thinking skills, and leads to self-respect. The humanities also alert us to the importance of other times, places, and belief systems, such as religious traditions that glorify neither sensationalism, wealth for its own sake, nor keeping up with anyone.

The practices I discuss here seem inevitable and so logical to me; I can't resist sharing them and feel glad to do so. Most men and women around the world have similarly ecological foundations by necessity or intuition, or have been converted to simple living by elder role models. Western civilization's present consumer-driven society is an anomaly.

Piously, I think about saving the Earth as I carry out projects.

Of course, it is more complicated than that because helping others is usually more important than saving stuff, and resource conservation can take time meant for enjoyment. I pray to walk the paradox-ridden median line between ecology and fullness of life successfully. Those tests of character aside, information shortages, or in some cases overloads, result in ecological conundrums: Should we choose paper or plastic bags at the grocery store? Is it worth the trouble to bring cloth grocery bags from home? Should we treat wood with common petroleum-based preservatives or vegetable oil? What are appropriately balanced approaches to gift giving, transportation, appliance ownership and disposal, material desires, and homemaking?

Please join me in the pursuit of sound choices and actions; it is even more fun with your company. Perhaps you will send me some of your findings in your efforts to be ecological.

Domestic Life

We can save the Earth, to the extent possible, in ways that give us a deep inner sense of joy. Said another way, homemaking, including housecleaning, cooking, sewing, entertaining, child rearing, spouse loving, and elder care, is more satisfying if ecological considerations are taken seriously. This is not to imply that everyone should do things in the same way. As St. Ignatius wrote in the 16th century, "If for any reason this idea is not right for you, do not act on it, find the action that gives you peace."

> **"If for any reason this idea is not right for you, do not act on it, find the action that gives you peace."**

Homemaking

Having no home, not even the tent and bedroll of a nomad, is an unsatisfactory state for most. Young men in overcrowded, underdeveloped cities sometimes rent bunks for a night to receive needed rest. Homeless men live under bridges, in boxes on the sidewalk, and in community shelters. Homeless women and children are more likely to end up in shelters. People sleep in cars; refugees and migrants sleep in forests and on roadsides. Most Americans end up with a place to call home most of the time: a dorm room, a hotel room, a rented apartment, or a house with a mortgage. We can hope and push for ecological practices in our workplaces and public spaces, but we have more freedom to practice ecology in our homes.

Having a traditional home means knowing how to rent, lease, buy, or build one, paying utility bills and taxes, and doing upkeep or hiring it done. Ownership demands decisions about lawns, floors, windows, walls, doors, furniture, and furnishings. In this section I share patterns and practices that have worked well for me; perhaps they will give you a few new ideas.

The Eastern decor style of Feng Shui—leaving much emptiness about the house—is very appealing to me, but unnatural. My husband Robert is always after me because I am apt to have every surface covered with some project. Feng Shui is helping me reform. All of our beds rest directly on the floor and consist of mattresses or futons with sheets and blankets. The absence of box spring mattresses seems to help our backs. Bypassing bed structures leaves more open space above and around the beds.

I like to use vegetable oils rather than paint on wooden window frames, doors, and furniture. I would prefer to give my painted outside window frames a natural wood surface by scraping away the peeling paint each year or so but my family and community can't stand the unsightly in-between look. Some say I should encase the old lead paint in new non-lead paint that would be safer. I adore the aesthetics of natural wood, old or new, too much to give up on it easily. I've seen wood from old barns provide real character as a new wall or floor covering. Robert makes rocking horses and toys out of old wood scraps. New wood products and wood substitutes can be relatively ecological too. My son David has installed a beautiful floor of fast-growing bamboo, and Robert and I installed a new, unfinished balcony railing made of long-lasting cedar that I wash down and oil.

I grapple with hiring outside help with home projects. Ethics dictates that we should not call on others to face health hazards we would not accept ourselves, so I try to avoid the use of hazardous lawn treatments, cleaning solutions, paints, and pest controls rather than having anyone apply them. Safer projects demand a balance of frugality and convenience. Sometimes a plumber must be called to fix a leaky pipe that has defeated amateur repairs. We hired a professional roofer recently, although 30 years ago Robert replaced the roof himself with great success. The pro left leaks. We had wood floors refinished on the second floor. Wood floors last a lifetime and look new after being re-sanded and varnished. Carpet made from recycled plastic is another option.

To keep the toilet bowl clean ecologically I scrub it daily and let vinegar sit in it for 30 minutes twice a week. I attack stubborn stains with laundry soap weekly; the soap is not very ecological but I have it around for ring around the collar and spot cleaning. If you have no animals that drink from the toilet and no children who might play in it, you don't have to flush it every time you pee—if you can cope with the aesthetics of that.

I have crocheted several throw rugs from cotton and synthetic knitted rags. Cross sections of old hosiery or plastic bags provide colorful loops for rug assembly. The oval rugs wear well and I am ready to make more. Braiding rugs is more work, I feel.

Window coverings are a good focus for art projects. We have commercial drapes in the living room but our own creations elsewhere. Homemade gathered curtains, some decorated with my daughters' childhood embroidery, hang in what were our two children's bedrooms. Plexiglas shelves holding plants and children's art adorn the dining room windows, as you see in the photograph below. In the kitchen are red nylon valences with antique lace and handiwork sown on. Beads hang on the front entry windows. Dark brown fiberboard with commercially cut designs covers plastic stained glass images stuck onto our bedroom windows. This combination brings a colorful glow into the

room through hundreds of patterned slits in the fiberboard—a nice effect for an inexpensive, no-maintenance window covering that will last indefinitely.

Quilts multiply here as wool and cotton blankets wear out. I cover one side of the aging item with a single layer of new fabric and the other side with quilted fabrics, old and new. I make potholders using similar techniques. Be careful to rip-check old fabrics to see if they will last. Our quilts do show wear and I make a lot of repairs these days.

I usually do some knitting in the winter. Lately for these projects—mostly scarves—I have wanted some big fat needles but couldn't find them in the local fabric shops or craft stores. Robert made some that work well by sanding the ends of wooden dowels to form points.

Cloth napkins are an aesthetically pleasing and ecological substitute for disposable paper products. Likewise, tablecloths and place mats help make a meal classy and avoid stains and scratches on wooden tabletops.

I give people kitchen supplies and all sorts of tools as gifts; they are cheerful symbols of future homemade productions. One of my favorite kitchen tools is a rubber spatula used to scrape cooking bowls and pans clean. They wear out and have to be replaced every few years. I keep two so that one is always easy to find, even with two cooks in the kitchen.

I save one-quart, one-pint, and eight-ounce bottles that share a single lid size. These become bug-proof containers for grains, holders for leftovers, pitchers for iced tea, and so on. I throw most other bottles into the recycling bin.

At the top of the cellar stairs I have three stacked milk crates: one for Robert's stuff to go downstairs (plumbing and electrical supplies, tools), one for some of Robert's running gear, and one for my stuff to go downstairs (laundry, Styrofoam to recycle, gardening tools, art supplies). Having a resting spot for items along the pathway to their final destination gives me more patience for managing a lot of projects and resource flows.

As U.S. homes become larger and more functional it is unfortunate that so many workers must divide their time between homes and offices, heating or cooling both places day and night and using time and energy to travel between the sites. It would be efficient in many ways for homes to double as workplaces, as has been common in other times and places. Robert's parents ran a general store out of their home and my parents ran a livestock auctioneering business out of mine. In impoverished countries it is typical for women to run recycling businesses out of their homes to supplement the meager incomes of their husbands. Some women in South American countries knit products for export, likewise crocheting is common in Asia. These home industries are relatively ecological sources of attractive and useful items that show up in U.S. homes and raise the standard of living both here and at the source, granted reasonably free and fair trade practices (considerate prices that make their way to the actual producers).

Cooking and Eating

Eating can be healthy and Earth-friendly or not. It was the norm during most of the 20th century for mothers to prepare 21 meals a week for their children and husbands, if not for their elders and guests. This continued for the children's years at home, which for some of us extended into adulthood. Now it is common to eat out, order in, or pick up meals. Nevertheless, our diets can be nutritional and ecologically sensible. To facilitate this ideal it is helpful to have trays of healthy food ready in the refrigerator to compete with junk-food snacks, know how to use frozen or canned foods to make inexpensive home-cooked meals, shop wisely, and maintain a good collection of suitable recipes. Consumers must also decipher from all the food advertisements and expert advice what types of foods are appropriate for people with differing needs.

Young children need fat, refined carbohydrates, and easily digestible proteins. For babies there is nothing as good as mother's milk, if physically possible. I found toddler nursing forbidden by our culture when we had our first child. I resented that very much. Seven years later when David was born there was no problem with nursing, thanks to La Leche League.

It is important for all of us to find healthy sources of protein. This is especially tricky for those dealing with diabetes or hypoglycemia, pregnant women, vegetarians, and vegans. Nuts, beans, and gelatin can complement meat, fish, eggs, and dairy. I use fresh soybeans, soy-protein powder, soy flour, roasted soybeans, tofu, low sugar soy milk, soy burgers, and soy cheese. Try mixing natural peanut butter with ground roasted, no-salt soybeans—Robert and I love it. We eat fish several times a week. Adding a little meat to dishes dominated by vegetables or whole grains may provide enough protein for most people.

I feel the best when I minimize the use of fats and refined carbohydrates (white grains and sugar, but also oranges, beets, potatoes, and corn). Whole grains and raw vegetables are essential foods for most adults and more ecological because they require less land and processing. If there is a loose bowel problem, refined grains and cooked vegetables may be necessary.

Fruits have a lot of sugar; fruit juices have even more. It is shocking to compare the volume of sugar we eat with the volume we should eat. Hypertension and high blood pressure is rampant among older adults and often significantly lowered by low-salt cooking, as Robert has found recently. Adults can cut the salt in a recipe and substitute olive oil for other fats without losing good flavor.

When baking desserts, one can halve the fat and use apple-sauce (raw or cooked) for some of the other half if one can cope with the sugar. Bake rather than fry! Adding nuts and milk to desserts increases their nutritional value and may help mitigate the excitability caused by the sugar. Use fruits as sweeteners, limiting the quantity to just barely enough to make the product sweet. I then offer more sweeteners (even decadent ones like sugar and honey) on the side as optional additions.

To create a calcium-rich and relatively sweet, cream-like sub-stance to drizzle over desserts, mix powdered skim milk with double the powder-to-water ratio recommended to make milk. I mix it in a blender. Some like it cold; room temperature is okay with me.

After a breakfast of proteins I feel energized throughout the day. I usually add one-eighth cup of walnuts or sunflower seeds and one tablespoon of soy protein powder (not soy flour) to my sugar-free breakfast cereal—oatmeal, shredded wheat, or Kashi. I should eat more egg breakfasts. I have three-to-five egg serv-ings a week. One serving is usually de-yoked by Robert, with olive oil and dried milk making up the difference. Robert's cho-lesterol is higher than mine. He tries not to have more than two servings (one de-yolked) of two eggs apiece each week.

Drink water. Tap water is generally healthy in North America.[1] Shipping water is a waste. Some households use filtered or dis-tilled tap water and we may experiment with that. Warm water cooled from a boiling tea kettle is comforting to me. For tea, I'

---

1   Municipalities provide free reports on the safety of water. Check yours to learn if there is need for concern. Usually there isn't.

slice and freeze fresh ginger root and use one slice at a time in hot water. One slice lasts me for many cups over several days. After that the ginger root still has enough flavor to go into a cooking project. Other fresh foods such as beans, greens, and cranberries can also be sliced and frozen for future use.

We buy skimmed milk when the price is reasonable. When it's cheaper to make milk from powder, we do that, except when we think visiting milk drinkers might be turned off by reconstituted milk. Nonetheless, milk made from powder is surprisingly good. Don't skimp on the powder and do refrigerate it before use.

I cook with leftovers often. Of course, if there is doubt about the safety or appetizing nature of a leftover, it should be thrown out. We freeze cut-up chicken and hamburger patties for convenience. Dessert bars and bread freeze well too. We can make a cooked turkey last a month.

It is fun to read the labels on packaged food to learn the ingredients and levels of salt (sodium), fat, fiber, protein, vitamins, minerals, and carbohydrates such as sugar. I notice beneficial effects on my body from taking in more fiber, more protein, or less sugar. I am hypoglycemic and my glucose cycles from too high to too low very rapidly unless I carefully balance my proteins, carbohydrates, and liquids. Popular diets emphasize the weight-control advantages from this balance. Check the latest fad diets periodically in the local bookstore; I feel it adds intrigue to the issue.

It is a challenge to treat the body well while eating out. Few restaurants cater to the health conscious and some cannot handle requests to hold the meat, white bread, or salt. I like to order hot water with my restaurant meals and usually do not have to pay for it. Most restaurants do have milk; McDonald's has one-percent milk, most have two-percent. Juices are too seldom available. I hate it when a restaurant serves only soda-pop.

Clothing

I tend to keep clothes even after they have gone out of style, and usually find that years later they are again in fashion. Skirts go up and down from mini to maxi, the toes of shoes are pointy and then squared. Men's lines are more likely to last from one generation to the next. I believe that styles parallel social patterns rather than simply the will of retailers to make money. Thus the rapidity with which women's clothes go out of style has to do with women's vacillating roles in society. When men's lives really do change, so will their day clothes.

We can resist the influence of advertising, but we cannot escape the historical period into which we are born. Male farmers, factory workers, and repairmen of the 1930s and 1940s wore practical uniforms—overalls and one-piece suits of denim, named after the southern French city of Nimes. Overalls were worn over other street clothes if weather allowed, so they were very loose. In the 1980s denim pants became a tight, girdle-like outer garment revealing much, and that sexy effect remains popular as an expression of the libertine attitudes of our times. The hip-hop generation of the 1990s wore very loose denim pants and jackets—the opposite of form-fitting styles—that could reflect confusion about sexuality, worklife, or life in general.

We are what we express or contradict with our fashion statements, and one can simultaneously be ecological and sensitive to the current meanings of fashion. Fixing up stylish clothes to wear, whether new or secondhand, is always a possibility. I do this to a fault. I know both women and men who depend on cleaners and tailors to do their sewing; most women in my generation have some sewing skills. Learning to sew is a pleasure and can be a great way to save resources and money.

The 4-H program was founded in 1902 to help young people develop practical skills such as sewing.[2] My son serves on the 4-H council in Danville, Kentucky. My mother, who earned a Home Economics degree, was a 4-H leader in Plainville, Connecticut. In that capacity she taught a group of my ten-year-old peers to make a sewing bag, a pin cushion, a three-sided thimble-and-thread holder, and a scissors case. I still make pin cushions and bags for odds and ends and passed the skill on to David during his childhood. I use a thimble and recommend getting used to one. With some practice they make sewing easier.

My present sewing bag is commercially made. I keep two smaller bags that I made nestled inside; one carries fabric pieces for patching, the other carries thread and scissors. I can take this kit into a conversation or on a trip, which is fun. In the outer, athletics-sized bag I have mending projects and little bags of recycled ribbon and elastic for use in mending projects. For example, if I decide a pair of underpants is too ragged to mend

2   There were initially three Hs to stand for Head, Heart, and Hands. A fourth H was added to stand for Hustle, and later came to stand for Health.

but the elastic is still taut, I take the elastic off and save it in the scrap bag for re-use when I need elastic to fix something. When I see how long certain kinds of mends keep an item in use, I learn whether or not to mend that type of item again. If a mended article gets a new hole the first time it is worn, I recycle it as a rag and try to remember not to mend the next one like it!

In my sewing bag I have a scissors case that Mother made. I also have a six-sided box, perhaps two inches square, with a flap at the top for access to the inside. In construction it resembles the three-sided thimble holder and the two-sided scissors case. Making this type of holder can be fun:

1. Decide on the shape you want.

2. Cut out two pieces of a cereal box or similar material for each side.

3. Using crisscrossing stitches, sew fabric onto one side of each piece, wrapping 5/8" of the fabric around to the other side of the cardboard.

4. With the fabric-covered sides facing outward, sew together the two pieces that make up each side of the holder. This involves dipping the needle into the fabric along the edges of the pieces. Do not put the needle through the cardboard.

5. Sew the sides together, again dipping the needle into the fabric along the edges of each piece.

I enjoy feeling I invented the cubic thimble holder. I made it while traveling and used the sides of a Saltines box to form my structure. As well as a thimble, in this square box I carry safety pins, needles, and some thread.

Early in my marriage an older married woman taught me that I could mend slacks. They last longer if, when the bottoms of the legs begin to show wear, I bring the hem in just a bit to carry the worn section up inside the pant leg and then apply binding tape to that inside section. When I catch slacks too late to make suitable repairs on the bottoms, I consider making them into shorts. These procedures seem worthwhile when the slacks are made of a good fabric such as wool.

I mend heavy socks with synthetic yarns. I mend cotton socks with three or four fibers of darning cotton. Anything less wears right through.

I was inspired by the youth of the 1990s, who cut the sleeves, bottoms, and necks off of T-shirts to make them more cool and comfortable. I take turtlenecks off knit shirts and hem the new, cooler necklines. I put skirts on T-shirts, inspired by comparable projects on display at art fairs. I have taken two matching T-shirts and cut one to be the skirt for the other. In Oxford, England I bought a big, secondhand, synthetic sweater that had elastic cleverly hand-threaded into the bottom to make it snug at the hip. This winter I stitched 8" matching bands on the waists of tank tops that were not warm enough to wear in dance classes when my navel showed!

Our daughter, a Certified Nurse-Midwife, once requested my thoughts on how to keep white cloth white. The short answer is to identify the source of the stain, apply the appropriate remedy (suggestions appear later in this discussion), and if the stain does not respond to the right process, consider dying the garment a darker color or placing decorations around the stains. The stain-removal question conjured up many memories for me—of the blueberry pie I spilled on a white chintz chair cover in a home where I was babysitting as an adolescent, the khaki sock of Robert's that marbleized over a winter when it was lost outside under our clothesline, and the pain in the neck that rust stains present. During the Great Depression my mother soaked the rags she used for her menstruation in cold water and scrubbed them clean, month after month. We were still using rags for this when I was a teenager! When battles with stains go through my mind, my hands feel itchy, tight, and dry. Although I have defeated many spots, the cost is evident in that feeling.

Over the years I have developed some systems for dealing with stains. The three basic remedies are scrubbing, chemicals, and sunshine. Timing is of the essence in making these procedures ecological and effective. First, if you're using anything besides water, wear appropriate work gloves. Even for safe substances I recommend applying cream to your hands before and afterwards. Soak the stain as soon as possible, but not for long in anything strong or the cloth will disintegrate. Information is needed about the fabric and the stain to know the temperature and chemical of the soak. On cotton and synthetic white fabrics, proteins such as blood, soy products, and egg dissolve in cold water and get worse in hot water. Fruit stains need hot water. Kitchen grease stains respond well to soap or synthetic detergent. Rust needs acid (lemon juice) and sunshine, but remains tough to contend with. Vinegar works well on mildew smells; mildew spots and blood are best addressed with heavy-duty detergent, bleach, several days in the sun, or all of the above. Body odor goes with fresh air. Bicycle grease and gum demand a dry-cleaning fluid. Hot water can shrink wool; stain removers can take some of the fabric's color with them. Do keep a good stain-remover chart handy for advice![3]

The overall whiteness of a piece of cloth is maintained by only washing it with other white or nearly white items. One can safely brighten-up light pastel fabrics that have been washed many times by sending them through with a white load. If there is a general griminess to white or light-colored items, add some bleach to the soap in a wash cycle with a 15-minute soak. Hours, even several days outdoors in the sun also help restore the original brightness to white cotton. When grimy white things do not respond to heavy-duty detergent, scrubbing, bleach, or sun, they can be dyed or tinted a color close to the color they have turned. That's not defeat, that's new life. I have dyed synthetic fabrics and cottons with varied success. Commercial dyes are expensive; I have not found onion skins or English walnuts to be satisfactory dyes. I usually take advantage of the irregular results of tie-dyeing to avoid the difficulty of achieving constant color tones across a large garment.

A splash of strong laundry soap on dirty collars, cuffs, and pockets disintegrates grease, bleaches the dirt, and carries both away in a normal washing. Be careful of bleach: it's lethal and ecologically unfriendly because it kills harmless and needed bacteria. Pure bleach will whiten most colors upon contact and dry human skin. Overnight soaks in bleach destroy many fabrics, although I have a white synthetic napkin that survives for several days in a solution of bleach, soap, and water. New, colored fabrics should be washed alone in a solution of one-quarter cup of salt to each gallon of water, and then washed with items of similar color.

The craft stores sell fabric paints that squirt from narrow bottle openings to form artwork. I have made red flowers and abstract designs over rust spots on our thermal "long johns." The decorated thermal tops even look okay at certain T-shirt-appropriate events. I also squiggled red paint on the faded side of a shoulder bag to make it presentable.

3   For example, see www.cleaning101.com/laundry/fact/staintable.cfm.

Recycling

Our city provides curbside recycling pickup for newsprint, shiny paper and magazines, junk mail, glass, tin, aluminum, and some plastics. We take our substantial volume of cereal and cracker boxes, as well as corrugated cardboard, telephone books, large metal pieces, and Styrofoam to recycling centers. The local Wal-Mart accepts washed and dried plastic bags. The availability of these recycling options is in constant flux and needs to be double-checked constantly. Fortunately, we can take control of many recycling opportunities by creating them at home.

Compost Vegetables, Reuse Minerals, Avoid Animals

Science and ecological reasoning guide the recycling of our material gifts. The old game of *Twenty Questions,* which has players label everything as either "animal" (animals and their by-products, such as leather, wool, and steak), "vegetable" (plants and their by-products, such as wood, coffee, and cotton), or "mineral" (everything else, including metals, plastics, and glass), provides broad and useful categorizations. Most items in the vegetable category decay quickly and can go into a compost bin or a mulch pile, including paper, bread, fruits and vegetables, coffee grounds, and yard trimmings. Do not place animal fats in the compost bin—they become smelly and attract pests. The composted items decompose into rich soil for the lawn and garden after a few months. Good information on composting is readily available.[4]

Most items in the mineral category can be reused or recycled. Success stories include aluminum can recycling: two-thirds of the aluminum ever produced is still in use today.[5] Chapter 7 discusses plastic recycling, which has yet to become a notable success story.

The good news about waste in the "animal" category is that people are relatively successful at avoiding it. The high cost of raising animals and the importance of protein in our diet lead to the relatively efficient use of animals' bodies. What might otherwise become waste turns up in catch-alls such as stews, hot dogs, dog food, and biodiesel fuel. Carcasses become leather, bones become bone meal, blood becomes fertilizer, fine feathers

4   See, for example, www.ct.gov/dep/cwp/view.asp?a=2718&q=325370&depNav_GID=1645.
5   For related information see http://earth911.org/recycling/aluminum-can-recycling.

become down, coarse feathers become feather meal, and so on. If only we could see this level of efficiency in the use of all resources. The sections below work in that direction.

Paper Goods

Junk mail with unused backs can be quartered and used for recipes, addresses, shopping lists, file cards, and scrap paper. Colorful greeting card envelopes can be recycled the same way. I enjoy the presence of color in my files and the opportunity to remember those who sent me the envelopes. I have a stack of large envelopes and a collection of paper bags grouped by size for reuse.

I cut out pictures of sculptures, paintings, and architecture from our magazines and newspapers and keep them in files; it's one of my hobbies. I also save pictures of cows, astronomical phenomena (planets, stars, galaxies), and famous people. I share them with friends who bring up relevant topics in conversation. Mostly I love looking at them when I can.

Many people are recycling gift wrap, gift bags, ribbon, and cards these days. Robert and David like to wrap gifts in the colorful comics section of the newspaper.

Plastic

The bottoms of plastic jugs that carried milk, vinegar, juice, etc., can become storage bins, water catchers below plants, sink-top compost receptacles, and countless art projects. The tops can be recycled. I use two-quart milk cartons to store art supplies and sewing paraphernalia.

Plastic eating utensils from fast-food restaurants are useful for family picnics and children's crafts. The knives cut clay and play dough well and the forks give nice texture to the same. For art projects I save fabric scraps, sawdust, bits of yarn, pieces of wood, and assorted collage ingredients. There is an arts center that recycles craft supplies four miles from my home. Perhaps there is one near you as well.

I have a good collection of small containers for whatever— boxes, cartons, bottles, jug-bottoms, bags, jars, mugs, plastic carry-out containers—and all come in remarkably handy.

To revitalize and expand the volume of play dough, mix in uncooked flour, salt, and sand (optional) in any combination so as to roughly double the size of the original dough ball. If you simply need to firm up some play dough that has become too moist after long storage, do the trick by kneading in white flour and salt. The flour-salt-dough mixture keeps well, and children enjoy the opportunity to help with the mixing.

The remains of candles can be melted together and poured into brass or ceramic dishes over a commercial wick from a craft store to make a new candle. I enjoy this project a lot. Wax can also be poured into a hole made in sand to make sand candles, or into a milk carton filled with ice to make a candle with amazing textures. I wish I could figure out how to make a wick from stuff around the house; so far my experimentation with string and other woven fibers has not been satisfactory.

Miscellaneous

My upbringing involved a lot of making do. Through my formative years my mother would say, "We will have to get along with what we have." Robert does not remember that message coming from his family but he lives that way. At the north end of our wild garden we have a grape arbor Robert made from two discarded lawn chairs. Before it was the grape arbor, one of the chairs had an extension that served as a footrest. The summer I had surgery for an acoustic neuroma and for three months could not sit up without getting a headache, he would strap that chair to our tandem bicycle and, with me on the back bicycle seat, take me to outdoor community events and seat me in great comfort. He made the poles for the pole beans in our garden out of old fencing, and fashioned extensions above the fencing out of bamboo tiki-light holders I found in local students' trash—they have illuminated parties.

With my homemade, four-sided, two-feet-square loom, I am experimenting with the use of elastic bands from worn clothing (shorts, underwear) alternated with yarn as warp, hand woven with strips of fabric to make rag rugs. I have made scarves with yarn warp and weft on the same loom by using only part of the loom's width; I wound two yards of the weft yarn at a time around an H-shaped spindle and conveniently passed it through the warp. For those projects I mixed natural and polyester fibers.

With a mind toward conservation there are many efforts we can make, large and small. As a few more examples: The use of rechargeable batteries saves our natural resources, junkyard space, and money. Office-supply stores sell erasers that can be put over the top of pencils with worn-out erasers. And when I know the water used to clean dishes or scrub floors is not too chemical-laden, I use it to water plants.

Gardens

Choose your plants carefully to avoid frail and fickle species. In Michigan we have particular success with begonias, Moses in the bulrushes, impatiens, moon flowers, hens and chickens, and geraniums. I put some out into the ground and others I leave in pots year round. I usually have way more in the fall than I can bring in. Vegetable gardens are a joy, although they are challenging without artificial fertilizers. We often have ample harvests of tomatoes, squash, pole beans, and peas. Garlic and chives grow voluptuously; the greens, the flowers gone to seed, and the roots are all great flavoring and contain antioxidants. I love to have parsley and crucifer greens grow in the yard. I buy peat moss, bone meal, and manure every spring and add them to the soil in all of my gardens.

When I was little, from the children's song "Oh Playmate, Come Out and Play with Me," I learned that rain barrels were once used, so I put some under our rain spouts. Throughout the growing season I set two cut-off gallon jugs near each barrel and we scoop out free water for our garden. Secondhand receptacles that make good rain barrels appear if you're on the lookout. We made a large rain barrel out of a trash can.

When the weather is dry during the growing season, running the dish and laundry water out to the yard and gardens is a satisfaction: it saves water, gives the runners some exercise, and gets us outside. Detergent bothers some garden pests and water spruces up wilting plants.

I convinced the lawn mower in the family to leave the east side of our house to grow naturally. I ask David to bring up a piece of the ubiquitous limestone from Kentucky every time he visits. We lay the pieces out as stepping stones and mementos of his whereabouts. In the same 10' x 20' area of our yard we have a great show of wildflowers, some of which I have brought in from local fields: milk week, mustard, daisies, several types of asters, and clover. At first I just wanted them everywhere in the yard to make it livelier, but now when weeds volunteer in the regular lawn I either transplant them to my wild garden or put their seeds in the wild section to maintain a sense of order elsewhere.

We put some store-bought perennial wildflowers up next to the house to add to the visual wonders—dramatic or subtle—with colors in the summer and quaint dried weeds the rest of the year. One summer those plants produced blossoms at sundown outside our dining room window. We put commercial birdseed into two feeders in the wild garden and see a regular parade of sparrows punctuated by an occasional mourning dove, chickadee, blue jay, house finch, cardinal, or nut hatch. Annually a few waxwings collect berries from shrubs that mark the line between us and the neighbors. Preschoolers love to visit my wild garden.

Yard Mulch

I once purchased a motorized shredder to turn branches into mulch, but it was embarrassingly noisy and a real hassle to work with. Natural solutions once more prevailed, despite the false promises of high-impact alternatives. We put the fall leaves over the gardens and up against the house to insulate it. Leaves ward off weeds and protect garden perennials from cold winters. We pile yard trimmings around the trees, behind the garage, and at the back of the yard. Trimmings that carry weed seeds are placed in plastic bags to await the city's free yard-waste collections in the fall and spring. Wild morning glories, asters, and dandelions come every year no matter how thoroughly we dig them up. I like it that gardened lawns with natural flowers are becoming popular. In the weeks of the free pickups we take the trimmed overgrowth from its resting places and bundle it. It is such a relief to have it taken away.

Wild Salad Greens

We eat dandelions, garlic mustard, violets, and sweet grass (the one with the darling little yellow flowers) from the lawn to celebrate the coming of spring. Natural tonics may be more necessary than we know. Libraries have books of wisdom on wild foods. I do not eat mushrooms because I don't care for them; if you're a fan, just know what you are eating! Purslane is among many common weeds with valuable nutrients.[6] For the truly adventurous, a variety of insects are edible.[7] All such lawn delicacies become available only in the absence of chemical applications.

---

6   See www.seasonalchef.com/purslane.htm.
7   See, for example, www.eatbug.com.

Scavenging

In the cities it is common to see people picking through trash. Once a friend from New York City described the trash there as a free secondhand store open 24 hours a day. Michigan State University had a "free store" for a short time in the 1960s where people could take what they wanted and bring in donations from home, but it did not last. I volunteered at a homeless shelter that had a free clothing bin where residents could help themselves. Townspeople contributed so profusely that we invited a thrift store to pick up remainders once a month. That system still works. East Lansing and Centre College, among many communities and schools, have offered free bicycles for temporary use. The idea has kinks in that cheap bikes do not hold up well and expensive bikes disappear. I put a "Take Me I'm Free" sign on items at my curb and passers by often snap them up. And, true confession of true confessions, on trash days I bring things home from other people's trash—treasures that include clothes, mirrors, umbrellas (I make skirt extensions for T-shirts out of them), bookshelves, and flower pots.

Money

Sometimes to save the Earth is to save money, sometimes not. Talking about costs was normal in my family. It seemed we had no money during the Great Depression. Nonetheless, my father felt we could have what we wanted and said so often, but was rarely around to hear the requests; mother heard the "I wants..." and had no tolerance for them. I did not know what to think of the problem until I took Family Economics and Consumer Education courses as part of my undergraduate Home Economics curriculum. It helps to keep a budget. Nothing motivates me to limit my spending like writing down what I spend each day, which I did early in our marriage and still do on some vacations. Robert did the same when we traveled abroad. I love not spending much and noting the accomplishment in my notebook. Dieters can do the same thing with food consumption to watch their caloric intake.

Money is one of the serious sources of altercations among people living together. Sooner or later it is bound to crop up. Shopping is unavoidable. Once a household is stocked with basic items, if its members are concerned about cash flow or trash flow, shopping slows down. The first time Robert and I went grocery shopping I bought a shocking $40 worth. I am still spending $40 at the grocery store roughly once a week, but it is not so shocking because inflation has brought prices up eight-fold between 1952 and 2008. We sometimes make purchases to freshen-up the home, for gift giving, and to restock the kitchen and bathroom cabinets. Robert does not mind buying things we can use up, but loathes buying things that require still more shelve and closet space. Better to buy apples than exercise equipment, for example, especially equipment that doesn't get used.

Shopping is an addiction for many Americans, particularly women. In the marketplace people will pay attention to us and try to hear what we are saying; we get to walk around, look at pretty things, touch pleasant things, satisfy needs and wants, and impress people with our acquisitions and gifts. Shopping is also tiring and over-stimulating. It is even more demanding to shop ecologically.

> In the market-place people will pay attention to us.

I talk freely about the costs of purchases. It can be touchy, and bragging is never appropriate, but getting our minds around prices and math is a good idea. Children can become depressed by somber money talk, but having them add and subtract is beneficial. Make a good-natured family exercise out of expenditure decisions. Lately I've been trying to project what savings I need to pay for my care over my last decade. If you've seen nursing home prices you know the cost is high.

The practice of comparing prices can get out of hand, but saving money is worthwhile, even entertaining, and permits pleasant fantasies of what good can be achieved with the money saved. I give myself small budgets. For a while I have not bought a pair of panty hose or a pound of meat for more than $1 without a lot of thought. Robert knows where to find cheap milk and bananas. He can remember prices and compares them at different stores for things like eggs and the *New York Times*. He also notices that the per-unit prices for bulk purchases are often no better than for smaller quantities. I do spot checks of prices, using as much time as I can without wearing myself out.

In comparison with most of the world's citizens, or with people in this country at the time of my birth, many North Americans now enjoy unbelievable prosperity. With household incomes capable of supporting multiple televisions, automobiles, and airline tickets come more opportunities to pollute the universe.

In contrast, most people in the world today, and too many in the United States, are so poor that pollution seems irrelevant to their existence. We are not really living humanely unless we are close to, and empathizing with, the people with the toughest lives anywhere. And the Earth needs everyone to protect it.

With greed rampant there are myriad frauds and fruitless temptations out there. Gambling is one; it is so addictive I do not partake at all. I do not even like to compete for door prizes or invest in stock. Once I had a phone caller claim I had to have some kind of credit union insurance. I went along until he asked for my credit card number, and then I hung up and called the credit union. They said it was a fraud. I have had my long-distance telephone account swiped from a small company by a large one. It took me three hours on the phone to get it straightened out. I find it scary to have people borrow money from me. "Neither a borrower nor a lender be, " wrote Shakespeare in *Hamlet*. It is a challenge to know whose lending requests to take seriously—mostly no one's, I believe.

Being Physical

Get and keep your body in shape as you care for yourself, your family, and your community! To travel by your own power and avoid needless calories is energy efficient.

Sponge baths can be sufficient washing-up for a few days between showers or baths, depending on how sweaty one gets in work and play. Daily baths were unheard of in my childhood; they do relieve strain and lessen the need for deodorants.

Isometric exercise involves a deliberate clinching of muscles. Where we are tense, as in the hands, shoulders, or forehead, clinching the area and then really relaxing it is healthy. Do not clinch the jaw, but make sure it hangs loose. Isometrics are helpful where we are flabby, for instance in the arms, thighs, stomach, and buttocks.

As you go through the day, move your legs and arms in all directions, combining the moves of aerobics, ballet, yoga, and whatever other types of exercise are appropriate for you. Be especially gentle and careful at first, but repeat moves with more vigor to increase the resulting metabolic energy dividend—more calories burned and more energy created. Slow kicks to the rear are a George Foreman recommendation for paring down the buttocks. Alternatively, lay on your back with your knees bent and your arms at your side and hoist your hips up while balancing on your upper back and feet.[8]

While standing, slowly stretch one leg at a time in each direction. Doing knee bends and standing on your toes help otherwise sedentary times become invigorating. Climbing up and down stairs and hills is good exercise. If you can still squat, do not stop; if you can't, work on it. During one-handed tasks such as filling a pan with water at the sink, move the free hand to your back and up to stretch the arm and perhaps scratch the back. Many chores are remarkably good for us physically: digging dandelions, push-mowing the lawn, cultivating, sawing branches, sweeping with a broom, scrubbing clothes and the bathtub, and so on.

Elderly people, among some others, lose their power to get up from the floor. That's another thing to keep working on and it's actually quite good exercise. Self-conscious concentration on correct posture improves it over time. It may be easy and unnecessary to get barrel-chested, pot bellied, bow legged, or bent over. Robert and I walk, jog, and bike often for exercise, and to avoid motorized transportation, which I find less pleasurable, less economical, and harder on the environment. We do drive distances that would be no fun to bike. We also cherish social dancing, which provides the double bonus of being social and being exercise.

Some cultures encourage people to carry things on their heads, shoulders, or backs. It may be strengthening. In Calcutta, India we saw individual men carry refrigerators—that is *not* healthy. Male dancers carry women. I love dances in which women carry men. Carrying babies is a joy. Pushing and carrying loads can be invigorating. I like to carry the trash out and to carry my own luggage, if it's not too heavy!

Healthy habits come more easily when they can be combined with other activities. For example, while reading I have more patience to floss my teeth and exercise. I will share the exercises I have developed with you. Start any of them slowly and concentrate on how you feel. Only do them to an extent that is appropriate for your present health condition. They should *not* hurt. You will get more and more flexible through practice, and

---

8   In Yoga this is called the bridge pose. Visit www.abc-of-yoga.com/yogapractice/thebridge.asp to view an animated illustration of this pose.

it may be best to prepare yourself with small, minimal, or part-of-your-body (isolation) versions of these exercises.

1. To simply lie on your back reading and hold the book above your chest provides exercise for your arms. Begin with a small book that you can hold up with either or both hands. Breathe in and out with your stomach held in.

2. To make a relaxing reading position that stretches the lower back, lying on your back, place a pillow under your lower back just above your waist and another pillow below your shoulders and head.

3. A torso twist can be done lying down, standing, or sitting. Slowly turn your hips in the opposite direction from your upper body. Do it on both sides and hold each position for a count of ten or so. This feels great when you're waiting in line, for instance in a supermarket. If you want to be inconspicuous, pretend you're too lazy to move your feet as you examine something to your right or left.

4. While reclining on my back or either side, I love to pull my thighs up into my stomach. It's centering for me.

5. While reading, consider sitting cross-legged, or with one foot up on the opposite thigh (the yoga half-lotus position), or with both legs up (the full-lotus position).

6. Lying on your stomach and hitching your shoulders up on right-angled elbows is a conventional reading posture. It is also a good stretch for the lower back.

7. Getting down on ones' knees for anything is great exercise. Some say praying there is good for the soul.

Opportunities to exercise are a gift, and a great substitute for boredom, fossil-fuel-fed transportation, ill health, and needless shopping. Some social groups even make a habit of taking long, brisk walks around the interior of shopping malls—a superior use of those buildings after all.[9]

Getting Along

Sometimes the act of treading lightly requires emotional strength and ambition, which makes it all the more important to avoid the strain of interpersonal conflict.

From my experiences it appears that many people, myself included, are hung up on self-defeating issues related to childhood. The most compelling book on the topic is *Letting Go of Mother* by James M. McMahon. The title may be sufficiently self-explanatory.

Only correct the behavior of others with great sensitivity. My friends in the field of social work tell me that every criticism one makes—even the most greatly needed and carefully delivered suggestion—should be balanced with perhaps two dozen positive comments to mend the receiver's ego and self-confidence.

Wise advice or requests are delivered in terms of "I" messages, such as, "I feel nervous when you play that loud music. Is there any way you can help me with that?" Or, "I feel upset when you don't respond to me because I feel ignored." I recommend *Sticks and Stones* by John Cooper to help the child within each of us receive corrections gracefully. Another key to getting along is to make it clear that you want to be kind and honest about difficult issues. Demonstrated respect will get you far. We may not need to correct things that annoy us as often as we do; drawing that line is hard, I know.

Do not hold grudges—find a way to release them! Learning one's weakness from one's enemies is something to finally be thankful for, if we can get over being defensive, even angry about it. Jealousy and other aggravations are always with us. If internal salves do not keep one from being unreasonable, counseling with friends, pastors, or other professionals is necessary. One should be alert to anger and anxiety as warning signs and mitigate them carefully. They can be unnecessary defenses needing special consideration.

Being kind, especially to people of lower physical or social stature, gives one a good opinion of one's self, but doing it for

9   See http://walking.about.com/od/beginners/a/mallwalking.htm, www.time.com/time/magazine/article/0,9171,956980,00.html.

that reward is not as comforting as doing it because it is there to be done. See Soren Kierkegaard's *Purity of Heart* for a nourishing though challenging read on related topics.

Adolescent awkwardness is repeated in elders' arthritic clumsiness and short-tempered states. Children and grandparents may thus understand each other better than children and parents. The more mutual acceptance and appreciation, the better.

Sometimes Robert and I cut our own hair, sometimes we cut each others'. My son David cuts his own and his children's hair. For an amateur haircut to go well requires self-confidence and some genius on the part of the cutter, and trust by the owner of the hair. I view it as a good opportunity to receive a scalp massage.

Male-female relationships seem to be more challenging than same-sex relationships, probably because of differences between men and women, both social and genetic. Twenty years ago I was taught that men want to be told how great their accomplishments are and that women want to be told they were loved. Recently the difference is being stated this way: women want to be validated, men want to be criticized minimally, if at all. Living amid the "battle of the sexes" is not easy, but it is necessary and worth it. To achieve the good life, recognize and accept inevitable differences with the wisdom of patience and hope, short of self-defeating decisions such as to accept abuse! Conceit changes nothing for the better. Strident fanatical attitudes such as misogyny (female hating) or misandry (male hating) are dangerous and harmful.

Newspaper stories often describe physical or emotional abuse of children, lovers, spouses, elders, prisoners, laborers, and animals. I suppose most people have endured some form of abuse. Self-abuse is also common. A great antidote for self-abuse is to learn not to have such high expectations—this makes life easier for everyone involved.

It is a major, though less-discussed challenge to explain things and give instructions to others. Patience and practice help. Realize that it is not simple to convey wisdom, and that procedures that are easy the second time can be very difficult the first time. Newer teachers have an advantage because they more-likely remember how hard it was to pick up the concepts they are teaching. Writing out instructions can help one explain ideas more effectively because information gaps become more evident on paper.

The practice of good manners is an element of success. Using napkins, holding doors and coats and chairs, saying please and thank you, and giving respectful introductions are great things to do with adults and children. These courtesies demonstrate respect and thereby lessen tension. Notice that we are most comfortable with our friends, in part because we are assured that they respect us.

At times it makes good sense to take the road less traveled. Doing unusual, eccentric, even weird things is sometimes incidental, sometimes Earth-shattering. If your friends do not tread lightly, you might be the first among them to recycle, have a natural lawn, breast-feed in public, or wear clothing from thrift stores. In safe settings it is fruitful to include among your acquaintances people who are mentally, physically, or social aberrant, grotesque in appearance, young, old, or in other ways unusual. We don't learn much from clones of ourselves. I am amazed by the gems of knowledge I pick up from people who are generally treated as outcasts.

I feel for the public officials who take moral responsibility for public money, power, and security. Running for election, holding office, hearing public concerns, and shaping public policy requires talent, skill, and hard work. As I vote, write letters, speak up, support, or boycott, I try to be grateful for what is being done by public officials that is holding our society together. To help them tread lightly, among other things, is to be a good citizen—a high calling.

Free and Almost-Free Joys

Reading is a joy. Organized book discussions allow that satisfaction to resonate. National Public Radio, newspapers, and magazines offer clues to wise living. This week I read of milk-based paint and a celebrity who does not paint or varnish her wooden floors, but leaves them "sandy." News articles about the dwindling natural resources are great motivators. As supplies of oil, fresh water, and aquatic species, for example, grow small enough to elicit conflict, I get ideas from the media on how to be a better steward of these blessings.

Robert and I have gone to lectures, concerts, plays, movies, poetry readings, and art shows since we began seeing each other in 1949. When we had no money and when we did have children, we went out less and enjoyed more hobbies, crafts, and board games at home. We try to expand our familiarity with culture; we discuss current events with friends. We have not watched TV much, but that may be in our future, particularly in mid-winter when traveling is difficult and we have colds. I particularly find that theatre, with its usual catharsis of emotions, clears my mind. It is trendy to listen to jazz and blues music in coffeehouses and pubic squares where the rhythms of our youth are revived. We love it. As a break from work and play, these public events are great fun, green, and free.

Try meditation, not "shop therapy," when you're feeling dissatisfied with your life: relax your body, clear your mind of what worries you cannot fix, figure out what the next steps are in the worthwhile projects that lie ahead, and then put them aside. Cool down your feelings and thoughts until they are where you want them—perhaps they are on hold, in a "happy place," or in a religious realm. Time for calm reflection is time well spent.

I want to spark your imagination with a few deeply satisfying opportunities that are free:

- Look at three-dimensional objects like an artist posed to figure out how to reproduce shapes and colors on a two-dimensional sheet of paper. On winter nights the sky can become a canvas of pastel tones with pink (even in the middle of the night!), orange, blue, lavender, purple, and green. It's wonderful. The concept of translating three-dimensionality onto flat surfaces was introduced to many of us in school; it is fun to rehearse the visual exercise. Notice where shadows fall and how they are in different places at different times of the day and year. The shadows to the north are much longer in the winter than in the summer. It is fascinating to see reflections and contrast them with reality. Keen visual observations feed rich thoughts, conversations, and artistic experimentation.

- To write poetry, one needs simply a pencil and paper and a belief in one's flow of consciousness. The writings may not sell, but they are heart rendering. You may enjoy sharing your writing with friends and family. Be sure to save it in a computer file or a drawer. It is incredible to reread poetry written through the years.

- It is great to keep a journal and Robert has done so since our youth; I'm ready to try my hand at fiction writing.

- Satisfaction comes from making music and listening to the beloved music of others. On my MP3 player I carry a recording of my granddaughter singing *The Twelve Days of Christmas*.

- Special joys come from shared affection at appropriate levels according to your relationship.

- I make our holiday cards with common art materials: ink, crayons, fabric, recycled paper, and paint. Robert makes cards for other occasions at home with a software program.

- Release the creativity inside you by designing, sketching, and assembling small masterpieces of art—it is frugal and worthy. Crafts such as knitting, embroidery, and crochet are taught in Community Education Centers, craft shops, and fabric stores.

- The intricacies of mathematics are entertaining to meditate on, as are all kinds of puzzles and brainteasers. It is healthy for the brain to learn new vocabulary and to concentrate on the correct spelling of words.

- In the winter it feels good to sit inside in the sunshine that is flowing through a window. In the summer it is pleasant to recline on a blanket outside in the shade.

- Complex situations can boggle the mind but feel good to work through, such as reading a map with a standard north-on-top orientation while traveling south, or turning a sewing project inside-out and keeping in mind how the outside will look as a result of what is done on the inside.

- Visually taking in the skeletons of trees in the winter is a quieting and absorbing project. To survey the colors and textures of trees in all seasons is satisfying. Listening to nature increases sensitivity to our surroundings.

- Our humanity is magnified when we savor every hello and goodbye, rethinking how it sounded, what it implied, and how it made us feel.

- It is a pleasure to walk, hike, run, or bike.

- For peace of mind, clean a junk drawer, sorting, reorganizing, and putting away misplaced stuff. The same goes for the car glove compartment, a cellar shelf, a pantry, a closet. Not only do I feel better to have things in good order, but I become so overwhelmed by reminders of all the junk I already own that I am pleased *not* to be out acquiring more.

- Local bus rides expose us to incredible people.

You may have a very different list of activities you enjoy, but whether it is playing charades, taking a bubble bath, caroling, or bird-watching, everyone can find true joys that are free.

Group Art

There are economical ways to enjoy participation in our communities. Churches, charities, schools, community education centers, and local governments all offer opportunities to be involved and help neighbors. My favorite form of community service addresses the tedium and tension of life by presenting art, writing, dance, and drama as healthier coping mechanisms than, say, alcohol, gambling, illicit sex, and drugs.

Setting children up to do art is a precious adult skill. It gives the children a chance to create things and puts them in touch with their self worth. Putting out art projects for families or adults is also fun. Assemblages of glued-together toothpicks, yarn pieces, felt bits, sand, macaroni, bottle caps, paper, etc., on cardboard are self-expression at its best. Little children can be taught to rip and glue paper into grand collages. Paper grocery bags can be flattened out for chalk, crayon, or paint artistry. Make useful artwork out of tin cans, cardboard boxes, cigar boxes, and similar containers by gluing on fabric, glitter, feathers, yarn, cut-outs from magazines, and colorful scraps of all types. The containers thereby become attractive pencil holders, photo boxes, marble bins, dice shakers, or whatever you please. We have a pencil holder of this type in nearly every room of the house.

Some families keep art supplies and construction toys in bags. I keep mine in boxboard or plastic two-quart milk or juice containers on the top shelf of my kitchen cupboard, bringing down a few at a time as needed and constantly replenishing them. At the homeless shelter where I volunteered there are gallon-sized bins lined up on shelves to hold scissors, play dough, wood for crafts, and scrap paper. I have added a fabric-for-sewing shoe box.

Save art projects in piles or files, framed or not on walls and shelves, or in scrapbooks. Assemblages and many painting projects can be brushed with a mixture of one part white glue and two parts water to help them last for decades. Children in the homeless shelter are preoccupied by whether their artwork is on display. Showcasing it is another costless joy. Paintings can be laminated and kept for posterity.

It is valuable to help children and adults see the virtues of abstract art. As with fashion, art reflect the times. Given the current instability of nature and humanity exemplified by ongoing global climate change and war, abstractions express the human search for reliability. Of course, toddlers begin their art lives with abstract scribbles. If adults do not join them in enjoying these expressions, the children become ashamed of their innate responses to life. Preschoolers advance beyond the abstract to make adorable people and objects that resemble drawings from societies whose art we call primitive. Teenagers can depict the physical world in great detail and may limit their art to replicating nature, sometimes with formal instruction, which is fine so long as the artists do not feel confined by that art form. Anything can be expressive in the art world. Vincent Van Gogh, for example, makes trees expressive. The history of art, with its great masters such as Van Gogh, can be yet another inexpensive and low-impact avocation.

Frustrations

Many questions remain about how to lead a satisfying life. To state a few of my own:

- How do I most ecologically clean tea stains from a teapot?
- How can I remove paint without breathing the toxins in the paint removers or the scrapings?
- How can I persuade my neighbors and city against herbicides and pesticides?
- How can we remind the business world of its reliance on the natural world for resources?
- When will we have community centers for all age groups that want them—good alternatives to shopping out of boredom!
- Does anyone really pickle hardboiled eggs for consumption? How?
- Where does one find literature on antidotes for know-it-all, bossy, controlling people?
- How can we get more community fun for kids?

Mimicking common trends, the playground across the street does not allow basketball playing except when a summer camp is in session, nor does the downtown allow skateboarding or teen loitering. I understand the drawbacks, but I believe ongoing talent shows of our teens and young adults playing sports and skateboarding are better than alternative sources of excitement for young people, which might involve sex, drugs, or various other crimes. Downtowns become entertainment centers by merely filling them with people. Manhattan exhibits that reality today. Fifty years ago people in towns large and small would congregate downtown on Friday nights to see and be seen. In Fulton, New York, the downtown place to be was called "dizzy block." In Madrid, Spain, in the afternoon after siesta time it is tradition for people of all types to take walks in their neighborhoods. Walking together as a community sounds good to me—it's good for the body and soul, and a lot better than watching television or going to the mall.

When tasks become frustrating, my husband's advice is to be content with a small amount of progress as we chip away at a problem. He had a full-time career for 42 years, plus some manual labor and service jobs in his second and third decades. Now in his 80th year, he is back teaching at Michigan State University part time. He has paced himself well. As part of every endeavor there are chores that are a bore or a pain. That's when it pays to do a little at a time and divide big jobs into daily doses. I cannot knit for hours at a time, but 30 minutes of knitting provides a good rest. I usually do not read a whole book in a day, but I chip away at one. Digging dandelions in the spring is not too bad for around an hour. I wash used sandwich bags out a few at a time, mend only when I'm in the mood, and bit-by-bit take worn-out items apart to recycle or discard—the defunct dehumidifier from our cellar, the old piano, the rocking chair. Each would cost a lot to have taken away whole.

> **Do a little at a time and divide big jobs into daily doses.**

Not so much to get things done as to make life interesting and avoid frustration, I find chores to fill brief waiting periods. I actually cook a lot in such budgeted times. Step by step, bread can be made over several hours, even days. As one gains exposure to bread recipes it becomes easier to pick varieties that can be made in the time available. If you want bread in half an hour, quick breads such as biscuits and muffins can be made on the spot. If you have ten minutes now and you want fresh-baked bread in a few hours and some more tomorrow, you can get the yeast, liquid, and flour together and knead it in that time for the first rising. Roll some of the dough out and bake little loaves from that; knead the rest and let it rise again overnight for another loaf or biscuits tomorrow.

Finally

Finally things wear out. A wonderful part of the last decades of life is the ability to see items we have mended and saved—sheets, clothing, shoes—disintegrate, just when we are not going to need them anymore. In the end, homes and bodies, like fabrics and paper goods, go beyond repair. The supplies are used up. "Junk" jewelry breaks and should be put into a child's dress-up set or a box of craft supplies. The bookcases, bureaus, tables and chairs do not need replacing but can be sold as rummage or given away. I find that a big relief. Cherish the release of responsibility for such possessions, just as you cherished capturing their vitality at an earlier stage.

Robert and Elizabeth express their objection to the Iraq war.

Photo by Frank Dennis (2008)

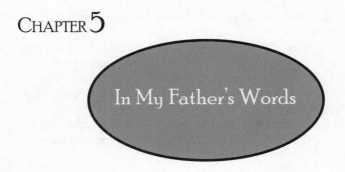

CHAPTER 5

In My Father's Words

The Ethics and Religion of Materialism

It is said that the Greek cynic philosopher Diogenes, "... on seeing a boy drink water from his hand, forthwith took his cup from his wallet and broke it, upbraiding himself with these words: 'Fool that I am, to have been carrying superfluous baggage all this time!' and then curled himself up in his tub and lay down to sleep ... ."[1] Diogenes, born in the late 5th century B.C.E., advocated the "simple" life and purportedly roamed the streets of Athens looking for someone who exemplified it. *Treading Lightly* explores the need, nature, and possibility of such a life, particularly in a highly affluent and complex culture.

Even the Bible seems conflicted in its talk about wealth. In the Hebrew Bible the title character in the Book of Job was a perfect and upright man as evidenced by the great wealth that God gave him.[2] God also rewards Solomon with great wealth. The Deuteronomic School that edited most of the Hebrew Scripture (Old Testament) emphasized the prosperity that will accrue to those who are good. But Ecclesiastes, the cynical Old Testament book, declaims the ephemeral significance of wealth as do many New Testament writers. James 5:1 warns, "Come

1   Seneca, *Epistulae Morales* 90:14-16.
2   Job, Chapter 1.

now, you rich people, weep and wail for the miseries that are coming to you."[3]

Material goods are indeed good and necessary. Diogenes needed the water if not the cup. At the same time they are detrimental and an obstacle to our fulfillment. We need to have goods in order to survive, but in the wrong combinations or quantities, they destroy us and leave future generations bereft.

I like the imagery in a curious passage in one of the apocryphal books that are esteemed, but not accepted as canon by some faiths:

> What can we show for all our wealth and arrogance?
> All those things have passed by like a shadow, like a
> messenger galloping by; like a ship that runs through
> the surging sea, and when she has passed, not a
> trace is to be found, no track of her keel among the
> waves; or as when a bird flies through the air, there
> is no sign of her passing, but with the stroke of her
> pinions she lashes the insubstantial breeze and parts
> it with the whir and the rush of her beating wings,
> and so she passes through it, and thereafter it bears
> no mark of her assault; or as when an arrow is shot
> at a target, the air is parted and instantly closes up
> again and no one can tell where it passed through.[4]

There are two important messages here. The first is that wealth is ephemeral—in the long run it does not mean much. The other is that our lives should move through our environment without leaving a mark. Neither ship, nor bird, nor arrow has hurt the environment through which it has passed. Each has treaded lightly. It is no longer possible to become wealthy or hold wealth without harming the environment. Hopefully we all arrive at meaningful fulfillment. Hopefully our harm to our surroundings is minimal in making that arrival, and hopefully fulfillment does not depend on the destruction of our pathway—the environment through which we pass. In fact, the pathway determines both our destination and a proper means of getting there.

Many friends and readers do not share this affirmation of simplicity. Many have thought it through and will not agree. I hope these writings will enrich a dialog that can be meaningful

3   James 5: 1-6.
4   Wisdom of Solomon 5:8-12.

to all of us. Many simply have been caught in the great swirl of our materialistic culture and are not particularly self-conscious or intentional in their attitudes toward the material world. Hopefully they will be drawn into a more intentional lifestyle.

Current Status

This book seeks to define a line between necessary and distracting consumerism. Part of the argument is that real fulfillment has little to do with material things. That is fortuitous because the other part of the argument is that we are experiencing a delicate balance between resources and demands. We begin with a look at the current status of resources and consumers. The ultimate goal is that the number of winners can be maximized and the number of losers can be minimized in the scramble for control of those resources. In contrast, while the United States creates 700,000 new millionaires each year;[5] four million newborn babies die annually in the developing world,[6] and three billion people live in dire poverty.[7] Let us consider different ways of playing the game of life—especially the basic game of human use of the Earth.

This chapter is grinding an axe, hopefully with sensitivity and good spirit. A value judgment has been made: There is a better way to use goods. That judgment comes from several experiences. I lived much of my life before the "disposable culture," so I was not accustomed to the waste that it entails, and I grew up with a natural disposition to make things last. My generation's tendency to conserve was augmented by the fact that much of our youth was lived in the aftermath of the Great Depression when a weak economy encouraged frugal use of resources. I think I also had a "graduate student" mentality for a fairly long period in my life—certainly longer than I was a graduate student. I spent ten years accumulating three degrees, and with minimal income, frugality was necessary. It was a hard mentality to shake.

Those reasons are practical rather than moral. The moral inclinations came more subtly. Pictures and talk about starving children made me sensitive to poverty in the world at a very young age. Between my undergraduate work and my entry into a Ph.D. program I went to a liberal theological seminary that was very social-action oriented. It gave articulation and new vistas to any propensity I had to be concerned about the world. The seminary was characterized by the *Readers Digest* as part of the "Pink Fringe" of Methodism. This was in the early 1950s during the McCarthy era. With some of my professors and some of my fellow students, I was catching the vestigial remnant of American socialism. Once I was part of a small group that chatted with Norman Thomas, the perennial socialist candidate for president of the United States. While I was not interested in the party, I did find the idealism meaningful.

In addition to Thomas there were other role models who inspired me. Those included several of the faculty at the seminary, Mahatma Gandhi in India, and missionaries who went on educational and health missions to deprived countries at considerable sacrifice given the lifestyles of the cultures in which they were raised. In India I met Father Fallon, a Belgian Jesuit priest who taught English literature at Jadawpur University. He lived in a small room in the midst of a Hindu neighborhood, sleeping on a wood plank bed beneath a Roault head of Christ. Daily he gathered the skirt of his priestly robes and bicycled seven miles to his university. Tourists sometimes live like the natives for a few days to have experiences to share with friends or feed into a book. His situation was different: for him there was no going back. He would never settle into a comfortable parish outside Brussels or seek fame as a writer or preacher. He had given up that life. For thirty years he had been in Calcutta bringing talent to people from whom he also learned.

> **A galloping materialism has made me increasingly concerned.**

That year in Calcutta and another spent in Cairo represented experiential meditations on the distribution of goods. In more recent years a galloping materialism has made me increasingly concerned about goods and their distribution.

What is the good life and what are the appropriate means of attaining it? It is rather startling that despite our culture's preoccupation with goods, almost no philosophy or theology holds material things to be the ultimate good. A rational definition of goods and the right way to attain them are subjects of ethics, a captivating discipline I studied at Syracuse University long ago under T.V. Smith, one of the founders of the *University of Chicago Round Table* program on NBC radio. I primarily studied the writings of Kant, Mills, Bentham, Rawls, Brunner, Ramsay and Niebuhr. They led me to ask, "What material goods are necessary as a means toward attaining whatever is ultimately 'the' good of goods? And what is the optimal amount of material goods that an individual or society can meaningfully and responsibly own?" Between too little and too much there may be two other definable amounts—the minimum amount required for life to be worth living and the optimal amount to make the most of life.

Then, how do we arrive at a fair distribution of at least minimal amounts of goods both across regions and between the present and the future so that all, or at least an optimal number of people, have at least the minimum amount? It is easy to question the fairness of the fact that people in the United States consume a grossly disproportionate share of the world's resources.

After both of my extended stays in developing nations it was a shock to return to the United States. Having become somewhat accustomed to the scarcity of goods in less prosperous countries, I was startled by the abuse of resources here in the West. Much of this centered around the ubiquitous automobile that demands so much paved land, burns so much energy, and saddles us with so much pollution. To return after a visit to impoverished areas of Asia or Africa is to be devastated by both the difference in lifestyles and the callous self-centeredness it reflects. I hold side-by-side the images of a bloated SUV and a severely malnourished child in front of a squalid hut.

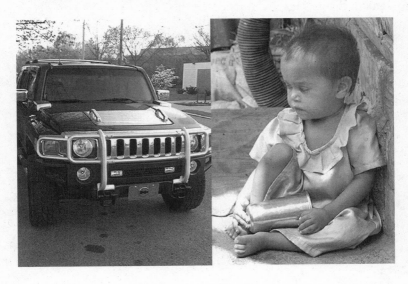

What percentage of the resources is it fair for the current generation to deplete? In order to survive it is necessary for the present population to use up some of the limited supplies. But can it claim any more resources than are demonstrably necessary or renewable? In the background is the serious possibility that critical elements of life on Earth will be irreplaceably lost on our watch. I hold that possibility in the back of my mind each time I turn off a light switch or turn the furnace thermostat down a notch. I feel I may be putting off the demise of resources just a little longer.

Ethos, the spirit or temper characteristic of our culture, is also relevant because ethos directs society's perception of the ultimate good. Material wealth need not be seen as that ultimate good. In the Middle Ages, theology could tout itself as the "Queen of the Sciences" with all the implicit affirmations that God and a religious life could lead individuals to a meaningful existence. In the early 19th century, Georg Wilhelm Friedrich Hegel saw the university as the center of culture, and philosophy as the focal point of the university and thus the focus of meaning. In the mid-20th century, Lionel Trilling could confidently assume that the depth of the human experience was best understood through literature. Indeed, "They who read best, live best and know the most."[8] Today, the disciplines of theology, philosophy, and literature claim barely any turf on an American campus, where the technical colleges, business school, and attendant disciplines are considered the main *raison d'être* of the university—or of humanity itself.

The priorities in academe are symptomatic of the current preoccupation with materialism (salaries and goods) in our culture as both the route and the goal of fulfillment. Religion, philosophy, literature, and traditional education are *passé*. Imagine the parody of a visit to the site of the Sermon on the Mount juxtaposed with the presence of contemporary values. The odor of diesels from tour buses would fill the air, venders would wander the grass hawking hot dogs and beer, stalls would sell T-shirts emblazoned with slogans like "My Folks Got to Touch Jesus' Robe and all I Got is this Lousy T-shirt." Jet skis would race up and down the Sea of Galilee. Television networks would argue over camera location. Small aircraft would pull trailing signs

---

8   John Sutherland in a review of Cynthia Ozick's *Quarrel and Quandary, New York Times,* October 8, 2000, Book Review section, p. 6.

reading, "Seek ye first Bob's Deli" or "Why walk the second mile when you could be riding a Panasaki."

Hegel ruminating in the park on the great issues of life would be no less humorous. His view would be blocked by his SUV which, for convenience, would be parked in front of the bench upon which he sat to meditate. The majestic mountains beyond him would be invisible behind a billboard advertising an elegant, smooth whiskey or an able plaintiff's attorney. Any meditation would be interrupted by frantic attempts to dislodge his ringing cell phone from his pocket. An unmuffled power mower would circle the park endlessly.

Literature as a pathway to insight has been eclipsed by a variety of electronic entertainment devices of ever increasing complexity. For better or worse, books themselves are being transformed into electronic forms such as audiobooks and e-books, but so far electronic books are not selling like Nintendo games.

Gabriel Marcel, a 20th-century remnant of both theology and philosophy, anticipated the power of the encroaching obsession with stuff: "We are tempted to think that no longer having anything is the same as no longer being anything: and in fact the general trend of life on the natural level is to identify one's self with what one has: and here the ontological [being, as opposed to having] category tends to be blotted out."[9]

After the necessity of having a body, where does one draw the line in terms of what one must have? That is the crucial issue. It seems that as our acquisitions increase arithmetically, our desires increase geometrically. The temptation is to feel that an infinite amount of goods is required for the protection and sustenance of the body. Drawing the line is an essential task of this book as it is of each individual and society.

How We Got Here

In large part money and material goods have been sucked into the vacuum created as religious, nationalistic, and cultural (aesthetic) institutions have eroded. The collapse of the Middle Ages was inevitable, but a monumental trauma nevertheless. Western culture had evolved a comprehensive culture of stories and symbols that made sense of human existence. Inevitably the internal adhesive of that culture deteriorated as the stories and symbols

9   *Being and Having,* Marcel Press, 2007, p. 84.

lost their power. This was unavoidable because societies are dynamic and finite, and *willy nilly* cannot last. I describe the implosion of the Middle Ages because it is relevant to the progression of society, but not as a call to relive that period.

More recently, "political correctness" has eroded narrow value systems such .as masculine business models, "Western art," and the "Protestant ethic," which are seen as intentionally or unintentionally imperialistic. "Male," "Northern European," and "Protestant" have been the dominant frames of reference and it is important that they, in particular, not exercise unfair influence in a pluralistic culture. Many past religious, philosophical, artistic, and literary values of our culture are products of some combination of privileged groups, so their sanction has appropriately been undercut.

Money and the material it buys are the only tangible "goods" that transcend virtually every subgroup in this country, in that regardless of their religion, political affiliation, ethnic group, or first language, everyone in America knows what a dollar is. Wealth-based prestige takes center stage and places us in our present dilemma of trying to establish non-materialistic values in a culture that has only one universally acknowledged good—materialism. All non-materialistic values carry the stigma of biases in that they are uniquely associated with a particular sub-culture—unless we can create a new value system that is a product of our new situation.

By law and societal consensus, schools cannot teach political, cultural, or religious values, but they can teach material success. Universities have become increasingly limited to vocational rather than cultural education. They collude with other parts of society in highlighting frequent polls indicating which jobs pay the most. The university is being transformed into a narrower institution that can safely affirm two major values: athletics and vocational education.

Vocationally focused training is legitimate, but it should not be equated with genuine education. One of the most impressive books I have read in the last decade is Gary Will's *Lincoln at Gettysburg*. Of relevance is his convincing case that Lincoln could articulate a vision for America because he knew the visions of great minds of the past—poets, philosophers, religious teachers, and politicians. Lincoln was not only vocationally trained, he was educated. A serious problem for so many institutions of our time, including our government and our universities, is that their representatives cannot articulate a vision. Often the reason is clear—they are cut off from the great minds of the past. They are not truly educated. That confusion facilitates thinking exclusively of material goods as means and ends to fulfillment.

Likewise athletics should not be passed over too lightly in any discussion of either the university or the society as a whole. Its importance is indicated by the extent of sports pages in the media, sports on television, contributions earmarked for sports at universities, and time spent discussing sports. They play a significant role in giving meaning and focus to lives. They transcend gender and ethnicity. But they can also detract from a balance in values, and more and more, the most remarkable aspect of athletics is the salaries paid to athletes. This preoccupation eclipses other dimensions of sports, including health, cooperation, skill development, loyalty, and self-discipline.

Responding to Critics

Many opinions differ from what is presented here. Most have been forcefully articulated. This book emerges as a voice that does not find those contrary positions compelling.

Some people want to say, "There really isn't a problem!" Peter Huber, in his book *Hard Green,*[10] wants to reassure us that the abuse of resources never was a problem and need not be one. His type has characterized people like me as "Chicken Little's" running about exaggerating the dangers of the world. He acknowledges that there have been some problems, but feels that they have been overcome. He knows that there will continue to be problems in the future, but is content that we will find ways to resolve them. Certainly science and technology have performed miracles and we can presumably expect more.

Before the 2000 election, the top environmental advisor for Republican George W. Bush, Christopher DeMuth, characterized Democratic candidate Al Gore as a "romantic" environmentalist and George W. Bush as a "practical" environmentalist.[11] The implication of the former accusation fits with the "tree hugger" label and other insinuations that people concerned about the environment are obsessed with a lifestyle that is not transparently the highest value. "Okay," they say, "so some people flee to

10 New York: Basic Books, 2000.
11 See http://findarticles.com/p/articles/mi_qn4155/is_20001023/ai_n13888435.

Montana because they want to live in the wilderness. But others flee to Manhattan because they want to live in the city. Neither group should impose their preference on all." There is even an implication that the romantic style is the lesser choice because it hinders production and wealth, the major values of our time. Of course, if one group exploits the environment, they preempt others from any choice.

On the issue of global warming, the line has already changed. The "contraries" in the 1980s were denying there was any global warming. In the 1990s they agreed that there was a natural warming, but claimed it had nothing to do with greenhouse gases. In 1995, university, government, and industry scientists predicted a worst-case scenario of a 6.3° F rise in global temperatures by 2100.[12] The worst-case prediction was raised to 10.8° F in 2000 when the Intergovernmental Panel on Climate Change, the most authoritative scientific voice on the issue, issued a report emphasizing that the problem is real and that the Earth is likely to get a lot hotter than previously predicted.[13] As we approach 2010, many of the contraries concede the involvement of humans, but grasp to shortsighted silver linings, such as the idea that climate change is a good thing because it will cause better crops. Don't count on it—scientists conclude otherwise.[14]

The contentions of the contraries on global climate change are corollaries of the "There really is no problem" stance on resource depletion. There is certainly hope and precedence for the development of new materials and energy by harnessing previously untapped resources. On the other hand, all resources are finite, and this solution, too, sounds short term. Huber is willing to consider an exhausted-resources scenario and says, "Cut down the last redwood for chopsticks, harpoon the last blue whale for sushi, and the additional mouths fed will nourish additional brains, which will soon invent ways to replace blubber with Olestra and pine with plastic. Humanity can survive just fine in a planet-covering crypt of concrete and computers."

The thought of an existence in a concrete crypt sounds pretty ghastly—quite apart from the possibility of even creating such an existence.

Particularly in the early stages of space exploration it was

---

12 H. Josef Hebert, Associated Press, *Lansing State Journal,* Oct. 26, 2000, 3A.
13 See www.ipcc.ch/press/sp-cop6-2.htm. Note that 10.8° F equals 6° C.
14 See, for example, www.sciencedaily.com/releases/2002/09/020919065913.htm.

possible to envision the National Aeronautics and Space Administration (NASA) as a new Noah, constructing a new ark that would deliver a doomed people from a dying planet. We could be delivered to the moon or Mars, which could have untapped resources. We might even develop a self-contained space ship. While these speculations can hold out glimmers of hope, most of us are condemned to a future on this planet.

Individualistic opportunism is still an option. "Greed is Good" is a slogan argued in the purported speech of Gordon Gekko in the movie *Wall Street*. Western capitalism sanctions an enormous system of focused personal acquisition and accepts and necessitates compromises with moral, cultural, and environmental values in the name of high-yield investments. Through intensive advertising, manufacturers glamorize the conspicuous gathering and consumption of material goods. These goods, it is held, provide the incentive to make people productive, disciplined, and moral—for example, it is argued that with more goods and money, people will be less inclined to steal.

It is questionable whether material goods are necessary or even the best motivators. There is plenty of evidence, ranging from *Survivor*-type reality television shows to the brutality of totalitarian regimes and corporations, that competition brings out the worst rather than the best in people. There is an increasing gulf between the rich and the poor, and even if the poor are doing better, there are too many Americans living beneath the poverty level. Perhaps of most importance, material goods distract us from the real good.[15]

One influential dimension of the "Protestant Ethic" is the notion that the "saved" are rewarded by God with wealth. That is one interpretation of Calvinism—not that works are rewarded with wealth, but that wealth is a mark of having been saved. One of the more dramatic expressions of it in this country was a sermon, "Acres of Diamonds," given many times by the evangelical preacher Russell Conwell. The main point of the sermon was not bad: we can look in all the wrong places for "wealth," only to find it in our own backyard. But Conwell meant wealth in a very literal sense and said that while he was sympathetic with the poor, it was God's will that the poor are poor and we should not interfere. He reiterated that wealth is a sign of Divine

---

15 A recent statement of the opposing position is found in Dinesh D'Sousa's *The Virtue of Prosperity*, New York: The Free Press, 2001.

approval and exclaimed, "So I say to you, "Get rich! Get rich! Get rich!" There is a lingering echo of this affirmation in reservations about the "welfare state." We can feel that the needy somehow deserve their fate because of a lack of ambition or bad habit, if not Divine Will.

The Judeo-Christian tradition which colors and sanctions much of the thinking of Western civilization on the issue of wealth (among other values) is ambiguous. The Deuteronomistic position, key-noted in the book of Deuteronomy and a permeating position of much of the editing of the Hebrew scripture, is basically that good behavior is rewarded and bad behavior is punished. The Calvinistic position that emerged as part of the Protestant Reformation essentially bought into Deuteronomistic thought, but concluded that it is God, and not humans, who decides whether humans are good. The unconditional demand of the Ten Commandments and the conclusion of the book of Job represent a significant counter theme that there is no reward for being good. Accordingly, one does good for the sake of the good alone. To do good for the sake of a reward constitutes idolatry, because one is valuing the reward above the good. The Danish philosopher Soren Kierkegaard conveyed the same position as a major point in his work, *Purity of Heart is to Will One Thing*. The consensus message from these sources is that there is no meaningful relationship between doing good and gaining material goods. Material goods are necessary for the sustenance of our material bodies, but they easily become idolatrous, as the next section will reflect.

Why Material Goods are Ultimately False Positives

Material goods present us with both agony and ecstasy. To paraphrase a cliché, "We can't live with them and we can't live without them." Material goods become bad when they preoccupy us to the exclusion of better alternatives. Recently a boy who was bagging my groceries told me that he would be content with the material goods he could purchase with a $100,000 salary, but the pursuit of a six-figure salary may cause him to abandon better options for contentment via family, nature, literature, religion, or the liberal arts. We have to find a meaningful balance between what we truly need and what unnecessarily preoccupies us. Trying to make material goods solve ultimate questions is idolatrous, in that it gives ultimate value to finite things.

Material goods are also bad when they give us a false sense of security. Apart from narrowing his vocational options, the boy in the supermarket will find minimal security in the $100,000 salary even if he achieves it. The people of ancient Byblos knew their city was a marvelous treasure, so they built a wall around it. But instead of making them feel secure about the city, they then had a city and a wall to worry about. So they built a wall around the wall. As you can anticipate, they now had a city and two walls to worry about. And indeed they did build a third wall. In fact, they built seven walls before an invading force cured their disillusionment about the security of walls, and made them realize what they gave up by becoming distracted by them.

Is it wrong, then, to want physical goods? According to a strict interpretation of Buddhist teachings, to eliminate desire is to eliminate pain and suffering. Perhaps the last of the Ten Commandments, "Thou shalt not covet . . . ," is a culmination of the previous nine, and the overarching wisdom is that desire should be eliminated. That would represent a position akin to Buddhism. In *Being and Having*, Gabriel Marcel argues that to be is to have a body and a need for some goods to sustain it. The challenge is to find the appropriate balance.

The Greek language may provide guidance. It has a multitude of words to help us analyze love/desire/wanting/coveting. *Eros, philia, agape,* and a kindred word, *epithumia,* facilitate the exploration of the subtleties of desire. Epithumia is lust, and by definition is not a healthy form of desire. The person feeling epithumia misuses the object of desire. Acting on epithumia, one does not savor a doughnut, but stuffs it down with a companion or two. Out of epithumia, one uses sex as a way of killing a boring evening, or worse, one depersonalizes another, as in rape.

Eros is in a sense selfish, like epithumia, but a person feeling eros uses the object of desire appropriately, savoring the smell of the flower or the embrace of the other. One who savors and reaches out for sensual gratification is caught up in eros. The object of desire may even be an ultimate value, like Truth or God. Plato used eros in that context.

People feeling philia seek something from the objects of their desires, but they are also willing to give something of themselves. Philia leads people into reciprocal agreements. I give you an apple and you give me some of your cheese. I will be with you in your time of need and you will be with me in my time of need. This is the nature of friendship.

People feeling agape are aware of self interest, but are willing to sacrifice for others. A parent's love is the typical paradigm. The saints are the non-familial model. They suffer for others. On occasion one might think of the other in the abstract. An illustration comes from the story of a man who left one new glove on the subway platform as he leapt onto a departing train.

> Sadly, he concluded that there was only one sensible thing to do. He leaned over to the open window and threw the other glove on the platform. At least someone would have a pair.[16]

Each of these terms sheds light on thinking about our complex desires for material things. Epithumia is a non-redeemable kind of wanting. It is associated with greed, abuse and gluttony. It should be defined in such a way that no one would defend it. It is the word to use for the misuse of the world. At least from our simplified view, Buddhism is saying that all desiring is really epithumia.

We can use the word eros to talk about a legitimate affirmation of the material (as well as any transcendent) world. It is a reaching out for material or spiritual values. One feeling eros requests fulfillment in a context of respect for material things.

With philia, the reciprocal love, there is recognition that the attainment of goods, and for our purposes let's say material goods, may result in a trade-off. I want something in my moment of eros, but a new element is introduced—you also want something, perhaps even the same thing. By reciprocity we may agree that I will give you some portion of what I have and you will give me some portion of what you have. Or we may share.

Agape is a selfless love probably as remote from the contemporary ethos as we can get. It involves concern for others. In terms of material goods, it fosters a concern that others get what they need. An understanding of agape and the other forms of love or desire can be instructive in our meditations on why people do or do not tread lightly.

Sustainable Approaches to Fair Distribution

Governments were established in good part to assure reasonable production, distribution, and protection of material goods. Theoretically, a government can see that all have access to what

---

16 "Metropolitan Diary," *New York Times*, October 1, 2000, p. 48.

they need and that no one abuses the material resources of the community. Practically, a government can have a vested interest in its own material prosperity and can be exploited to the material advantage of those in power. So there is a two-level issue: How can governments be held in check? And how can governments facilitate the distribution of material goods?

The first issue requires a study in political science sufficiently secondary to the focus of this book that it need not be part of the discussion. The just distribution of wealth is relevant to our discussion and a potential societal response to problems of materialism. Some people argue that the promotion of societal welfare is not an appropriate function of government. Social welfare programs are idealistic, they say, due to their focus on the good of all members of society rather than on the individual.

Social welfare can be addressed without government sanction as evidenced by a multitude of utopian communities and the collective farms of present day Israel. Socialism, in its many forms, is the most explicit governmental attempt at a societal solution to problems involving the production and distribution of material goods. It was very popular in western culture, including in the United States, in the early part of the 20th century. Russia embraced it most strongly, and many of its programs have endured in China, northern Europe and Canada. Its influence was felt in the political parties in the United States, particularly among more liberal Democrats.

Socialism is an idealistic and altruistic system that should continue to influence all governments, but for various reasons the idealism continually breaks down and cannot be the continuing solution.

Probably the main cause of the continuous breakdowns is the finitude of human nature. In that sense the socialists are more realistic than the utopians. The utopians in a sense say, "Let us good people go off by ourselves and build a just society," not sensitive to the fact that they bring with them the same elements of human nature that beleaguer society as a whole. Socialists at least realize that all are saved or none are saved. But socialism was strongly influenced by the extreme optimism of the late 19th and early 20th century, including the belief that reason prevailed and that humans were basically good and could build a just society with new freedoms and technologies. The sciences seemed destined to unravel the problems of the human community, from healthcare to poverty. Another problem with

socialism in practice was that it required a strong central government, which easily led to authoritarian regimes. Some utopian
communities have had significant lifespans, showing that they
have at least temporary viability. But it seems clear that while
the philosophy of socialism can affect any society, it is not going
to be the ultimate form of government anywhere.

Variations of local communal structure are sometimes successful. There has been a noticeable increase in cooperative
housing developments in the United States and elsewhere.[17]
The Findhorn ecovillage in Scotland has been one model.[18]
Economics, ecology, and cooperation have been the focuses,
rather than political or religious philosophy. The Ten Stones
Community in Vermont is a successful cooperative community
in the United States. Thirteen energy-efficient homes on half-
acre lots surround a large green. Each of the homes has its own
unique style. The green provides opportunities for community
events and shared activities like gardening.[19]

A second societal approach to resource scarcity would be a
serious campaign for population control. A smaller population
would make fewer demands on the finite Earth. In parts of the
western world the population is decreasing without any conscious effort on the part of governments. On the other hand, Asia
and Africa are still growing at an alarming rate. Government
programs, from the provision of family planning services to limits of one child per family, have been instituted as counter measures. Sometimes they are questioned as inhumane or immoral.
Seldom are they overwhelmingly successful. Such campaigns
are underway in countries including China and India with mixed
success to date.[20]

There is also an increasing sensitivity to the need for sustainable agriculture around the world. The same land can produce
more food if planted with crops for human consumption rather
than with forage crops for cattle grazing, because the cattle burn
a lot of the calories from the plants and pass relatively few on
in their meat. Sturdy plants, such as onions and avocados rather
than peaches and celery, require fewer chemical pesticides that
endanger farmers and consumers.[21]

17 For a list, see http://directory.ic.org/iclist/.
18 See www.ecovillagefindhorn.org/.
19 See www.sover.net/~dogstar/10stones.html.
20 See *The New York Times Almanac: 2006*, New York: Penguin Group, 481-2.
21 For a ranking of pesticide dangers, see www.foodnews.org.

A societal shift in values could also lead to less abuse of resources. The incomes of so many in the West are far beyond what any individual or family can responsibly spend. What other values could compete—what is a moral equivalent of wealth? There are cultures for which money and goods are not the ultimate goal. There have been successful collective farms in various parts of the world, notably the kibbutzim in Israel. Religious communities, among them the Shakers, the Ephrata Cloister, and the Oneida community, have sustained relatively large populations without preoccupation with a market economy. Stories regularly appear about individuals and families that have left the stress and waste of the corporate world for greater involvement with family and personal interests.[22]

We have not discovered the key to selling any of these societal approaches to the masses. The pursuit is still worth encouraging with the stakes so high, and such dents as can be made, should be made. We turn to the individual, who has far more control over personal responses than any collective has over societal responses.

In a cartoon by Eldon Dedini, a stick figure sits back leisurely on a fully drawn park bench amid a lush three-dimensional-looking environment remarking to a startled full-figured man, "I got rid of all the excess in my life."[23] The cartoon expresses the ideal of recognition that life can be more meaningful with more modest ownership of goods.

The Bible, too, speaks of the dismissal of excesses. The most compelling biblical story is found in Exodus (16:12-36) in which God provides manna for the fleeing Israelites. They found just enough for everyone's need for each day, as echoed in the prayer: "Give us this day our daily bread" (Matthew 6:11), and it would not last overnight. It could not be stored. There was no payoff to hoarding it.

Often the call to a simple life is understood to mean a return to the land in the sense of a simple rural home where one can be largely self sufficient with a garden and a few solar panels. That is one option, but the more generic call is to a simplicity that does two basic things: it considerably lessens dependence on material goods and it is sensitive to the finite natural resources of the Earth. On one hand, simple living leaves little room for

22 See, for example, http://noimpactman.typepad.com/blog/.
23 *New Yorker,* September 4, 2000.

superfluity—there is recognition that any excess one has is at the expense of someone else. More telling is the reality that preoccupation with the attainment and maintenance of the superfluous distracts from things that can really make life meaningful.

At a minimum, the simple life can mean living within one's means. In *The Millionaire Next Door*, Thomas Stanley and William Danko argue that most millionaires are inconspicuous because they live within their means—that's how they save money. Conspicuous consumers are usually living beyond their means. As a young man I conceived the idea that as my income grew, I would try to budget so that I would not be in debt. I would not have the big items, but I would be able to buy all the orange juice I wanted and all the magazines off the rack that interested me. Some people are said to be "house poor" because they have so much invested in their lavish houses that they always feel the pinch of money—and don't feel comfortable buying a magazine on a whim.

I suspect we all have anecdotes confirming that the meaningful moments of our lives may have little to do with pricey material goods. The classic, of course, is the child more intrigued by the cardboard box than the expensive toy that came in it. I recall things that I enjoyed as a child: a cart, a baseball glove and bat, and roller skates. There were also some pretty modest toys—little cars and paper models built from plans in the Sunday comics. The most enjoyable experiences were those with other people, including going to parks, playing games such as marbles and cards, and participating in athletics.

As an adult it has been harder to stay away from material things, in part because our culture has become more materialistic and in part because adulthood requires more direct ownership of things. Some of the things, like a house or a car, are substantial. Big items can be major sources of stress, while detachment from those items can provide comforting freedom. Two brief stories illustrate my point:

In 1965 the street we lived on underwent radical change. It had been a tree-lined dead end residential street. Rather quickly developers purchased the surrounding land. The woods at the end of the street were cleared and student apartments were built. The sprawl of new apartment buildings made its way up the street toward our house. There were no longer any single-family houses across the street. That's when the developer came to our door. Initially he sent an agent who happened to be a friend of ours and there was a friendly offer and a friendly rejection. After three such visits, the developer himself came and applied pressure. His main pitch was that the houses on either side of us had been bought (which was not true) and if we did not sell now we would not be able to sell our property. On a map he pointed out a house in another part of the city that was marooned amongst development and said that was us in a few years.

It was scary. We had more money invested in that house than in anything else. The thought of it being worthless was certainly something to reflect on. After a difficult period of anxiety I had an epiphany and felt a sudden, genuine sense of relief. The next time the developer came around with the question, "What will you do then?" I was ready with a response: "I'll give the property to the city and they can plant flowers on it."

I had a similar experience while eating in a Cincinnati restaurant with my car parked nearby. Two men at the next table were talking about auto thefts in Cincinnati. Slowly they raised my concern and I wondered if I should go out and check the car. Then the moment of relief came when it dawned on me that the theft of the car would not be the end of the world.

When my then-fiancée and I visited our pastor's home for pre-marital counseling, the pastor was obviously having real problems with his wife—among them his anxiety about her spending habits. He took us to her closet and showed us an array of dresses far in excess of what he thought she might need. He might as well have opened any of our closet doors—too many of us have too many garments, not to mention gadgets, machines, and possessions in general.

Nature itself is inefficient in its production. Most of the seeds produced by plants are superfluous, as with the thousands of acorns produced for every one new oak tree. Annie Dillard tells of many such instances in *Pilgrim at Tinker Creek*. At least nature's excesses are biodegradable and quickly recyclable.

The thrift stores that sell secondhand items, such as the Goodwill and Salvation Army stores, offer ample evidence of superfluity, their stocks coming from overstuffed closets thinned to make room for new additions. The major thrift stores receive so many T-shirts that they are compacted into bales and shipped to developing countries. The fact that almost every type of clothing can be found in profusion in thrift stores is a testament to the broad scope of our excesses.

The secondhand stores are praiseworthy as well. They are

a better destination for surplus clothing than the landfills with their glut of trash, and a better source of needed clothing than the malls and their glut of garments. The secondhand stores also offer many a tale of benefits for their customers. Dressed up for church recently, I was aware that my "best" suit had been purchased at the Salvation Army for $14 and my shoes for $4.

Many items are so unnecessary they are sold only as gifts—virtually no one would buy them for themselves. These items proliferate over the holidays: joke plaques and cups, mustache grooming kits, fruitcakes, gigantic candy items, and kitschy paintings and figurines. I do not mean to suggest that anyone who *does* receive lasting joy from these items should not have them; I just worry that most of them receive little use.

Other examples of waste include food discarded by supermarkets, restaurants, dining halls, and homes; newspapers and magazines that are read once and tossed; and manufactured items such as cars and refrigerators that are junked quickly in developed countries, but maintained much longer in underdeveloped countries. And then there are the throwaway bottles, cameras, cigarette lighters, food trays, flashlights, bags, and diapers.

Good intentions lead to the ownership of a plethora of other items that seldom or never get used: things like exercise equipment, books we intend to read, hobby supplies, bread machines, and mountains of toys. When everyone on the block owns a lawn mower, a snow blower, and a weed whacker, neighborhood cooperation would be much more ecological.

There is waste in the ease with which we abandon or tear down schools, shops, factories and homes that could simply be adapted or remodeled. Even building renovation recurs with wasteful frequency. We are obsessed with disposal and the perceived need for a new look.

By contrast, I was meaningfully impressed during short stays in the developing world, and particularly in Calcutta, India, where I spent several months. Many manufactured goods had to be imported into India, and there were high tariffs to protect the Indian currency. As a consequence, such goods that came into the country were well maintained. There were many vintage automobiles. The refrigerator that we rented was an old model with an unconcealed motor on top. I hadn't seen a refrigerator like that since the 1930s. It took surprisingly little effort to maintain the old machines. Repairmen were adept at creating and installing replacement parts with minimal tools, usually simply pliers, screwdrivers, and wire. I've since learned the term *bricoleur* to describe this type of handyman who cleverly uses the available items to maintain the material parts of the world. Bricoleurs and their employers are to be commended for helping to protect the environment. Like cobblers, mechanics, and electronics repairers, bricoleurs reduce the need for replacement and make ecological reuse of scrap materials. A bricoleur might use a discarded coat hanger to fix a door latch, cola to clean a toilet, or duct tape to mend broken fixtures.

When the Concorde airplane crashed in 2000 I was surprised to learn that thirty years is not an unusual length of time to keep a commercial aircraft in use. Compare that with the length of time that most people use their automobiles. If anything, a huge craft that flies miles above the Earth would seem to need more attention than a vehicle that does not have to struggle so constantly with the forces of gravity. I am inspired to keep my automobile, along with other manufactured items, longer. Our automobile recently passed the 100,000 mile mark—a record for me. For more inspiration, consider the Freegans, who dismiss corporate culture and practice "urban foraging" or "dumpster diving" to live, not off the land, but off the waste. Their website states that

> Freegans embrace community, generosity, social concern, freedom, cooperation, and sharing in opposition to a society based on materialism, moral apathy, competition, conformity, and greed.[24]

Their lifestyle is extreme, but from what I've read, it brings them considerable contentment.

Rewards

Treading lightly can involve sacrifice. Ethically we should do the good for the sake of the good alone, whatever the consequences. That moral argument can be hard to sell. Reinhold Niebuhr convincingly argued that neither people nor corporations change their behavior on the basis of moral argument.[25] For example, I received an e-mail today from a woman who is trying to convince everyone in our neighborhood to walk to

24 See http://freegan.info.
25 *An Interpretation of Christian Ethics*, San Francisco: Harper and Row, 1935, 62-83.

our neighborhood grocery store and take a bus when we need to travel farther rather than polluting our air or necessitating more pavement with more cars. Her argument is impeccable, but there is a 100 percent guarantee that it will fall on deaf or unwilling ears.

We are moved to do good by some payoff—much of our moral behavior is really pragmatic in that we like the results. Consider the Boy Scout who helps the old lady across the street to get a merit badge, or the virgin who abstains from sex to avoid pregnancy and disease. In such cases the moral outcome has little to do with moral judgments, which would weigh right against wrong rather than benefits against costs.

I find it appropriate to make sacrifices for the sake of other people who live in our time or who will live in the future. We have no moral claim on more resources than we can reasonably use. The exact line between reasonable and unreasonable use may be difficult to draw, but with the United States using far more resources than the Earth could provide if the world population consumed as we do, it should not be hard to find excesses in our volumes of clothing, furniture, home and yard machinery, plastic toys, and other possessions. The argument for sacrifice in the service of others is not well received. For example, people have not stopped buying big automobiles in spite of highly publicized health and environmental concerns.

> **The sacrifices of simple living may be more imagined than real.**

The sacrifices of simple living may be more imagined than real. It is often a misconception that we would be better off with greedy pursuits of more possessions, as is a lesson from the Tales of the Arabian Nights. In one story a blind beggar, Baba Abdullah, tells his tale of woe: While he still had his sight, he led a caravan of 80 camels. Upon returning one day with no load on his beasts, he met a curious fellow traveler who led him to a secret cavern filled with gold, silver, diamonds, and other riches. Baba suggested they load his 80 camels with treasures and each take 40 camel loads. But at the time for parting, Baba could not bear to see even one camel load of wealth walk away. With slick talk, Baba convinced the other traveler that Baba should have every camel load. Not content even with that, Baba noted a tin of ointment that the other still had, and asked for it. The other said it was a magic potion that, when rubbed on the right eye, would reveal wealth, but when rubbed on the left eye, would render him blind. Baba tried it on his right eye and was awed by the vision of wealth. He could not believe that it would not be doubled if he rubbed it on his left eye. When he did, he became blind, and the other traveler went off with all the camels, leaving Baba to beg for his living. Our desires can ultimately blind us to real treasures.

Whether or not the sacrifice is significant, there is a payoff for treading lightly. Ecologically sound cars, furnaces, and power sources cost more up front than relatively abusive alternatives, but many of these "green" purchases save money over the long term. To reduce, re-use, maintain, and recycle is more economical than to dispose of and replace. Treading lightly, even out of a sense of responsibility, will bring unexpected rewards as well. This is suggested in the Bible story in which God asked Solomon what gift he would choose if anything were possible (I Kings 3: 3-15). This is a rather primal question because many of us don't know what we ultimately want. Solomon asked for wisdom to govern his people. God was so surprised that Solomon had not asked for wealth or fame that he gave Solomon those things as well.

Many of the unexpected rewards center on new freedoms. When our son was a child we took him to a modest festival on the local college campus. He eagerly sought out a person who was giving away balloons. The child smiled and gleefully carried his balloon. Then he noticed children having fun tossing a ball around and he wanted to join them, but possession of the balloon limited his freedom. He implored his parents to free him from the balloon so he could join the more exciting game.

The children's story of Hans in Luck[26] offers an impressive repudiation of the value of material-based "success." In the story, Hans works hard for seven years and is given a chunk of gold. He heads off for town and finds the gold a heavy burden. Fortunately, a passing farmer is willing to trade his horse for the gold. The horse bucks and throws Hans off. A dairyman offers to trade a cow for the horse. The cow kicks when Hans tries to milk it. Then a herdsman trades him a pig for the cow. A passerby warns Hans that someone has stolen the mayor's pig and if he walks into town with a pig in tow, he will be a suspect. The passerby has a goose that he is willing to swap for the pig. Hans arrives in town and watches a man sharpening knives on

26 *The Complete Grimm's Fairy Tales*, New York: Pantheon, 1944, pp. 381-388.

a grinding wheel. He thinks it would be wonderful to have such a wheel to make his living. The man has an old wheel that he gives to Hans in return for the goose. Hans carries the wheel down the road. It is very heavy so he stops to rest. He sets the wheel on the edge of a well and turns to sit down for a rest, but in so doing he knocks the wheel into the well. Hans peers down the well and suddenly a big smile crosses his face. He has had to deal with a heavy gold piece, a bucking horse, a kicking cow, a purloined pig, a goose, and a heavy stone. Finally he is free of all encumbrances!

I am struck by the simplicity of Japanese houses. They are minimal in their size and furnishings, yet very satisfying aesthetically. Simplicity has its own rewards. The cost, maintenance and cleaning of simple homes free the occupants for more meaningful pursuits, and for a life focused on being rather than having.

What are these more meaningful pursuits? What is sauce for the goose is not necessarily sauce for the gander, but there are so many sauces that it is hard to believe there are not free delicacies enough for all—delicacies that do not deplete our environment and that lead us into deeper arenas of fulfillment.

> Flower in the crannied wall,
> I pluck you out of the crannies,
> I hold you here, root and all, in my hand,
> Little flower—but *if* I could understand
> What you are, root and all, and all in all,
> I should know what God and man is.

> —Alford, Lord Tennyson

The study and experience of nature, literature, art, music, dance, theater, and relationships are quick routes to what God and humanity are. These are the great resonating experiences in which people with various tastes tend to have their peak experiences. The Danish philosopher Kierkegaard commented that just as material experiences are not ultimately fulfilling, so aesthetic experiences are not ultimate either. Rather than taking that as a warning, we can take it as a guideline to thread our way from necessary material possessions through the great symbolic experiences of nature, arts and relationships to discover communication with whatever provides us with moments of ultimate transcendence.

Finding Meaning on Mountains

Ancient Greeks knew the good stuff was "up there," transcendent. Their gods were assembled on Mount Olympus. Ancient Mesopotamians had no mountains to ascend in their broad valleys, but they knew the importance of ascension for perspective. They built their temples on artificial mountains called Ziggurats from 40 to 300 feet high. Moses climbed Mount Sinai to transcend the chaos of his disgruntled and disparate community and was met with a brilliance still reflected in his face when he descended the Mount. Seekers scale Himalayan peaks in search of gurus who will illuminate their needs for direction. Martin Luther King, Jr., carrying the burden of poverty and discrimination, could nevertheless say that he had been to a metaphorical mountaintop that still had the power of illumination and guidance. People climb mountains not just because they are there, but because they lift us out of irresponsible ruts and redirect our lives.

During a break from her work for Doctors Without Borders in Africa, our daughter Rondi set out to climb Mount Kilimanjaro. She provides the following glimpse at the wonder of mountains and the thrill of challenges that do not involve material pursuits:

> We stayed at a tiny lake at the base of the sub-peak of Kili called Mwenzi. It is a much more dramatic peak than Kili, rising sharply with many rocky points. The next morning we moved over what is called the saddle—a flat, desert-like area between the two peaks—to the base of the steepest ascent of Kili. There were enormous lava rocks everywhere and masses of solidified flows. At midnight we plodded off for the final ascent. Scorpio was above us in the sky, pulling as we moved through the lava scree. After four hours we stood on the rim of the crater. As we circled around the crater edge to the summit the sun started to rise. It was as if we had gone through the closet door and were in Narnia—a vast magnificent land came into view with glaciers taller than the tallest building and deep craters and expansive views. It would have taken days to explore, but we were in Arctic-like cold and I was drunk on the altitude. We headed down as the mountain slowly changed colors from purple and pink to the brilliant reflection of daylight.

Mountains provide perspective on the levels of reality in which people can exist. That perspective makes life meaningful. It also gives direction for how to live. When we aspire to higher levels of intellect, aesthetics, and morality, we gain not only a richer life for ourselves, but for others as well, by releasing material goods to those who are in need of basic necessities.

A popular bumper sticker challenges this move away from a materialistic preoccupation: "Whoever Ends Up with the Most Toys Wins." Even if you end up with the most toys, there is evidence that you are actually less happy. Americans reached their peak of happiness in 1957, well before the current boom of economic wellbeing.[27] The high alcoholism and suicide rates in "wealthy" nations may be a symptom that wealth is not fulfilling.[28] The break between wealth and happiness is underscored in places like China, where a very high poverty rate is coupled with a high percentage of people reporting that they are happy.[29]

In a *New Yorker* cartoon a seeker of happiness climbs the mountain to ask wisdom of a guru. The guru responds: "If I knew the meaning of life, would I be sitting in a cave in my underpants?"[30] Paradoxically, there is an authenticity or credential in sitting in a cave in your underpants. The seeker senses that the guru has found a secret—simple living. Those who conquer the urge to seek more toys than they need may find that they already have what they need. If you are at that point, sit back and relax. It is like the driving lesson I learned from an experiment many years ago: two cars took off at the same time to drive across the city of Syracuse from north to south, a distance of about seven miles. One driver was instructed that his goal was to see how quickly he could arrive at the other side of town. He was to feel free to drive at any speed—with the usual concern that he try not to get stopped by the police. The other driver was told to relax and not worry about the time of arrival. He was not to exceed the posted speed limit or to interpret yellow traffic lights loosely. The difference between the arrival times of the two cars was less than a minute and a half.

Much of the anxiety I feel at traffic lights and stop signs is

---

27 See www.bbc.co.uk/pressoffice/pressreleases/stories/2006/05_may/03/happiness.shtml.

28 See, for example, www.mailmanschool.org/news/display.asp?ID=551 and http://fathersforlife.org/health/who_suicide_rates.htm.

29 See www.china-embassy.org/eng/xw/t233974.htm.

30 December 11, 2000, p. 84.

strangely misplaced. That is, I have no idea why I don't just relax. It is a truism that I will get to my destination when I get there. Why not relax and "enjoy the trip"? Likewise, because there is scant evidence that amassed toys, social status, or salaries add meaning or happiness to life—and there is ample evidence to the contrary—why not enjoy the relaxation of not competing? That is a first reward.

The Pleasures of Frugality

Items that turn out to be "worth it" are those we really use. There is a certain joy when something actually wears out. It has been used admirably, and not simply warehoused in one of the storage facilities that dot the countryside as a testimony to overconsumption and underuse. Indeed, there is contentment in knowing that we got our money's worth out of what we have.

Some things may still be in use, but we are pleased because they are used so well or so often. My wife bought a little plastic golf set for a dollar a few years ago. It turned out to be a real winner with our under-five guests and has been highly utilized. I had a Winston dictionary in college that both my wife and I have appreciated for half a century. Its pages are dog-eared and it has been rebound with duct tape.

Sometimes individuals are forced into non-materialistic lifestyles by layoffs, imprisonment, health problems, or financial trouble, only to find themselves comforted by the new aspect of simplicity. I have a painting of an Italian countryside that reminds me of two stories of people exiled to rural Italy—both, it happens, from the city of Florence with its epitome of wealth, art, and luxurious life. The first is Machiavelli. Toward the end of his life, Machiavelli was imprisoned, tortured, and exiled to a farmhouse in the Italian countryside. He says he was able to relive something of the nobility of his life as it had been. His secret? Some great books and an active imagination:

> When evening comes, I return home and enter my study; on the threshold, I take off my workday clothes, covered with mud and dirt, and put on the garments of court and palace. Fitted out appropriately, I step inside the venerable courts of the ancients, where, solicitously received by them, I nourish myself on that food that alone is mine

and for which I was born; where I am unashamed
to converse with them and to question them about
the motives for their actions, and they, out of the
human kindness, answer me.[31]

The other story concerns the fictional exiles of Bocaccio's
Decamoron. In it, a little party of ten has fled the plagues of
Florence and settled in an Italian villa removed from the distrac-
tions of Florentine life. To occupy their time they choose the
cost-free, no-impact art of telling stories to one another, and
the book is composed of ten rounds of ten stories each. There
is much to be said about storytelling as a life enhancer. We entertain ourselves in our interstitial time—the unoccupied mental
spaces between the tasks of our lives—by telling stories. We
hold our lives together with the fabric of our national, religious,
vocational, romantic, and athletic stories, none of which is expensive or hurts the environment. In the process we tell the part
of the story that defines ourselves in terms of the goals we seek
and how that affects our relationship with our environment.

We look to nature (sky, water, greenery, fresh air, food), the
arts (poetry, music, painting, theater, dance, sculpture), relationships (with children, friends, relatives), and creativity (the arts)
to find happiness. Of course, they each lure us back to material things—a collection of stones or artworks or books or photos—and we continue the process of finding the right balance
of things in our lives.

Recreational vehicles often sport bumper stickers with some
version of the line, "Using Up our Kids' Inheritance." That's
probably okay. Usually our children want us to enjoy our later
years, and our greatest legacy to them is not the possessions we
leave for them, but the healthy condition of the world and its
resources. That bequest, and the associated gratification, comes
from treading lightly.

---

31 Letter from Machiavelli to Vettori, 10 December 1513, quoted in Patapan, Haig,
Machiavelli in Love: The Modern Politics of Love and Fear, Lanham, MD:
Lexington Books, 2006, p. 33.

CHAPTER 6

The Thin Foundation of Truth

"There's a sucker born every minute." Did you know that P.T. Barnum did *not* say that? It was David Hannum, who in 1869 thought the fossilized human giant attraction he invested in was real, while Barnum's similar attraction was fake. It turns out that Hannum was yet another sucker—his was fake too. Did you know that former vice president Al Gore never said he invented the Internet? Or that the popular pictures of former president George Bush holding a book upside down and Senator Barack Obama holding a telephone handset upside down are fakes? We are suckers for misinformation, which has started many a war[1] and ended many a friendship. Half-truths, exaggerations, and fantasies entertain us, but we are too far immersed in baloney to get out when it's time to draw conclusions about people, policies, or the environment.

Did you know that the *National Enquirer* tabloid, with current cover story "Hot Babes want You to Dump Dubya," has a circulation of 2.7 million, while the *New York Times*, with cover

---

1 The 2004 Deuffler Report indicates that misinformation led the United States into a deadly war against non-existent weapons of mass destruction in Iraq. For a discussion of other wars that resulted from misinformation, see David A. Anderson, *Economics By Example*, New York: Worth, 2007, p. 88.

story "Study Says U.S. Should Replace States' High School Standards," has a circulation of 1.1 million? Our love-affair with fiction has few bounds. Consider how many of our beliefs and behaviors have roots of tenuous veracity.

Think about health issues. A medical doctor who helps write the certifying exams for U.S. physicians told me recently that even the most accepted correlations among circulation, exercise, and health are not well understood. Saccharin, asbestos, DDT, silicon breast implants, and "defective" medicines such as Fen-Phen and Vioxx are on the long list of products that have been deemed safe and then not.[2] Health solutions such as antioxidants and oat bran have been held up and shot down.[3] Perhaps that is why teachers and clergy topped physicians and scientists in a poll about the most trusted people in America.[4] Although I wish I could claim one of those top two categories for myself, I'm down in sixth place as a professor, but pollsters were in tenth place, so can we really trust these rankings?

Think about religion—a renowned source of explanations for the unknown. The *World Christian Encyclopedia*[5] identifies more than 10,000 distinct religions. To the extent that the religions have contradictory teachings, at most one can be correct, but a 2001 Gallop poll found that over 60 percent of Americans believe religion "can answer all or most of today's problems."

Supporters of 5,000 colleges, 193 nations, and umpteen sports teams speak of their own as the best. One can consider them all above average in the spirit of Garrison Keillor, who jokes of a fictional community called Lake Wobegon where all the children are above average, but policy setting deserves a different level of truth. In reality, there is much to gain from mutual respect and much to learn from the successes of others.

Think about how we fill in the blanks about other people with fiction. Think about how often people who worry us are simply misunderstood. Think about how often people who appear arrogant are really just boasting out of insecurity. Think about the last rumor you heard about yourself. The ones I hear about me

---

2   See, for example, www.fda.gov/cder/drug/infopage/COX2/default.htm.

3   For a discussion of the ups and downs of antioxidants see www.cancer.gov/newscenter/pressreleases/antioxidants. For a discussion of the oat bran controversy see http://en.wikipedia.org/wiki/Bran.

4   See www.aaeteachers.org/pros.shtml.

5   David Barrett et al., *World Christian Encyclopedia: A Comparative Survey of Churches and Religions - AD 30 to 2200*, Oxford, U.K.: Oxford University Press, 2001.

are hilarious. They say that I never went to a basketball game while in college and that I never give high grades as a professor. Not true! I gave an A once. Well, it was almost an A—it was a B+. No—that's *all* complete fiction. I took my head out of the books and watched many ball games while in college, and my students earn, and receive, all sorts of high grades.

Risky Assumptions about People

*"Nothing can be believed
unless it is first understood."*

—Peter Abelard,
12th Century Philosopher

Do you know the real color of your grocer's hair? Or whether that hair is even real? As they say, believe none of what you hear and half of what you see. Consider the popularity of breast implants, reductions, and lifts, lip augmentation, face lifts, liposuction, chemical peels, facial implants, fat injections, collagen implants and Botulinum toxin (Botox) injections to remove facial lines, hair transplants and laser hair removal, microdermabrasion to remove age spots and "crows feet," micropigmentation as permanent make-up, sklerotherapy for spider veins, ear reshaping, eyelid surgery, rhinoplasty (nose reshaping), skin resurfacing, soft tissue fillers, abdominoplasty (tummy tucks), upper arm reduction, hair dye, make-up, perfume, and clothing in general. These procedures and cover-ups are fine if they make people happy, but they do obscure truths about the recipients. As people watchers, we seldom know whether we're seeing the real thing, and we're often wrong when we make judgments on the basis of appearance.

According to the American Society for Aesthetic Plastic Surgery,[6] the top five surgical procedures in 2007 were: breast augmentation, 348,000; liposuction, 302,000; rhinoplasty, 285,000; eyelid surgery, 241,000; and abdominoplasty, 148,000. The top five nonsurgical procedures were: Botox injection, 4.6 million; hyaluronic acid fillers, 1.1 million; chemical peel, 1 million; laser hair removal, 906,000; and microdermabrasion,

---

6   See www.plasticsurgery.org/media/press_releases/Plastic-Surgery-Growth-in-2007.cfm.

897,000. Between 2000 and 2007 there was a 59 percent increase in the total number of cosmetic procedures. Again, this is not to say that cosmetic changes are inherently bad. They can be rational responses to physical abnormalities, and adjustments can bring the appearance-based assumptions of other people more in-line with the truth. For example, frown lines might obscure the truth about a happy person and excess weight might make an active person with a slow metabolism look lazy.

More broadly, dangers lurk in the limits of knowledge when judgments are based on assumptions and limited observations. Those who seemingly slight us may simply be overwhelmed by other tasks. Those who appear unreasonable may well be misunderstood. Plausible appearance-based assumptions may simply miss the mark. The truth is more than skin deep, and to fill in the blanks about others on the basis of appearance or short-term behavior is to chart a course toward mistruths and mistakes.

Philosophers debate the meaning of "truth" in contexts such as: if Madonna's head were grafted onto Eminem's body, which singer would the resulting body become? At a more realistic level, if members of a community in Appalachia received Beverly-Hills-style makeovers and wardrobes, would we still level the mountains they live on to obtain coal? Actual site selection for mountaintop removal, landfills, and power plants tends to follow mistruths about the value of communities that lack the look of the affluent. For instance, a study of power plant locations chosen by the California Energy Commission found that 16 out of 18 plant sites were in areas with predominantly minority populations and 15 out of 18 plants were in predominantly poor areas.[7] It is unfortunate when decisions are driven by cosmetic differences among populations or by assessments of purely financial costs, which omit psychological, community, and environmental costs.

Fallout from Careless Judgments

The combination of discomfort with uncertainty and fluency with imagination tempts people to fill voids of information with conjecture. Speculation can cast undue shadows. An inordinate number of employees think their bosses are against them.[8] It

---

7 See www.lif.org/download/power_rpt.pdf.
8 See, for example, Bruce L. Katcher and Adam Snyder, *30 Reasons Why Employees Hate Their Bosses*, New York: American Management Association, 2007.

is natural to fear strangers who approach on a deserted street. Many Americans assumed that Saddam Hussein had weapons of mass destruction. Stereotyping depicts the rich as greedy, the poor as needy, the famous as arrogant, and the uneducated as obtuse. We have been warned against this. We know that we should metaphorically walk a mile in our neighbor's shoes before passing judgment on that neighbor, but we don't, and our misunderstandings cause unnecessary strife.

Mistaken assumptions can detract from efforts to tread lightly. Consider environmental policies, the adoption of which rests on the assumed credibility of those issuing warnings or dismissals. A few examples: Senator James Inhofe (R-Oklahoma), chairman of the Senate Committee on the Environment, stated that "man-made global warming is the greatest hoax ever perpetrated on the American people."[9] Trust in such statements slowed U.S. policy responses to global climate change. In regard to policies on neurotoxins, a state official told me that the chemical chlor-pyrifos in the pesticide Dursban is safe *because it is legal*. That reasoning would deem smoking, drinking, sky diving, and the consumption of mass quantities of lard to be safe as well. At the city level, an official said that spraying chlorpyrifos would not cause problems "unless you put your mouth over the nozzle." Government officials such as these are trusted to make policy decisions about dangerous chemicals and environmental risks. It is our duty to hold a higher standard for "truth" and collect information from independent sources to influence our beliefs. That is not hard to do with today's information technology! In a matter of minutes I determined that the Environmental Protection Agency, the Centers for Disease Control, and the Agency for Toxic Substances and Disease Registry all warn that chlorpyrifos poses serious health risks, especially to children.

One cannot look at the fancy suits and advanced degrees of politicians, executives, professors, or anyone else and assume that the well decorated are always right. No one is omniscient or infallible. Excellence in one area does not imply reliability or moral standing in other areas. There may be a few renaissance men and women out there, but I would not trust an oil executive to estimate the effects of drilling on arctic wildlife populations, and I would not count on politicians with corporate backing to perform comprehensive cost-benefit analyses of environmental

9   See www.tulsaworld.com/NewsStory.asp?ID=060722_Ne_A1_Heatw72040.

policy proposals. "Question Authority" was a popular slogan in the 1960s. In the face of complex issues with important ramifications for the planet, it is wise to look beyond assertions and double-check claims.

Pressure and haste to approve questionable products lead to further information failures and policy missteps. Yesterday's accepted substances, including lead, asbestos, and DDT, are banned today, and today's mercury in flu shots, chlorpyrifos in mosquito spray, and chemical preservatives in foods might be banned tomorrow as we adjust the "truth" to fit new evidence. With greater care during the initial examination and approval stages for potentially dangerous products, deadly surprises would become less common.

Working against public awareness are policies veiled by their own facelifts of sorts. Like people, policy proposals can be dressed up or misrepresented by cosmetic changes. Consider recent legislation that some might judge by name alone:

The *Healthy Forests Initiative* has expedited logging on 20 million acres of federal lands and limited anti-logging injunctions.[10] Supporters say that logging helps to avoid forest fires. Environmentalists point out that loggers seek large trees, which happen to be relatively fire-resistant, rather than smaller tinder. To hear an expert opinion and a new perspective, I invited veteran forester Glen Datillo to join me on a visit to a forest thinned by loggers. Large discarded remnants of trees littered the forest floor. Datillo said that the debris left by loggers could *increase* the risk of fire, and that, in an operation involving millions of acres of forest, it would be impossible to enforce requests to remove small trees and discarded limbs that increase fire risks.

The *Clear Skies Initiative*[11] would lower targets for emissions of sulfur dioxide, mercury, and nitrogen oxides from U.S. power plants relative to the implementation of existing law. As reported by the National Resources Defense Council,[12] the Clear Skies legislation would allow three times more toxic mercury emissions, 50 percent more sulfur emissions, and hundreds of thousands of additional tons of smog-forming nitrogen oxides. It would also delay pollution abatement by up to a decade relative to the existing Clean Air Act.

10 See www.sierraclub.org/forests/fires/healthyforests_initiative.asp, www. healthyforests.gov/.

11 See www.sierraclub.org/cleanair/clear_skies.asp, www.epa.gov/clearskies/.

12 See www.nrdc.org/air/pollution/qbushplan.asp.

The frequent and successful use of euphemisms in titles and descriptions demonstrates that we fall for these semantic gymnastics. Clever names are less common on the pro-environment side. For example, "bottle bills" use the incentive of a nickel or dime deposit to encourage consumers to recycle beverage containers. The name *bottle bill* obscures the remarkable environmental benefits of recycling. Who would know that to recycle an aluminum can is to save 95 percent of the energy required to make a new can?[13] That's enough power to operate a television for three hours. Perhaps bottle bills would be more successful if they were re-named *Initiatives to Avoid Strip Mining, Roadside Trash, and Mountaintop Removal*.

At election time, prospective policymakers immerse voters in a haze of deceptive advertising. One of the most common and successful smear campaigns in recent elections has been to say that the opponent "flip-flops" or wavers on her or his positions. Of course, knowledge is accumulated over time, and a rigid adherence to initial stands is equivalent to a stubborn refusal to benefit from new information. I like a policymaker who wavers.

It takes time, though not a lot, to delve into the implications of proposed policies. The realities behind environmental legislation are often as close as the nearest computer.[14] It would be prudent for voters to take a few moments to study proposed laws, and if the laws do not sound wise, that we take a bit more time and write to our legislators. In your next letter, tell your elected representatives to prioritize health, the environment, and truth.

Yardsticks for Truth

The standards for truth in this society are eminently important but disturbingly low. The ancient philosophers debated standards for truth. The great academic institutions emphasize truth. Yale's motto is *Lux et Veritas,* meaning "light and truth." Harvard's motto is *Veritas*—truth. In the 1600s, Harvard's "truth" was related to Christianity, but that changed to a broader interpretation in the 1800s, influenced by the rationalism of the enlightenment. There are philosophical questions about what truth is and whether anything is in fact "true."[15] For practical purposes the question

13 See www.eia.doe.gov/kids/energyfacts/saving/recycling/solidwaste/recycling.html.
14 Even if you don't have one, you local public library probably does.
15 See www.christian-faith.com/philosophy/truth.html and www.gotquestions.org/

is whether our actions are based on a *reasonable standard* for truth. Decision makers must filter important claims with a few questions of their own: Are the claims corroborated? Do they make sense? Are they consistent with observed behavior? Does the source have a selfish interest in misleading the public?

One can think of standards for truth falling along a scale from one to ten, with one being the lowest standard and ten being the highest (realistic) standard. For example, the criteria for the numbers in this scale could be as follows:

Something is to be believed if:

1) It is convenient or attractive to believe, but no particular evidence supports it.

   Example: None of the many species of wildlife that go extinct every year holds the cure for cancer.

2) You have a hunch.

   Example: A new, clean fuel will be developed soon.

3) You heard it through the grapevine.

   Examples: Urban legends (for example, there are crocodiles in the sewers), gossip.

4) It was stated as fact on a personal website or you heard it first-hand from someone you don't know well.

   Examples: The alleged success of pyramid schemes; tabloid news.

5) It came from an authority who makes more money if people believe it.

   Example: *"We support healthy lifestyles by serving a variety of nutritious, high-quality food products and portion sizes."* —www.McDonalds.com

6) You heard it from a trusted friend who says she or he is sure about it.

   Example: Better gossip.

7) It came from an independent and respected expert.

absolute-truth.html.

Example: Information read directly from refereed journal articles or well documented books.

8) Many independent and respected experts concur.

Examples: The Earth is round; antioxidants seem to have no beneficial effect on cancer.[16]
Formerly: The Earth is flat, antioxidants seems to work against cancer.

9) You observe it first-hand.

Examples: The Dixie Chicks are great singers.
Formerly: Milli Vanilli are great singers. (After winning a Grammy Award in 1990, it was revealed that the purported singers did not actually sing on their debut album and lip synched during their concert performances.)

10) It is evident from your own first-hand experience and verified by a consensus among independent experts whose techniques have been closely scrutinized.

Examples: The moon revolves around the Earth.
Formerly: The sun revolves around the Earth.

Even a stab in the dark can turn out to be true with a lot of luck, and the highest standards of truth can turn out to be false, but examples of mistakes under higher standards are harder to come by. The appropriate standard for truth depends on the importance of getting things right. We can readily accept gossip that only matters to our own amusement, while thinking twice about using lawn care products that may or may not cause miscarriages. It takes extra diligence to question assertions we want to believe. What is our standard for truth about the dangers of mercury in fish, arsenic in water supplies, chemical preservatives in popular foods, or pollution created by the cars we drive?

Rather than quibble about which standard is appropriate, let's lament the standards most people actually employ. None of the standards on the list represents proof, but too often people stoop to the rock-bottom standards of convenience, hunches, and hear-

16 See www.cancer.org/docroot/NWS/content/NWS_1_1x_Major_Study_Debunks_ Aspirin_Vitamin_E_for_Cancer_Prevention.asp, *Cancer Research* (Vol. 63, No. 15: 4295-4298), www.cancer.gov/cancertopics/factsheet/antioxidantsprevention, particularly item 3.

say. Despite persistent media reports to the contrary, over a year after the invasion, a majority of the U.S. population still believed that Iraq had weapons of mass destruction when the United States began its war there and that there were strong ties between Iraq and al-Qaeda.[17] If you start counting the number of outrageous claims you hear stated as fact in the course of a day, you may well lose count.

Myths Swallowed Whole

On the symptom list for excessive gullibility in our culture is the popularity of urban legends. There's a new one every week —taxes on e-mail messages, teddy bear viruses, frogs allowing themselves to be slowly boiled, Paul McCartney being dead, Elvis being alive—you know the type. Some of the bogus stories are widely believed and have been for decades. Many of us have heard that Walt Disney was cryogenically frozen with hopes that revival would be possible after the advance of medicine. According to www.urbanlegends.com, the best available information says that Walt Disney was cremated, and www.snopes2. com/disney/ includes a photo of Disney's burial site. To dispel environmental folklore, Snopes.com cites a "rice expert" and a Berkeley biologist who say that the consumption of dry rice is in fact not harmful for birds, so we can go back to throwing rice and not rose pedals (as recommended by Ann Landers) or bird seed at weddings. The same site explains that mother birds are not likely to reject eggs or babies that have been touched by humans, opossums don't hang by their tails, the combination of Coke and aspirin won't make you high or amorous, and lemmings don't routinely commit suicide by jumping off cliffs.

Myths, lies, distortions, and exaggerations influence environmental activism. It is common to hear that recycling isn't worthwhile,[18] an argument that characteristically fails to mention the *environmental benefits* of recycling alongside the commercial value of recycled materials.[19] The benefits of hybrid cars are likewise couched in terms of fuel savings with little mention of their contributions of health and environment benefits.[20] Information about problems such as global climate change and secondhand

17 See www.commondreams.org/headlines04/0422-09.htm.
18 See, for example, www.pittsburghlive.com/x/pittsburghtrib/s_384807.html.
19 For more on recycling myths, see www.grn.com/library/5myths.htm.
20 For example, see www.cnn.com/2006/AUTOS/08/22/bc.autos.hybrids.reut/index.html.

smoke is delayed, shrouded, or laughed off. Important concerns about extinction are dismissed.[21] Optimism abounds for new discoveries or technology that will make current levels of materialism sustainable, as if science fiction fantasies became realities by virtue of wishful thinking and poorly funded research programs.[22] When policymakers gloss over the facts, keep them in line. Check the sources. A few mistakes are inevitable, but in this information age people should not be so easily misled.

Convenient Beliefs

Human nature includes a remarkable capacity to dismiss factual or ethical arguments that go against short-term interests. Executives for some companies that make tennis shoes and soccer balls seem to lose little sleep over the chemicals used in the manufacturing processes, not to mention the low wages paid to their production workers. Many coffee company executives accept coffee-growing practices that are neither organic nor fair-trade certified. Fast food promoters ought to know that heart disease is the leading killer in the United States, but they adjust their beliefs to justify their work. Approximately 282,000 retail outlets sell cigarettes.[23]

> **Approximately 282,000 retail outlets sell cigarettes.**

Just as businesspeople neglect moral imperatives to do the right thing, consumers miss their own opportunities to effect change. Albeit with tremendous influence from advertising campaigns, it is often consumer demand that drives destructive industries, and it is the consumers' right to choose their poison that helps workers in health-damaging industries rationalize their behavior. Manufacturers can argue that if they didn't provide dangerous products, someone else would. But if consumers didn't buy tobacco, manufacturers wouldn't make tobacco products, and if consumers only purchased fair trade, organic coffee, that's all that would be made. It is wrong to place all of the blame on customers for their submission to aggressive and misleading marketing efforts, but when it comes to solutions, it is more realistic to expect customers to push corporations in the right direction than the other way around.

---

21 Several popular myths are addressed at www.nepenthes.dk/files/Pimm2002.pdf.
22 A website on anti-environmental myths appears at http://info-pollution.com/myths.htm.
23 See www.tobonline.com/ArticlePages/ArticlePagesVol95/vol95p36.htm.

Businesspeople and consumers share the blame for societal problems that would be resolved if we were all better informed and honest with ourselves. Fast food isn't a device of the devil, but perhaps everyone who eats fast food should read *Fast Food Nation* by Eric Schlosser or talk with someone in the industry to learn what goes on behind the scenes to make the food fast and cheap. Eating meat isn't always bad, but perhaps we should all have to see the slaughter of the types of animals we eat and understand about the extra land, water, and energy that goes into meat production so that we can weigh the true costs and benefits for ourselves.[24] Some manufactured goods serve society quite well, but perhaps everyone should see images of the factories, working conditions, pollution, and disease brought about by consumers flocking to big-box retailers. We should all be shown pictures of the felling of trees for our newspapers, magazines, catalogs, and books (unless they're printed on 100% recycled paper, like this one), the mining of ores for our metals, and the disposal of waste from our discards.

In Michael Moore's movie *The Big One*, Nike chairman Phil Knight admits that he has never visited the factories in Indonesia where his company's shoes are made. He ought to grant himself a look at those realities and run an operation he is proud to display to his customers. When choosing which labor and environmental practices, pay scales, and factory conditions to condone with our purchases, the Golden Rule of treating others as we would like to be treated is a fitting guide.

It would be a dream to have more corporate leaders who are focused on environmental truths, but it is more realistic to expect executives to serve stockholders and to expect stockholders to pursue short-term profits. With their hands on the wallets that serve up those profits, consumers should acknowledge the true repercussions of their decisions and act accordingly. Knowing more of the truth would allow us to make more appropriate cost-benefit decisions, and for those who understand the joy of treading lightly, changes will be easier to accept.

Beer drinkers don't want to think that Anheuser-Busch is the largest producer of sulfur dioxide in St. Louis, which is among the worst 20 percent of cities in terms of sulfur dioxide pollution, and that Anheuser-Busch is among the worst 10 percent of U.S.

24 For a rich discussion of these issues, read Michael Pollan's *The Omnivore's Dilemma*, New York: Penguin, 2007.

facilities in terms of total environmental releases.[25] Cigarette smokers don't want to believe that they inhale 4,000 chemicals and cause approximately 3,000 lung cancer deaths among non-smokers and over 150,000 lower respiratory tract infections in young children each year.[26] Commercial fishers don't want to be reminded that 47 species are overfished,[27] or that one-quarter of the global catch is made up of fish, birds, turtles, and marine mammals that are subsequently discarded because they are inappropriate for commercial trade.[28] Those who burn gasoline in unnecessarily large vehicles don't want to acknowledge their role in global climate change, oil spills, or the loss of pristine wilderness areas to drilling rigs. Those who illuminate vacant rooms with electric lighting and heat their homes to 70 degrees Fahrenheit in the winter prefer to pretend they are not causing unnecessary levels of filthy coal mining and combustion. It is natural, though the downfall of nature, to turn a blind eye to the truth about our own interests. Those who suit their beliefs to convenience live in a fantasy world, and that includes most of us much of the time. Amid our blissful ignorance, we fail to see how much better we could serve ourselves by treading lightly.

Respect for High Standards

Standards for truth determine more than the probability of being right—they influence respect and social status. It is an insult to be called gullible; it is an honor to be called trustworthy. The most trusted professions named in the Louis Harris poll mentioned in the opening section of this chapter: teachers, clergy, doctors, scientists, and judges, are among the most respected as well. Society clearly reveres those whose information can be relied upon. Nobel Laureates command tens of thousands of dollars for a single lecture. Americans pay $120,000 or more to give their kids a good college education. And critical thinking—that process of careful deliberation over the acceptability of claims—has become prominent in school curricula and corporate training programs.

---

25 See www.scorecard.org.
26 See www.epa.gov/iaq/pubs/etsbro.html.
27 See www.flmnh.ufl.edu/fish/InNews/overfished2007.html.
28 See http://archive.greenpeace.org/comms/fish/part6.html.

Conclusions

Weak environmental policy is the result of flaws in ethics, communication, education, and politics, and the overarching problem of a low standard of truth. Fictional assumptions spawn unfortunate outcomes in the usual way: garbage in, garbage out. To resolve the problem of fiction-based behavior, consumers and policymakers can seek greater understanding. Rather than disliking people in countries with differences we don't understand, we can open our classrooms to international awareness and tune in to what the differing ethnicities, religions, genders, preferences, and perspectives are all about. Rather than pretending that an unsustainable lifestyle is unproblematic, the well-to-do can experience the thrill of helping others and be more personally fulfilled by contributing to the betterment of the planet. Decision makers will never be omniscient, for perfect information comes at no small expense, but society could certainly raise the bar. What is your standard for truth?

> My parents befriend people from places Americans are taught to fear, and learn both sides of the stories.

Additional Reading

Why People Believe Weird Things: Pseudoscience, Superstition, and Other Confusions of Our Times, by Michael Shermer, W. H. Freeman and Company, 1997.

The Demon-Haunted World: Science as a Candle in the Dark, by Carl Sagan, Ballantine Books, 1996.

The Betrayal of Science and Reason: How Anti-Environmental Rhetoric Threatens Our Future, by Paul and Anne Ehrlich, Island Press, 1996.

Websites on Environmental Myths

"Anti-Environmental Myths"
www.info-pollution.com/myths.htm

"Global Warming - Fact vs. Myth"
www.environmentaldefense.org/documents/382_Myths.htm

"Ten Popular Myths About Global Climate Change"
www.sierraclub.ca/national/climate/ten-myths.html

"Ten Popular Myths About the Kyoto Protocol"
www.sierraclub.ca/national/climate/ten-myths-kyoto.html

"What the Skeptics Don't Tell You"
www.whrc.org/globalwarming/warmingearth.htm

"Countering the Skeptics"
http://archive.greenpeace.org/climate/industry/reports/sceptics.html

"Forrest: Myths and Facts"
www.chesco.com/~treeman/nfpra/zerocut/maf.html

"Eight Pesticide Myths"
www.ewg.org/pub/home/reports/myths/industry_myths.html

"The Five Most Dangerous Myths about Recycling"
www.grn.com/library/5myths.htm

"NRDC: Too Good to Throw Away"

www.nrdc.org/cities/recycling/recyc/recyint.asp

"Dispelling Common Myths about Wind Power"
www.environmentaldefense.org/pdf.cfm?ContentID=2
881&FileName=MythsWindEnergy%2Epdf

"Missouri River Myths and Facts"
www.environmentaldefense.org/pdf.cfm?ContentID=2
172&FileName=MissouriRiverMythsFacts%2Epdf

"Anti-Recycling Myths"
www.environmentaldefense.org/documents/611_
ACF17F%2Ehtm

"The Endangered Species Act: Fact vs. Myth"
www.environmentaldefense.org/documents/611_
ACF17F%2Ehtm

"Anti-Environmental Myths Answered"
www.monitor.net/rachel/r406.html

Additional Information to Dispel Environmental Myths

"GreenpeaceUSA Fact Sheets"
www.greenpeaceusa.org/bin/view.fpl/15576/cms_
category/22.html

"Sierra Club Environmental Update"
www.sierraclub.org/environment/

National Resources Defense Council
www.nrdc.org/

CHAPTER 7

Our Plastic Lives

S tandard enumerations of our pollution problems have become cliché. Instead of repeating those numbers, this chapter sheds light on the extent of our problems with a case
study and related examples that arise close to home. If you are
sufficiently compelled by the problems, do skip the gory details
later in this chapter, which are primarily intended for skeptics,
information junkies, and the uninitiated.

The Fisher-Price Power Wheels Cadillac Escalade EXT is one
of the most popular toys in America.[1] "This realistic Cadillac
Escalade EXT riding toy is just as luxurious and sporty as the
real thing!" or so the product description boasts. In mid-2008 this
51" beginner's SUV sold for $299.88 at Wal-Mart. As I once
read on an enormous tractor at the county fair tractor pull:

*The only difference between men
and boys is the size of their toys.*

Consumers young and old may overlook the ramifications
of their toy purchases. This is unfortunate, because purchasing
decisions that neglect associated health and environmental costs

---

1 This product was ranked among the 10 most popular toys by PriceGrabber.com in
November, 2006. Six similar toys were among the 200 most popular in March, 2008.

will inevitably lead to excessive consumption. Nineteenth-century American author Henry David Thoreau wrote, "The cost of a thing is the amount of what I will call life which is required to be exchanged for it, immediately or in the long run." Economists refer to costs that aren't included in the retail price of a good as "externalities." Some of the less-known costs of buying Escalades and similar toys stem from the products' main component—plastic. How much do you know about the most used material in the world?[2]

The first human-made plastic debuted in 1862, but civilization went on largely without plastics until the 20th century, when products such as Cellophane (1913), Teflon (1938), nylon stockings (1939), and Silly Putty (1949) paved the way for mushrooming popularity in the second half of the century.

Plastic production usually begins with the extraction of non-renewable crude oil or natural gas from the Earth and the transportation of that resource, often over great distances, to a facility where it is heated and refined. The resulting "intermediaries" of methane, ethylene, propylene, styrene, and butenes make up plastic "feedstock" which is shipped to the plastic manufacturer. Chemical units of carbon, hydrogen, chlorine, nitrogen, and sulfur, among other elements derived from the feedstock, are bonded into long chains called polymers, the foundation of most plastics. The polymers are then blended with chemical additives such as phthalates, bisphenol A, or p-nonylphenol to provide strength, pliability, color, and texture.

The Environmental Protection Agency's National Partnership for Environmental Priorities aims to reduce the levels of 31 "priority chemicals" found in U.S. products and wastes. Several of them are banned substances, such as polychlorinated biphenyls (PCBs). Others are used to make plastic, including

> acenaphthene, acenaphthylene, anthracene,
> benzo(g,h,i)perylene, fluorine, hexachloroethane,
> phenanthrene, and pyrene.[3]

Additional priority chemicals—dioxins and furans—can be released when plastic is burned. Plastic production and disposal

---

2 According to the American Plastics Council (www.americanplasticscouncil.org/ s_apc/sec.asp?CID=310&DID=920), plastic has been the most used material in the world since 1976.

3 See www.epa.gov/epaoswer/hazwaste/minimize/chemlist.htm.

can also involve hundreds of other potentially hazardous chemicals including

> antimony oxide, bensoquinone, benzene, benzoyl peroxide, carbon tetrachloride, chromium oxide, cumene hydroperoxide, cyclohexane, diaszomethane, ethylene, hexane, lead oxide, methanol, nickel dibutyl dithiocarbamate, phenol, polystyrene, polyvinyl alcohol, propylene, tert-butyl hydroperoxide, and 2,6-di-tert-butyl-4-methyl.

Danger Zone

The use of hazardous chemicals begets exposure to hazardous chemicals. An infamous example was the Love Canal toxic dump near Niagara Falls, New York,[4] which was a byproduct of Hooker Chemical and Plastics Company's manufacture of PVC plastic, pesticides, and PCBs used as plasticizers, fire-retardants, and insulators. Plastics and pesticides share similar hazardous ingredients and produce similar hazardous wastes. It becomes difficult to avoid human and environmental exposure when toxic substances are used in large volumes. Emeritus Chemistry Professor Paul H. Connett[5] and his wife Ellen put it this way:

> Those who work in the production of the chemicals necessary to produce plastics have been the hardest hit. They are exposed, almost unconscionably, to toxic and hazardous chemicals. Many have had their health impaired; many suffer illness and cancer; too many have died. Similarly, people who live in the communities where these chemicals and plastics are produced; who live near the incinerators and cement kilns where they are burned; who live next to hazardous waste landfills; and the firefighters who brave toxic fires, are also put at grave risk for cancers, illness and death. Shouldn't we be asking: "Are plastic food wraps, plastic packaging, plastic furniture, plastic construction materials, and plas-

---

4   For more on this story see www.epa.gov/history/topics/lovecanal/01.htm.
5   Prof. Connett received his Ph.D. in Chemistry from Dartmouth University and his B.S. in Natural Sciences from the University of Cambridge.

tic toys worth the cancers, illness and deaths their production, manufacture and disposal cause?"[6]

The American International Group of environmental insurance underwriters lists the following potential sources of environmental problems at plastic industry sites:[7]

- Fuel storage – including old storage yards with spills
- Underground storage tanks
- Waste materials
- Surface and groundwater contamination
- Historical – past spills and releases
- Decommissioning old processes
- Electrical equipment and PCBs
- Asbestos
- Loading/unloading of product
- Former on-site disposal practices
- Wastewater, cooling water and storm water runoff
- Fire and explosion dangers

In addition to health problems in locations where plastics and their additives are made, stored, burned, and disposed of, there is reason for concern among consumers and the general public. As one example, phthalates—plasticizing additives mixed with plastic to make it flexible—are among the most abundant man-made pollutants in the environment. More than 18 billion pounds of phthalates are produced each year.[8] Phthalates go into cosmetics, perfumes, pesticides, wood finishes, insect repellents, lubricants, and solvents. Because phthalates are mixed with plastics rather than being chemically bonded into the polymer chains, they separate from the plastics with relative ease. When

---

6　See www.mindfully.org/Plastic/Dont-Buy-Plastics.htm.

7　See www.aigenvironmental.com/environmental/public/envindustries/0,1340,63-11-330,00.html.

8　See Blount, B.C. et al., "Quantitative Detection of Eight Phthalate Metabolites in Human Urine using HPLC-APCI-MS/MS," *Anal. Chemistry* 72 (2000): 4127-34.

present in toys, phthalates can sometimes be released by chewing or sucking.[9]

The most abundant phthalate, di(2-ethylhexyl) or DEHP, is classified as a probable human carcinogen by the Environmental Protection Agency (EPA),[10] and has caused cancer in laboratory animals.[11] Detectable levels of phthalates have made their way into the air, water,[12] and food.[13] The European Union restricts the use of phthalates in products for children, and some U.S. cities and manufacturers are adopting similar safety measures.[14]

The Place for Plastic

Despite its inherent risks, we owe much to plastic. Without it, healthcare would be impeded, cars would be heavier and burn more fuel, and harvested trees would be in greater demand. Nobody I know is trying to outlaw plastic, although lightweight plastic bags have been banned in several cities and countries.[15] Small amounts of plastic and pollution are well justified by benefits that exceed the costs imposed on people and the planet. A good case can be made for plastic products that serve society well and could not be easily replaced. Plastic valves in artificial hearts are a no-brainer. Plastic products that can be used over and over, such as bowls, coat-hangers, and computer keyboards, are easier to justify than single-use non-essentials, such as Styrofoam cups and plastic bags that could be replaced by multiple-use ceramic mugs and fabric bags.

Might the Escalade and many of the other $25 billion worth of annual toy purchases produce happiness that warrants the costs? Surely some plastic superhero figures and Barbie dolls pull their own weight in terms of environmental and health damage, but are more and bigger plastic toys the best source of happiness? The toy advertisements would have us believe so. Thanks to fancy camera angles and enthusiastic child actors, one

9   See www.earthresource.org/campaigns/capp/phthalates.html.
10 See www.epa.gov/enviro/html/emci/chemref/117817.html.
11 See www.epa.gov/iris/subst/0014.htm#woe section II.A.3.
12 See Agency for Toxic Substances and Disease Registry, *Toxicological profile for Di-2ethylhexyl) phthalate*, Atlanta, GA, 2000. Available at www.atsdr.cdc.gov/toxprofiles.
13 Peterson, J.H. and Breindahl, R., "Plasticizers in Total Diet Samples, Baby Food and Infant Formulae," *Food Additives and Contaminants* 17, no. 2 (2000): 133-141.
14 See www.besafenet.com/pvc/.
15 See www.commondreams.org/headlines04/0721-04.htm.

would think orange plastic roadways brought heaven to Earth. Another possibility is that the perceived need to earn money at all costs—to enable us to "shop until we drop"—has driven a wedge between consumers and the real sources of happiness. Consider an alternative perspective:

The African country of Sierra Leone is among the poorest in the world. The children of Sierra Leone have virtually no conventional toys. While visiting several villages there in 2006 I saw no plastic dolls, no monopoly sets, no Rock 'Em Sock 'Em Robots, and no beginner's SUVs. It was also clear that the children of Sierra Leone were some of the happiest children I had ever met. They sang, danced, swam, explored, and drew pictures. They played hop-scotch on dirt paths and soccer with tin cans. They enjoyed good food and spent a lot of quality time with family and friends. What toys they had were crafted from sticks or old bicycle wheels. They thrived on their own creativity.

The simple pleasures in the lives of Africa's children reach an extreme that Americans might not want to approach, but could we be missing the boat with our emphasis on consump-

tion? Might it be that mass-produced toys sometimes distract kids from the real joys of life? Might it be healthy for children to use their imaginations to occasionally craft toys from non-toys? Might exploring wooded trails be more fun than pulling out the plastic Escalade for yet another excursion to the end of the driveway?

We don't need to prohibit toys or plastic, but we could improve the quality of our lives, and the lives of many others in the present and future, by becoming more mindful shoppers. Common sense guides us to weigh the gains and losses from our actions, make sure that affluence isn't standing in the way of happiness, avoid the unnecessary use of plastics and other resources, and feel good about ourselves when we take the extra steps to send a bottle into a recycling bin or re-use a plastic bag. If the Power Wheels Cadillac Escalade EXT would bring your family tremendous joy, buy it. But if it might become a large piece of clutter in your garage, don't forget the product's long path from the oil refinery, the trail of toxins it leaves behind, and the centuries that will pass before it turns to dust.

Plastic by the numbers

The plastics industry uses a numbering system to categorize plastics according to their composition. Look for the number inside the triangle of arrows on the bottom of many plastic products. Although these arrows resemble the symbol for recycling, the presence of these arrows does not guarantee that the plastic product can be recycled. Some types of plastic pose few known risks at the consumer level; others are of greater concern. What follows is a guide to the numbers for those who have puzzled over their meaning:

1 Polyethylene Terephthalate (PETE or PET)

PET is a common material in soda and water bottles, cereal box liners, boil-in-the-bag pouches, microwave food trays, and boat sails. In a summary of research on PET, the International Plastics Task Force (IPTF) notes that at least 19 compounds including acetaldehyde (a probable human carcinogen)[16] can leach out of PET food containers, although the levels were generally low

16 See www.epa.gov/ttn/uatw/hlthef/acetalde.html.

relative to those known to cause health problems.[17] PET is easy to recycle.

2 High-Density Polyethylene (HDPE)

HDPE is used to make many detergent, milk, and juice bottles, among other products. It, too, is easy to recycle. The IPTF reports that compounds such as 2-hydroxy-4-octoxy-benzophenone can leach out of HDPE, but at levels below those known to cause health problems.[18]

3 Polyvinyl Chloride (PVC, V, or "vinyl")[19]

PVC has been used to make a wide variety of products including bottles, water pipes, flooring, rainwear, toys, car seats, gutters, insulation, credit cards, blood bags, food wraps, and Barbie dolls.[20] Perhaps the most problematic of plastics, PVC is difficult to recycle, its manufacture and incineration can release dioxins,[21] and PVC products themselves can leach hormone-disrupting chemicals.[22] Di-2-ethylhexyl phthalate (DEHP), a rodent carcinogen[23] and suspected human carcinogen,[24] is a common ingredient in PVC.[25] American toy manufacturers voluntarily substitute diiso-heptyl phthalate (DIHP) for DEHP in pacifiers, rattles, and baby teething devices.[26] A study published by the National Institutes of Health Sciences found MEHP, a marker for DEHP exposure,[27] in 78 percent of the 2,540 human urine samples studied.[28] The same study explains that phthalates can be absorbed through the skin, inhaled, ingested, or received during healthcare

17 See www.ecologycenter.org/iptf/plastic_types/petmigration.html.
18 See www.ecologycenter.org/iptf/plastic_types/HDPESCIENCE.html.
19 For more on PVC, see www.mindfully.org/Plastic/Polyvinylchloride/PVC-Health-HazardPWG25oct01.htm for a summary of negative aspects, and www.vinylinfo. org/pressmaterials/factsheets/glad.html for a summary of positive aspects.
20 See www.webmd.com/content/article/27/1728_60731.
21 See http://archive.greenpeace.org/toxics/html/content/pvc1.html.
22 See www.breastcancerfund.org/site/pp.asp?c=kwKXLdPaE&b=83848.
23 See www.atsdr.cdc.gov/toxprofiles/tp9-c3.pdf.
24 See http://ehs.ucdavis.edu/ftpd/ucih/CarcinogenList2006.pdf.
25 See www.when.org/DEHP.html.
26 In 2002 the U.S. Consumer Product Safety Commission rejected a proposed ban on toys with DIHP because releases of DIHP, cadmium, and lead from PVC made with DIHP were not considered dangerous given the short periods that children spend sucking on plastic products. For a full report on this decision, see www.cpsc.gov/ LIBRARY/FOIA/FOIA02/brief/fiveyearpt1.PDF.
27 See www.ehponline.org/members/2003/6663/6663.html.
28 See www.ehponline.org/members/2003/6723/6723.html.

that involves PVC medical devices such as intravenous (IV) feeding tubes. Another study detected lead releases from imported PVC mini blinds.[29] The Center for Health, Environment & Justice[30] and the Environmental Health Strategy Center[31] have asked companies to phase out PVCs, and several manufacturers, including Microsoft, Hewlett-Packer, Toyota, and Kaiser Permanente, are making efforts to do so.[32] Nonetheless, PVC is the second-most-used plastic in the world and over 14 billion pounds of PVCs are made in North America annually.[33] Is the Power Wheels Escalade made of PVC plastic? The consumer help desk at Mattel, the parent company of Fisher-Price, told me they have no idea.

4 Low-Density Polyethylene (LDPE)

LDPE is common in produce bags, bowls, squeezable bottles, pipes, and toys. I found no studies indicating that dangerous chemicals leach out of LDPE. The bad news is that LDPE is difficult to recycle.

5 Polypropylene (PP)

Polypropylene is used to make products such as drinking straws, clothing, ketchup bottles, and yogurt containers. As with LDPE, it is difficult to recycle, but I found no studies indicating direct risks at the consumer level.

6 Polystyrene (PS)

Styrofoam cups, opaque plastic cutlery, to-go containers, and packaging "peanuts" are made of PS. This plastic is hard to recycle and can leach a colorless, sweet-smelling chemical called styrene into food and beverages.[34] The Environmental Protection Agency classifies styrene as a possible human carcinogen, and styrene exposure may increase the risk of leukemia and lymphoma.[35] Long-term exposure to styrene can also cause liver

---

29 See Norman, Ed, *Imported Plastic Mini-Blinds Identified as Potential Source of Lead Poisoning*, North Carolina Department of Environment, Health, and Natural Resources, 1996.

30 See www.besafenet.com/pvc/.

31 See www.preventharm.org/camp.toxi.shtml.

32 See www.ecocenter.org/releases/20051207_pvc_phaseout.shtml.

33 See www.vinylinfo.org/materialvinyl/material.html.

34 See www.epa.gov/safewater/dwh/c-voc/styrene.html.

35 See www.epa.gov/ttn/atw/hlthef/styrene.html.

and nerve damage. Short-term styrene exposure can affect the nervous-system, resulting in depression, weakness, and nausea, among other maladies.[36]

7 Other (Includes polycarbonate and mixed plastics)

Polycarbonate is found in many baby bottles, water cooler bottles, sports drink containers, eating utensils, and liners in metal cans. Polycarbonate is hard to recycle and leaches an endocrine disruptor called Bisphenol-A (BPA). BPA releases from food and beverage containers are a source of widespread human exposure.[37] Researchers reviewed 115 published BPA studies and found that 94 of the studies reported significant effects from low-doses of BPA.[38] These effects including changes in behavior, male and female reproductive systems, the immune system, and brain chemistry and structure.[39]

> 94 of 115 published BPA studies found significant effects.

Fossil Fuels

Additional health and environmental costs result from the extraction of petroleum and natural gas to make plastic feedstock, and from transportation, such as that of fossil fuels to refineries, feedstock to manufacturing plants, manufactured goods to retailers, consumers to and from retailers, and the resulting waste to landfills. A customer relations operator at Mattel told me that Power Wheels vehicle components come from Mexico and Asia; so, like most toys, the plastic Escalades are transported across the globe to reach retail shelves.

Every gallon of gasoline burned causes the release of 20 pounds of carbon dioxide, a greenhouse gas that promotes global warming.[40] Thus, a car that gets 20 miles per gallon generates one pound of carbon dioxide emissions per mile. Exhaust from the

---

36 Agency for Toxic Substances and Disease Registry, *Toxicological Profile for Styrene,* Atlanta, GA: U.S. Public Health Service, U.S. Department of Health and Human Services, 1992; and U.S. Department of Health and Human Services, *Registry of Toxic Effects of Chemical Substances*, Bethesda, MD: National Toxicology Information Program, National Library of Medicine, 1993.

37 See www.emcom.ca/summaries/vomsaal.shtml.

38 See www.ehponline.org/docs/2005/7713/abstract.html.

39 See www.coopamerica.org/pubs/realmoney/articles/plastics.cfm.

40 See www.epa.gov/emissweb/about.htm in the 2nd paragraph under Fuel Economy.

petroleum-fueled engines that move our raw materials, products, consumers, and waste around also release the following:[41]

Particulate matter (PM)

Fine particles of carbon and an assortment of toxic acids, metals, and organic chemicals (chemicals that contain carbon) make up particulate matter. According to the EPA, particulate matter is of concern because the particles are small enough to "easily reach the deepest recesses of the lungs."[42] The EPA also indicates that "batteries" of scientific studies link particulate matter to premature death, respiratory related hospital visits, aggravated asthma, acute respiratory symptoms including aggravated coughing and difficult or painful breathing, chronic bronchitis, and decreased lung function, not to mention work and school absences.

Volatile Organic Compounds (VOCs)

Gasoline and diesel engine exhaust contain VOCs that evaporate into the air and are present in approximately one-fifth of U.S. water supplies.[43] VOCs can include acetaldehyde, acrolein, benzene, 1,3-butadiene, formaldehyde, naphthalene, and polycyclic aromatic hydrocarbons. Some VOCs are known to cause cancer in humans. Other health problems resulting from VOC exposure can include damage to the liver, kidney, and central nervous system; eye, nose, and throat irritation; headaches; nausea; and loss of coordination.[44]

Sulfur Dioxide (SO2)

Sulfur dioxide is emitted from diesel engines and coal-burning power plants. Diesel engines are used in the large trucks, planes, boats, and trains that transport products and materials. Coal provides 52 percent of the electricity used in the United States.[45] In China, where $322 billion worth of goods were manufactured for the U.S. market in 2007,[46] approximately 75 percent of the power supply comes from coal.[47]

41 See www.energyindependencenow.org/pdf/fs/EIN-WhatToxicAirPollutants.pdf.
42 See www.epa.gov/ttn/oarpg/naaqsfin/pmhealth.html.
43 See www.bae.ncsu.edu/programs/extension/publicat/wqwm/ag473_5.html.
44 See www.epa.gov/iaq/voc.html.
45 See www.nema.org/gov/energy/supply/.
46 See www.census.gov/foreign-trade/balance/c5700.html#2008.
47 See http://english.people.com.cn/200312/02/eng20031202_129540.shtml.

Sulfur dioxide emissions are a cause of acid deposition, also known as acid rain. Lifeless trees and lakes in formerly pristine areas of North America and Europe are among the casualties of acid deposition.[48] Environment Canada, the federal agency established to oversee environmental policy and programs, reports that the United States emits six times as much SO_2 as Canada, and that 95,000 lakes will remain damaged by acid deposition even after control programs are fully implemented in 2010.[49] Acid also speeds the decay of buildings and paint, among other exposed materials. The resulting costs include $61 million spent annually in the United States on acid-resistant paint for new automobiles.[50]

Carbon Monoxide (CO)

CO is a tasteless, colorless, odorless toxic gas, the breathing of which inhibits the blood's ability to carry oxygen to vital organs including the heart and brain. Depending on the level and length of exposure, CO can cause problems from dizziness to death.[51] Most CO emissions come from gasoline engines and are intensified in cold weather and at high elevations as the result of less complete fuel combustion.

Nitrogen Oxides (NO$_x$)

Tailpipe emissions from gasoline and diesel engines are the largest source of NO_x emissions in the United States. NO_x compounds are a source of particulates, acid deposition, strong acid aerosols, and ozone pollution.

Ozone (O$_3$)

NO_x, CO, unburned hydrocarbons, and evaporative emissions from gasoline react in sunlight to form ground-level ozone, the principal component of smog. The EPA describes O_3 as a "potent irritant" that causes respiratory problems and lung damage.[52]

---

48 See www.epa.gov/acidrain/effects/forests.html and www.angelfire.com/ks3/ acidrainreport/acid.html.
49 See www.ec.gc.ca/acidrain/acidfact.html.
50 See www.epa.gov/airmarkt/acidrain/effects/materials.html.
51 See http://biology.about.com/library/blco.htm.
52 See www.epa.gov/OMS/invntory/overview/definitions.htm.

Waste

At the manufacturing and packaging stages, and at the end of a product's lifecycle, there is waste. The Power Wheels Escalade runs on a lead-acid battery which the toy's manual says might "explode or leak" if not disposed of properly. Plastic can take centuries to biodegrade because the molecules are bound so tightly together that bacteria, fungi, and other decomposers have a hard time breaking them down.[53] Sunlight is an effective decomposer as well, but plastics typically end up buried in piles or landfills where the sun can't reach them. The volume of waste is a problem in the United States, where the average resident generates 4.6 pounds of municipal solid waste daily, not including industrial waste, agricultural waste, or sewage. Between 1988 and 2006, as smaller and older landfills reached capacity, the number of operating U.S. landfills decreased from 7924 to 1754.[54]

It used to be that milk jugs were made out of glass rather than plastic, and after the jugs were emptied, consumers would return them to be cleaned and re-used.[55] Glass soda bottles could fol-

53 See www.rco.on.ca/factsheet/fs_g04.html.
54 See www.epa.gov/garbage/facts.htm.
55 As mentioned in Chapter 9, the Legacy Dairy in Nebraska still uses glass bottles.

low the same "closed loop" recycling system of re-use for their original purpose. Even when plastic bottles are recycled, however, most do not go back into use as plastic bottles. Rather, the plastics become carpets, eco-fleece, synthetic lumber, or various other recycled products. It's nice that they are recycled, but the failure to close the loop in recycling means that virgin resources are used to make new bottles. Sometimes the open loop results from a degradation of plastics during recycling that prevents them from being re-used for the same purpose. The technology exists to make recycled #1 plastic back into bottles, but that is not yet common practice.[56]

Recycling is not the only practice with room for improvement. Petroleum-based plastics and plasticizers could be replaced with versions made from corn and soybeans that biodegrade with relative ease.[57] Manufacturers are in the business of making what consumers will buy, so progress on the plastics front will be made when consumers demand it. For the time being consumers are demanding, among other things, a lot of petroleum-based plastic Escalades. As for the full-sized model, the 2008 Cadillac Escalade 2WD gets 14 mpg and emits an estimated 13.1 tons of greenhouse gases annually.[58] It is made of its share of plastic and about 5000 pounds of steel. Steel production begins with the mining of coal, limestone, and iron ore, mixtures of which are brought to high temperatures by burning fossil fuels .... As you might imagine, that's yet another story of environmental destruction and threats to human health. Clearly, the benefits from moderated resource use are plentiful.

> My parents recycle plastic grocery bags.

56 See www.ecologycenter.org/recycling/recycledcontent_fall2000/plastics_qa.html.
57 See www.unitedsoybean.org/feedstocks/fsv3i3g.html.
58 See www.fueleconomy.gov/Feg/noframes/24564.shtml.

CHAPTER 8

The Real Problem with Wal-Mart

Wal-Mart Stores, Inc., operates 7,266 discount stores, Supercenters, Sam's Clubs, and Neighborhood Markets in 14 countries.[1] The 971 Wal-Mart discount stores in the United States are each the size of two football fields—about 98,000 square feet—and sell 62,500 general-merchandise items. Each of the 2,447 Wal-Mart Supercenters covers about 187,000 square feet (more than three football fields) and sells 116,000 items of general merchandise, groceries, and pharmaceuticals. Each of the 591 Sam's Clubs offers about 127,000 square feet of general merchandise and bulk items, and the 132 Neighborhood Markets average about 43,000 square feet and sell 38,000 items each. Net sales for these combined operations amount to about $375 billion annually.[2]

More people shop at Wal-Mart stores than anywhere else. Some people shop with a guilty conscience. The world's largest company typifies the good, the bad, and the ugly of corporate culture and gives people reason to resist. Wal-Mart is a target for boycotts because the company's aggressive discounting is

---

1 See http://walmartstores.com/FactsNews/FactSheets/ and http://walmartstores.com/ Investors/7610.aspx, accessed March 29, 2008.
2 See www.wal-mart.com and www.standardandpoors.com.

a death-knell for smaller shops. Like other "big-box" retailers, Wal-Mart has been accused of predatory pricing, which entails toppling competitors with below-cost prices and then sometimes charging more than did the victimized stores. Wal-Mart is blamed for closing small pharmacies, groceries, and specialty shops, and for bankrupting bigger foes like toy-seller FAO Inc.[3] Their benefit package is small, their environmental footprint is enormous, and we love them to death. Some of the blame for the downside of Wal-Mart rests with us as consumers, and some of it doesn't.

Shoppers Vote for Stores with their Wallets

The demise of beloved family-run businesses is a problem, but as strip malls and superstores dismantle downtown shopping districts, it is shoppers who choose between the service and charm of smaller stores and the lower prices and one-stop shopping of new retail developments. A growing number of city centers are endangered by the contest of big vs. small in which shoppers "vote" with their pocketbooks. Mega stores would not and could not stay on the scene without the supporting vote of the public. It would seem that the existence of superstores demonstrates their desirability. Wal-Mart gives consumers another choice and consumers acquiesce. If consumers cared more about the mom-and-pop soda shop than the quarter they save buying Dr. Thunder (fake Dr. Pepper) at Wal-Mart, they would support mom and pop, right?

Alas, it's not that simple. There are countervailing forces in the retail market that may prevent a fair "election." Pocketbook voters who cherish quaint downtowns, unique shops, and the availability of repair services from hardware stores, jewelers, tailors, cobblers, and the like may consider their individual support inconsequential and rely on others to support Main Street while they pay lower prices on the interstate. Ernst Crown-Weber, a bicycle retailer on Main Street in Danville, Kentucky, finds it is common for people to buy a cheap bike at Wal-Mart and then expect him to fix it. The closing of full-service shops makes throwaways out of goods such as bicycles and lawn mowers that could be maintained for decades with professional service. Of

3   See www.consumeraffairs.com/news03/fao.html and www.time.com/time/
    magazine/article/0,9171,1006375-3,00.html.

With the loss of full-service shops that offer repairs, products that could serve for years are instead discarded and replaced.

course, the sustenance of full-service shops, and of any vibrant downtown, is patronage. Economists refer to the natural desire to benefit from amenities and let others pay for them as the *free rider* problem.

If consumers voted admirably by supporting the types of businesses they most appreciate, the businesses that survived would reflect the choices of the masses. However, the private incentive is to free ride. As we decide where to shop and what to pay, it is easy to suppose that others will protect the treasures of vibrant downtowns, green space, service-oriented retailers, moderated resource depletion, well-paying jobs, and products made under high environmental standards. For that reason, collectively but unwittingly, consumers unravel the core of their best interests.

The detrimental temptation to free ride is a reason for society to act collectively in defense of the common good. Parks, roads, and police protection would be in short supply if individuals were asked to fund them voluntarily, for it is rational for each individual to pay nothing and benefit from the generosity of others. Communities remedy this free-rider problem by working together with pooled tax dollars to target the optimal provision of public goods. A community-wide decision to fund a road with public money removes the option for some people to benefit from the expenditures of others. When prospective retail developments threaten existing green space or charm, communities can work together to protect these amenities from analogous free-rider problems by voting collectively for zoning restrictions. According to WakeUpWalMart.com, "In town after town, average Americans are coming together to stop Wal-Mart from destroying their way of life." It is never easy to work against the deep pockets of Wal-Mart, but Sprawl-busters.com reports that 277 communities have battled successfully against a big-box retailer or pressured a developer to withdraw.

Wal-Mart isn't always a bad choice. In some cases there is more to gain than to lose from a Supercenter. But the decision to accommodate a new Wal-Mart should be approached at the community level, not at the individual level, because incentives to free ride work against individuals doing what's best for their communities *or* for themselves.

Corporate Culture

> *"Wal-Mart isn't building this store for people on Main Street; it's building it for investors on Wall Street."*

—Al Norman[4]

Part of the ugliness of corporate culture stems from obligatory efforts to please stockholders' narrow interests. Corporate leaders are generally expected to maximize the bottom line, whereas smaller producers have less pressure to limit their pursuits to profits alone. When neither stockholders nor cutthroat discounters are breathing down their backs, individual entrepreneurs can take pride in paying employees well, serving customers ethically, producing products of fine quality, and doing the right thing for the environment. After discounters enter, downward pressure on prices inhibits the mutual joy of commerce between

4   See sprawl-busters.com.

proud sellers and proud new owners of products. Big-box retailers have spelled the end of department stores like Jacobson's, where sales associates would take the time to adjust the length of customers' new slacks or teach the uninitiated how to tie a bow tie. The big stores are also effective at running pharmacies off Main Streets and farmers' markets off squares.

Discounters do allow people to buy more stuff, so the question becomes: Do we really need more stuff than we could buy in a traditional town? I tend to think of material goods in the same way that I think of meat—both should be enjoyed as garnishes rather than as main courses. A modest piece of meat complements a well-rounded meal of, say, seasoned rice, local vegetables, and homemade rolls. Likewise, a modest amount of shopping complements a well-rounded week of work, exercise, entertainment, gardening, and conversation. A modest number of gadgets complements a practical kitchen and a modest toy chest complements a platter of options for children's activities that might include crafts, sports, sandbox play, and reading. To be happy we need everything in moderation, not everything in Wal-Mart.

Serving the Underprivileged

What about the poor? Let's make sure that everyone has enough healthy food to eat, ample clothing, and enough of every essential item to live comfortably. But rather than doing that with big-box retailers that encourage overconsumption and tempt everyone with aisles of excess, let's use methods targeted for those who need assistance. There is no shortage of terrific clothing at thrift stores such as Goodwill and the Salvation Army. I make most of my clothing purchases at those stores. The prices are lower than at the big-box retailers, and the re-use of the products saves virgin resources and conserves landfill space. Thrift stores also sell toys, kitchen appliances, dishes, and other essentials. The purchase of brand new clothes and toys could be reserved for special occasions.

Starvation is rarely a problem in the United States.[5] Obesity and unhealthy diets, both of which can be encouraged by Wal-Mart's low prices on processed foods, are tremendous problems.

---

5   See, for example, www.wfp.org/country_brief/hunger_map/map/hungermap_popup/map_popup.html.

Indeed, heart disease is the leading cause of death in this country. For anyone who doesn't get enough to eat, let's support food banks, soup kitchens, meals on wheels, food stamp programs, and other safety nets. If our goal is to embrace and serve the poor, rather than taking the Wal-Mart approach, let's improve Head Start programs, volunteerism, and access to education and training programs. Let's openly and proudly wear second-hand clothing, available at thrift stores for less than the cost of Wal-Mart clothing, to fight the stigma of re-using garments. And let's honor those who don't go overboard with their materialism, rather than making anyone think they must have an abundance of manufactured goods to gain respect.

If the goal is to help the disadvantaged, U.S. citizens and policymakers could study income distribution problems and reconsider tax policies that cater to the rich. Income equality in the United States ranks 71st among nations as measured by the Gini index.[6] Denmark is ranked first, and like most of the countries that do a relatively good job sharing the riches of development with the poor, they do it without the help of Wal-Mart.

Aren't They Just Maximizing Profits?

This is a typical response to the suggestion that conscience should play a larger role in business decisions. Are most providers simply seeking profits? And what if all that anyone cared about were gaining as many dollars as possible? This is a valuable thought experiment.

In markets not pressured by large discounters, pride and conscience are important elements of what motivates people. If they were not, every doctor would diagnose every patient with the most expensive diseases that the patient and her insurance company could possibly afford. Never mind that the patient might be a picture of health. Never mind that she might quit her job, sell her house, spend her children's college money, and lose her hair due to needless chemotherapy treatments.

If it were all about money, to the extent possible, every pharmacist would water down drugs, every antivirus software company would propagate viruses to promote its sales, every grocer would bleach the old fish and chicken to make it look new, every student would cheat on exams to improve his or her

---

6   See http://hdrstats.undp.org/indicators/147.html.

grades and marketability, every prospective professional athlete would use performance-enhancing drugs, every butcher would have her thumb on the scale, and every gas station owner would set the flow monitors to read high so as to overcharge customers. If it were all about money there would be no interest in relatively expensive alternative energy, recycled paper, or hybrid cars. There would be no participation in recreational activities or religion. There would be no volunteerism, no charity, and no child rearing unless the children would provide cheap labor. Manufacturers and restaurateurs would use whatever deadly products and poisons necessary to minimize their costs. There would be no foundation for trust, no faith, no reluctance to commit crimes that would go unpunished.

> **If it were all about money ... there would be no volunteerism, no charity.**

If it were only money that mattered, we would work every waking hour and think nothing of blackening all of the skies in

the name of productivity. That is not the case. There are elements of blind greed in our world, but they are neither virtuous nor victorious. It is the morality in our society, the kindness of strangers, the generosity of neighbors, and the acceptance of friends that enables and sustains our happiness. Without a foundation of morality we would wallow in filth and corruption, and we have not reached that point. Profit maximization is a useful simplifying assumption in economic models, but to suggest that it is the only important purpose in the real world is absurd.

Regretfully, aggressive discounters make it increasingly difficult to take the high road and pursue multiple goals. It is hard to sell goods made by workers who earn fair wages and benefits when competitors do not. The story is similar for sellers of fairtrade coffee, organic food, high-quality products, and products made with recycled fibers, all of which cost a bit more.

Skeptics will say: "But they're just doing what is individually rational." How can one argue with that? Here's how: If we accept all individually rational behavior then we must accept murder, rape, incest, spousal abuse, theft, and every atrocity imaginable whenever the acts are rational for the party committing the acts. Let's not go there.

The Real Problem

The real problem with Wal-Mart is that their prices are *too* low. They lead us to buy too much. We purchase piles of plastic goods destined for obsolescence. This planet cannot sustain the resource depletion, pollution, or subsequent levels of municipal solid waste encouraged by artificially low prices that foil the moderating effect of prices that reflect true societal costs.

Consider the question of how many kitchen gadgets to buy. For about $50 at Wal-Mart one can choose among the Presto Pizzazz Pizza Oven, the George Foreman Lean Mean Grilling Machine, and more fryers, toasters, poppers and processors than one can shake a stick at. Suppose that on the basis of the products' usefulness, the Doe family would pay up to $65 for a fryer, up to $55 for a food processor, and no more than $45 for any of the other gadgets. We can expect them to buy the two gadgets that are worth more to them than the $50 price.

Here's the rub: The price doesn't reflect the full cost of a gadget. It doesn't include, for starters, the pollution costs imposed by the production, packaging, transportation, use, and disposal of these products. Taxpayers cover some of the health costs via Medicare and Medicaid, pollution victims bear some of the medical and insurance costs, and the ozone layer, global climate, wildlife species, and future generations all bear some of the burden. Then there are the costs of resource extraction, which degrades the Earth with strip mines, mountaintop removal, oil spills, and deforestation. Add to that the depletion of non-renewable resources. These costs are paid by society, but they are generally not part of what the Doe family pays at the cash register for its gadgets.

The hidden costs of manufactured goods are substantial. In the material-intensive U.S. economy it takes approximately 660 pounds of natural resources to create $100 of income.[7] The U.S. Environmental Protection Agency reports that in 2006, 105.6 million Americans lived in counties where air pollution levels exceeded the National Ambient Air Quality standards.[8] And with the help of temperature fluctuations and the expansion of human territory, in this, the Quaternary Period of mass extinction, the Earth may be losing 30,000 species annually.[9]

Wal-Mart prices may be artificially low for reasons beyond pollution and predation. In 2005, raids of 60 Wal-Mart stores in 21 states turned up alleged illegal aliens from 18 different nations who had been hired by subcontractors to clean the stores.[10] Wal-Mart paid $11 million to settle federal allegations in that case. The company also paid $50 million to settle one of several lawsuits alleging that executives failed to pay overtime and forced employees to work "off the clock."[11]

If hidden costs, include unpaid environmental, health, and labor costs, bring the gadgets' toll up from $50 to $60, only the fryer worth $65 should be purchased. To purchase the ones

---

7   See www.umich.edu/~indecol/materials.pdf or Albert Adriaanse (ed.), *Resource Flows: The Material Basis of Industrial Economies*, Washington, DC: World Resources Institute (1997).

8   See www.epa.gov/air/airtrends/2007/report/trends_report_full.pdf.

9   See Edward O. Wilson, *The Diversity of Life*, Cambridge, MA: The Belknap Press of Harvard University Press, (1992); Niles Eldredge, *Life in the Balance: Humanity and the Biodiversity Crisis*, Cambridge, MA: Princeton University Press (1998); David A. Anderson, *Environmental Economics and Natural Resource Management*, Danville, KY: Pensive Press (2006), p. 227; www.whole-systems.org/extinctions.html; www.actionbioscience.org/newfrontiers/eldredge2.html.

10 See www.cbsnews.com/stories/2005/03/18/national/main681593.shtml.

11 See http://query.nytimes.com/gst/fullpage.html?res=9C04E7DC163EF936A15755C0A9649C8B63.

worth $55 and $45 would lower societal well-being by impos-
ing more costs than benefits. Due to deceptively low prices, our
representative family would purchase twice the quantity that
would best serve society. With about 176 million Wal-Mart
shoppers susceptible to this type of mistake each week, what
follows is a colossal level of excess consumption.

The disease of neglected costs can be infectious. Wal-Mart
allegedly bullies suppliers and competitors into adopting similar low-cost, low-concern-for-the-planet practices. Protests
erupted in California in 2004 when the threat of Wal-Mart's
cut-rate groceries led to proposed wage and benefit cuts by
competitors trying to stay afloat.[12] In rural America that's nothing new. Now the retailer is bringing its wage-suppressing
tendencies into urban markets where wages have traditionally
been higher.

Wal-Mart is not all bad. Some of Wal-Mart's price cutting
is made possible not by lower compensation for workers and
suppliers, but by efficient distribution and retailing practices.
Kudos to Wal-Mart for its advancements and innovations that
include merchandise tracking systems[13] and motivational techniques.[14] Wal-Mart has also responded to consumer interest in
health food, organic cotton clothing, and waste reduction,[15] and
the company is experimenting with biodegradable packaging[16]
and less damaging construction practices.[17]

Conclusions

Although retailers can be too short-sighted and narrow-minded
to recognize the importance of ethics, consumers hold the purse
strings. Like Wal-Mart, most retailers will ultimately supply
what consumers demand, be it plastic items one use away from

12 See, for example, www.now.org/nnt/winter-2004/wal-mart.html.
13 See http://news.zdnet.com/2100-9584_22-5202240.html.
14 To learn the Wal-Mart cheer, visit here: www.walmartstores.com/
    GlobalWMStoresWeb/navigate.do?catg=259.
15 See www.walmartstores.com/GlobalWMStoresWeb/navigate.do?catg=217.
16 See www.smithsonianmagazine.com/issues/2006/august/pla.php.
17 See http://greenermagazine.blogspot.com/2005/07/will-green-work-for-wal-mart.
    html.

usurping landfill space, Earth-friendly necessities, or repair services that keep the old jalopy going and going. A few suggestions to help guide the market toward offerings that are in our best interests:

1. Tell store managers that you would purchase low-impact products if they sold them.

2. Avoid impulse purchases. Bring a shopping list to the store and don't buy more than you need. That is, pass on the counter-top pizza oven and the Lean Mean Grilling Machine.

3. Consider paying a bit more for a product that will last longer, or better yet, have your old one repaired.

4. When possible, buy locally made or grown products rather than products shipped long distances using fossil fuels.

5. Invest in aesthetics, service, and ethics.

Our shopping patterns matter to our quality of life. For the sake of local charm, ecosystems, manufacturers who pay good wages, shopkeepers who provide important services, and future generations who will benefit from the resources we leave behind, let's think outside the (big) box.

My parents walk to downtown shops.

Further Reading

John Dicker, *The United States of Wal-Mart*, New York: Tarcher (2005).

Charles Fishman, *The Wal-Mart Effect: How the World's Most Powerful Company Really Works—and How It's Transforming the American Economy,* New York: Penguin Press (2006).

Nelson Lichtenstein, *Wal-Mart: The Face of Twenty-First-Century Capitalism*, New York: New Press (2006).

Al Norman, *The Case Against Wal-Mart*, St. Johnsbury, VT: Raphel Marketing (2004).

Greg Spotts and Robert Greenwald, *Wal-Mart: The High Cost of Low Price*, New York: The Disinformation Company (2005).

Sam Walton and John Huey, *Made In America*, New York: Bantam (1993).

Related Websites

www.walmart.com

http://walmartwatch.com

www.walmartmovie.com

www.fastcompany.com/magazine/77/walmart.html

www.1worldcommunication.org/Walmart.htm#sweatshop

www.pbs.org/wgbh/pages/frontline/shows/walmart/

http://factchecker.purpleocean.org

http://walmartworkersrights.org

www.alternet.org/story/40784/

CHAPTER 9

Morality Matters

The focus of the citizenry changed as wars, corporate ethics scandals, and political misdeeds ushered in the new millennium. Bill Clinton was elected president in 1992 with a motto about the most important issue of the time: *It's the economy, stupid!* The economy is never passé, but more recently another issue has returned to the spotlight: *It's morality, stupid!* Moral values trumped jobs, terror, taxes, education, and everything else as the most important issue to voters in the 2004 presidential election.[1] Corruption topped terrorism, the economy, and the Iraq war as the most important issue in the 2006 midterm election.[2] In 2007, reports that Bush-administration appointees had pressured 150 scientists to suppress evidence of global climate change[3] helped pull President Bush's popularity down to levels not seen since the Nixon era.[4] And in 2008, New York governor Eliot Spitzer resigned two days after revelations of his involvement in a prostitution ring. Waning tolerance for immoral acts is a healthy sign that voters recognize the benefits of higher moral standards, even if some voters disagree about what is right

---

1   See www.cnn.com/ELECTION/2004/pages/results/states/US/P/00/epolls.0.html.
2   See www.cnn.com/2006/POLITICS/11/07/election.main/index.html
3   See www.csmonitor.com/2007/0131/p01s04-uspo.html.
4   See www.abcnews.go.com/Politics/PollVault/story?id=2811599&page=1.

and wrong. This chapter discusses the value of morality and provides perspectives on the question: "Is my behavior moral?"

The Value of Good Behavior

It is difficult to overstate the potential gains from honorable conduct. In an ideal world in which everyone could be trusted, citizens would avoid, for starters, the $2 trillion annual burden of crime in a typical year. This includes $600 billion worth of stolen goods, $36 billion spent on corrections, and $100 billion spent on preventative measures such as security fences and alarms.[5] The quality of our lives hinges on the extent to which we can trust the myriad people to whom we are vulnerable, including friends, family, bankers, doctors, teachers, clergy, and providers of water and food. The ability to open our homes to visitors, put our children in the hands of care providers, and put faith in government is invaluable, but we could not do these things if greed truly became paramount.

It is our good fortune that we can trust many people to some degree and some people to a large degree. To follow up on a thought experiment from Chapter 8, imagine if we lived in an ethical void—a true financial-gain free-for-all. Virtually everything that wasn't nailed down would be stolen. Gas would be siphoned from cars at night, assuming the cars themselves couldn't be hot-wired. In stores, salesclerks would steal everything customers did not. Assassinations and kidnappings would become routine. Children would be sold into slavery or prostitution. Even now these things happen in small pockets of moral bankruptcy, which should help us appreciate the relative amity of most places and times. Indeed, it is a mistake to assume that strictly selfish behavior pervades our society or to view corruption under the pretext that it is common for people to do whatever they can get away with. Culprits cannot rationalize corruption with the adage that if they didn't do it then someone else would, because in so many cases no one else would.

What Behavior is Acceptable?

Several points of view on right and wrong have withstood centuries of debate. Unfortunately, these exemplary perspectives and

---

5   David A. Anderson, "The Aggregate Burden of Crime and Distrust," *Journal of Law and Economics* 42, no. 2 (1999): 611-642.

approaches are not taught in schools. This section highlights a sampling of prominent ethical theories that anyone can consider during crises of decision making. The consequentialist theories of ethical egoism, utilitarianism, and the common good focus on the consequences of actions and the achievement of a desired end, such as the maximization of happiness. The nonconsequentialist ethical theories of virtue, rights, and justice focus on the duties and intentions of the decision maker. It is up to individuals to decide which of the underlying principles to incorporate into their own pursuits.

Ethical Egoism

Ethical egoism or individualism is about looking out for "number one." The idea is that an individual's moral obligation is to pursue personal interests, regardless of the effects of these pursuits on others. Author Ayn Rand embraced egoism as part of her larger philosophy of objectivism.[6] Rand summarized her view this way:

> My philosophy, in essence, is the concept of man as a heroic being, with his own happiness as the moral purpose of his life, with productive achievement as his noblest activity, and reason as his only absolute.[7]

Critics of ethical egoism argue that excessive inward focus can result in needless interpersonal conflict, neglect of the environment, and outcomes that are inferior to cooperative outcomes for everyone involved. In their dismissal of society's interests, ethical egoists must be careful not to let their desire for personal freedom cause personal losses. For example, the freedom to pollute can backfire, damaging property values and causing illness and environmental degradation that harms the polluters themselves. Often that which is best for society is also best for the individual.

Cooperation turns out to be a key ingredient in the recipe for prosperity. Consider the following non-cooperative lose-lose scenario: Ten residences and a vacant parcel of land lie side-by-side along a road in a county with no zoning ordinances. The opening of a rifle range on the vacant parcel would generate

---

6   The Objectivist Center Web site at http://ios.org/ provides detailed explanations of objectivism and Ayn Rand's views.

7   See http://www.aynrand.org.

long-term total profits of $50,000 for the owner.[8] In that event the values of the other parcels would fall precipitously due to the disturbing noise and the risk of stray bullets. If the rifle range would cause the values of the other ten parcels to fall by more than $5,000 each, the rifle range would create a net loss.

An alternative to selfish development at the peril of neighbors would be cooperative support for zoning standards that would make everyone's property more valuable. Property governed by strict standards appreciates in value because potential purchasers don't face the risk of windfall losses from nearby eyesores and nuisances. In rural Kentucky where I live, land with strict zoning restrictions sells for over 25 times the price of loosely zoned or un-zoned land. Thus, although the market price for the un-zoned parcel in our story might be $4,000, the owner would stand to increase the property's value to over $100,000 by working with other property owners in support of zoning. For similar reasons, neighborhood associations and county zoning boards frequently decide to restrict the behavior of ethical egoists by banning the likes of billboards, livestock, junk cars, large fires, and commercial developments in residential areas.

Critics of ethical egoism also point out that a narrow focus on self-interest can lead to even greater damage than that from rifle ranges. An example is the opportunity to kill one's rich relative in order to obtain his or her wealth. Indeed, many an act of violence and destruction is carried out for personal advancement or satisfaction, with neglect for the impact on others. Children really have been known to kill their parents for their wealth,[9] pharmacists have watered down chemotherapy drugs to reduce their costs and raise their profits at the expense of human lives,[10] landowners have preemptively destroyed endangered species and their habitat to avoid the need to comply with environmental regulations,[11] and manufacturers have dumped deadly chemi-

---

8 In economic terms, this is the discounted present value of net earnings, meaning the value today of all future earnings of the rifle range.

9 For example, Red Baron heiress Suzane von Richthofen killed her wealthy parents in 2002 (see http://news.bbc.co.uk/2/hi/americas/5207124.stm), as did the Menendez brothers in 1996.

10 For example, in 2002 a pharmacist admitted diluting cancer drugs for more than 30 patients, many of whom died shortly thereafter. See www.usatoday.com/news/nation/2002/02/26/pharmacist.htm.

11 This is called the *scorched earth* technique for avoiding regulations. See Dean Lueck and Jeffrey A. Michael, "Preemptive Habitat Destruction under the Endangered Species Act," *Journal of Law & Economics* 46 (2003): 27–60.

cals into the air and waterways to avoid the cost of safer disposal.[12] Ethical egoists could disavow hideous self-serving acts by operating within a broader ethical framework that provides boundaries for behavior. The challenge is to define and defend this outer set of boundaries. Guidance is available from the ethical theories that follow.

Utilitarianism

Under utilitarianism it is a moral obligation to steward the greatest good for the greatest number of people. Promoted by 19th-century economic philosophers Jeremy Bentham and John Stuart Mill, this criterion brings into the picture everyone who would be affected by a contemplated action. Rather than focusing inwardly as advocated by ethical egoism, Mill wrote that "the liberty of the individual must be thus far limited; he must not make himself a nuisance to other people."[13] Bentham's utilitarian calculus called for a maximization of the sum of everyone's happiness or "utility." Although it may be impossible to make comparable measures of different people's happiness, the goal of maximizing public welfare is sufficiently straightforward to provide guidance for many individual and public decisions. According to Bentham, we are to let individuals define what "good" means to them, examine policy options with regard to their effect on every person, and subscribe to those policies that provide the most beneficial balance of what the public perceives as good and as evil.[14]

Utilitarianism is implicit in everyday deliberations. When a plan for a new wilderness area is evaluated in terms of its benefits to nature lovers, its effect on nearby property values, and the resulting losses to those who would otherwise develop the

12   As one of many examples, GE legally dumped over a million pounds of chemicals into the Hudson River; see www.cnn.com/2000/NATURE/12/06/hudson.pcb/.
13   John Stuart Mill, *On Liberty*, Arlington Heights, IL: Harlna Davidson, Inc., 1947, 55.
14   Jeremy Bentham, *An Introduction to the Principles of Morals and Legislation*, Oxford: Clarendon Press, 1907, Chapter 4, paragraph 14.

protected area, this is a utilitarian exercise. In regard to the case study in the previous section, utilitarian guidelines would not permit the construction of a rifle range that caused more overall harm as a nuisance than good from profits, whether or not the range owner would benefit personally. The utilitarian approach is egalitarian in its equal consideration of each person's interests, and appealing to some because it does not rely on tradition, superstition, prejudice, or religious doctrine. It does not, however, follow a strict egalitarian tenet that each individual should receive the same allocation of goods or happiness.

Detractors point out difficulties with the classical interpretation of good and evil as pleasure and pain. The satisfaction of selfish and sadistic preferences could be consistent with a goal of utility maximization even if the preferences involved were, say, the torture of animals or the burning of forests. For this reason, utilitarians often speak of a limited range of acceptable preferences, or define good and evil in terms with less room for immoral pleasures. For example, good can be defined as the production of intrinsic goods such as health, beauty, or knowledge, which have universal appeal.

Utilitarianism is also criticized for permitting the unjust distribution of resources. Discrimination, exploitation, and the concentration of wealth among a small number of individuals can all be justified under this theory, so long as the result is a maximization of total utility. If people who are rich were found to receive more happiness per dollar spent cleaning up nearby toxic dump sites than people who are poor, no dump sites would be cleaned up near the homes of the poor until every site had been cleaned up near the homes of the rich.

As an alternative to utilitarianism, contemporary philosopher John Rawls advocates a *maximin* approach that targets utility improvements for those who are the worst off. [15] Rawls suggests that we devote resources to better the lives of the poor and downtrodden first, and continue to do so until they are on equal footing with the rich and privileged. Rawls stresses the goal of providing everyone with equal opportunities, rather than equal income levels, for the latter would create incentive problems in practice. The maximin approach might serve well in the context of public school systems, public transportation systems, and environmental clean-up projects.

15 John *A. Rawls, Theory of Justice*, Cambridge, Mass.: Belknap Press, 1999.

The Common Good

Having originated in the ancient writings of Plato, Aristotle, and Cicero, the notion of the common good is that society is a community whose members share the pursuit of common goals. The welfare of individuals is inextricably bound to the good of the community. John Rawls wrote, "The common good I think of as certain general conditions that are in an appropriate sense equally to everyone's advantage."[16] Likewise, common-good policies are focused on outcomes that are beneficial to all, examples being clean air and water, healthcare, public safety, and stable global temperatures. Followers of this approach generally respect and encourage individuals' freedom to pursue private goals, but seek recognition and advancement of those goals we all share in common.

Like many of the ethical theories, this approach leaves ambiguities. Exactly which outcomes are for the common good? When may individual freedoms be exercised at the expense of others? How do we assess activities that benefit some people and harm others? While this approach may involve few absolutes, those who favor it clearly advocate a greater sense of community, awareness of the interconnectedness of everyone's happiness, collective action, and cooperation in the interest of social welfare. Plato stressed the social benefits of education in this regard. Further examples of activities for the common good in the environmental realm include the maintenance of soils and aquifers suitable for agriculture, the protection of wildlife species whose mere existence provides widespread benefits, and conservation efforts that substitute renewable resources for non-renewable resources.

Virtue

With roots in the writings of Plato, Homer, and Sophocles, the nonconsequentialist theory of virtue is the oldest ethical theory in Western philosophy. This theory asks us to reflect on the types of people we intend, or have the duty, to be. According to Aristotle, "That which is the prize and end of virtue seems to be the best thing in the world."[17] Aristotle explained a moral virtue as the mean between two vices. For example, courage is a moral virtue between the vices of cowardice and rashness. Modesty falls

16 John A. Rawls, Theory of Justice. Cambridge, Mass.: Belknap Press, 1999, 217.
17 Nicomachean Ethics, New York: Penguin, 1955, Book I, Section 9.

between the vices of arrogance and low self-esteem. Aristotle's theory of virtue enjoyed great popularity during the Middle Ages with the endorsement of philosopher Thomas Aquinas. Despite the rise of competing approaches, virtue theory remains among the most prominent ethical theories of modern times.

Virtues are character traits, attitudes, and dispositions that influence our goals and actions. Examples include generosity, courage, compassion, temperance, fortitude, honesty, fairness, and self-control. Virtues must be learned and practiced, and virtue theorists place special emphasis on education and the exercise of self-discipline. The theory of virtue holds that once a character trait is obtained, it becomes characteristic of the acquirer. Those who have formed the virtue of benevolence tend to practice benevolence with regularity. Those who have developed plentiful virtues are predisposed to act broadly in accordance with moral principles. For these reasons, the theory of virtue equates a virtuous person with an ethical person.

Critics argue that the virtue approach to ethics fails to address several issues relevant to the quest for right and wrong.[18] The lack of specific behavioral guidelines leaves common ethical dilemmas open to interpretation, such as whether to recycle or whether to contribute to habitat preservation. Well intentioned people might engage in questionable behavior for lack of specified criteria. Is it moral to hunt? Is it moral to drive an SUV? There is little in virtue theory to assist with such determinations. There is also the possibility of moral backsliding. If virtues are maintained only with practice, individuals might fall out of practice, or temporarily deviate from the standards their character traits imply. A focus on traits rather than on conduct might foster approval for activities that would pass few other tests of morality.

Rights

Eighteenth-century German philosopher Immanuel Kant, like Aristotle, argued that it is adherence to moral duties that determines the morality of an action. Kant taught that moral duties include the treatment of individuals with dignity and respect. Consider the U.S. Department of Health and Human Services'

---

18 See, for example, Robert B. Louden, "On Some Vices of Virtue Ethics," in *Virtue Ethics*, edited by Roger Crisp and Michael Slote, New York: Oxford University Press, 1997.

determination that larger-than-expected portions of the nation and world were blanketed with nuclear fallout from Cold War nuclear testing, causing at least 15,000 cancer deaths in the United States alone.[19] One could make an "ignorance is bliss" argument that withholding information on this irreversible environmental disaster would permit higher levels of happiness and do more for the common good than its revelation. Kant argued that individuals have the right to learn the truth, and would have applauded the U.S. government's report of these findings as duly honest treatment, regardless of the consequences. Other fundamental moral rights in Kant's theory include the rights of individuals to choose freely what they will do with their lives, to have privacy, to be free of punishment, and to receive what has been promised in a contract or agreement.

Kant advocated two additional principles that are relevant to society's treatment of the Earth. According to the *Principle of Ends*, one should never treat humanity as a means to an end, but always as an end in itself. One implication is that individuals should not be exploited in the pursuit of profits. Kant taught that people are obligated to act out of respect for the human worth of others. Environmentalists tend to advocate the same principle of respect for wildlife.

Kant's *categorical imperative* states that one should choose only those actions that one would put forth as universal laws of nature. If we would not want everyone to build rifle ranges in residential areas, we should not choose that behavior for ourselves. If we would want everyone to bicycle more and throw away less, we should do so as well. The view of moral behavior as that which we would rationally recommend to others provides a criterion for specific actions that would be difficult to classify as moral or immoral under other deontological theories.

Justice

Rawls, Aristotle, and Plato saw fairness and justice as compelling measures of morality. These criteria for behavior have a firm intuitive foundation. Even young children call attention to actions they do not perceive as fair, with acuity that the actions are therefore not right. Aristotle's teaching that "equals should be treated equally" supports modern antidiscrimination

---

19 See www.usatoday.com/news/nation/2002/02/28/usat-nuke.htm.

and comparable-worth movements.[20] In regard to the environment, justice theory calls for decisions that are fair to present and future generations of humans. In the same way, justice for animals and other wildlife is central to the ethical stance of environmental organizations including People for the Ethical Treatment of Animals (PETA) and Citizens for Responsible Animal Behavior Studies (CRABS).

Those applying the theory of justice are challenged to determine which actions are indeed fair and just. For example, the theory makes it clear that citizens of the United States should have equal access to national wilderness areas, but it is not clear how much pollution it is fair to impose on one's neighbors or how the cost of environmental clean-ups should be distributed.

Environmental Ethics

Ethical theories are useful for guiding human decisions that affect other humans. Human decisions that affect the environment, and in turn affect humans, are also within the purview of these theories. However, with the exception of some modern adaptations, the theories are anthropocentric (human-centered). The approaches explained in this section shed more light on ecocentric morality and the importance on ecological interests that go beyond human interests.

Deep Ecology

Norwegian philosopher Arne Naess defined shallow ecology as the fight against pollution and resource depletion in order to improve the health and affluence of people in developed nations.[21] Deep ecology, he said, adds to this fight the elements of ecocentrism and sustainability, and the intrinsic value of nonhuman nature. Naess and other deep ecologists believe that moral evaluations should rest on ecological principles and scientific insight into the interrelatedness of all systems of life. They feel that greater respect for the environment is morally right, in part, because environmental peril could mean the end of us all. In other words, that which is good for the environment is good

20 The comparable-worth doctrine states that those whose jobs are deemed equally important should receive equal compensation. See www.scu.edu/SCU/Centers/Ethics/publications/iie/v3n2/comparable.html.

21 "The Shallow and the Deep, Long-Range Ecology Movements: A Summary," *Inquiry* 16 (1973).

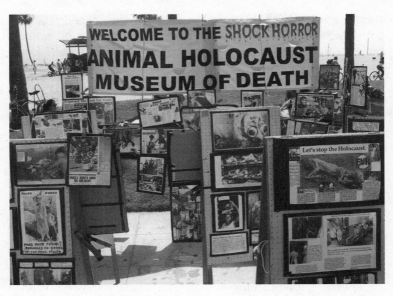

A display on Venice Beach, California, condemns animal cruelty.

for humans and all living things. Those who would prioritize business interests should be reminded that without the support of viable ecosystems there would be no labor force, no consumers, no economy, no happiness, and nothing to justify the acts that led to environmental collapse.

In contrast to ethical egoism, which is about individuals focusing on themselves, Naess suggests that people should identify with the ecosphere and the plants and animals therein. Such a focus would encourage behavior that is consistent with what science tells us is necessary for the well-being of life on Earth. In contrast, Australian philosopher John Passmore, among other critics of deep ecology, feels that its emphasis on environmental concerns is unnecessary, and that the risks of environmental neglect are less important to ego-based choices than are individual rights.

Social Ecology

Ecoanarchist Murray Bookchin criticized deep ecology for its lack of emphasis on society as the source of ecological problems. Bookchin's theory of social ecology promotes social equality and ecological interests within a framework of revolutionary libertarian socialism.[22] To social ecologists, the concentration of economic and political power, the homogenization of culture, and the strengthening of social hierarchies inhibit freedom and are the principal causes of an ongoing ecological crisis. Social ecologists ask people to play an active role in social evolution that will help remedy what they see as imbalances of power, diversity, and equality.

Ecofeminism

A term coined by French feminist François d'Eaubonne,[23] ecofeminism links environmentalism with feminism. Ecofeminists see a common thread of immorality in varying levels of disrespect for women and for wilderness, and link the unethical domination of women with the unethical domination of nature. Disregard for the feelings of other human beings and disinterest in the state of the environment may be rationalized in similar ways, and conversely, the virtue of compassion may carry over from compassion for humans to compassion for animals. With a focus on the interconnected spheres of feminism, development, and community, ecofeminism has become a popular grassroots activist movement.

The respect for living things and the environment inherent in ecofeminism comes at a price. The expense of keeping livestock increases with the quality of the animals' food and the size of their living quarters, thus making the ethical treatment of animals a financial commitment. Products made from recycled materials can likewise cost more to manufacture than products made from virgin resources. Theological ethicist Reinhold Niebuhr argues that corporations can only be coerced into respectful behavior by another entity that threatens their survival.[24] For example, the Roman Catholic Church has said in effect, "We represent the second-biggest block of consumers in the United States [after the government], and we will no longer do business with any corporation that is not an equal opportunity employer." When consumers take stands such as this, even businesses that only

---

22 For more on Murray Bookchin, see http://library.thinkquest.org/26026/People/murray_bookchin.html.

23 See François d'Eaubonne, "The Time for Ecofeminism," trans. by Ruth Hottell, in *Ecology*, ed. by Carolyn Merchant, Amherst, New York: Humanity Books, 1994.

24 Reinhold Niebuhr, *Moral Man and Immoral Society: A Study in Ethics and Politics*, Louisville: Westminster John Knox Press, 2002.

respect the bottom line can be brought to address a broad range of concerns.

In keeping with the deep ecology and ecofeminism models, Swiss dairy farmers take great pride in their treatment of livestock. Switzerland, like the rest of the European Union, Canada, Australia, New Zealand, and Japan,[25] restricts the use of a lactation-enhancing growth hormone for cows called recombinant bovine somatotropin (rBST). There is apprehension about the possible effects on cows, humans, and the ecosystem from hormones and the antibiotics used to cure hormone-induced mastitis (udder enlargement).[26] Some American dairies are concerned as well. The website for the Crescent Ridge Dairy in New England states, "Our farm manager does not feel it is in the best interest of the animals to inject our herd with rBST."[27] At the same time, the Monsanto Corporation reports that rBST is the best-selling dairy animal health product in the United States.[28] The decision by some farmers to forego hormones out of respect for the well-being of other living things, fully aware of the resulting 10 to 20 percent decrease in milk production, suggests the existence of business objectives beyond profit maximization.

Photo by Dr. Jeff DeFrain (2006)

The Legacy Dairy in Nebraska uses no rBST and provides milk in reusable glass bottles.

Resolving Ethical Dilemmas

Would you be able to sleep at night after dumping hazardous waste where it might reach drinking water supplies? Is it conscionable to wash your car during a drought, to discard recyclables, to throw trash out the car window, or to buy unneeded

---

25 See www.organicconsumers.org/articles/article_4034.cfm.
26 For a collection of news items on this issue, see http://organicconsumers.org/ rbghlink.html.
27 See www.cresentridge.com/growth.html.
28 See www.monsantodairy.com.

material goods? The daily ethical dilemmas of individuals, business owners, and policymakers are simplified by the application of decision rules. Almost any behavior can be rationalized with such arguments as, "Other people do it," "It's legal," "It provides a product that people demand," or "Someone else will do it if I don't." However, these statements take no account of the harm caused by the activity, possible alternatives to the activity, or the effect of the behavior on one's conscience.

Economic theory provides the guidance that behaviors should be continued until the additional cost of going on would exceed the additional benefit.[29] Unfortunately, dilemmas still arise regarding which costs and benefits to consider. For example, ethical egoists weigh their own costs and benefits, while utilitarians consider a comprehensive collection of costs and benefits received by everyone involved.

A boiling down of the predominant ethical theories for the purpose of comparison yields the following criteria to assist with decisions:

Ethical Egoism: Is this action good for me?

Utilitarianism: Does it bring the greatest good to the greatest number of people?

The Common Good: Is it good for society as a whole?

Virtue: Does this action reflect balance between vices?

Rights: Does this action respect the moral rights of everyone?

Kantianism: Would I want everyone to do it?

Justice: Is this action fair and just? Does it treat equals equally?

Deep Ecology: Is this action sustainable and ecocentric?

Social Ecology: Is it consistent with social equality and ecological interests?

Ecofeminism: Does this action show due respect for living things?

29 For details on this theme, see David A. Anderson, *Environmental Economics and Natural Resource Management*, Danville, KY: Pensive Press, 2006, 18-20.

The sections that follow explain three more criteria worth noting for their ability to cull right from wrong.

Would You Like to See It in a Headline?

The front-page-of-the-newspaper test promotes consideration of what other members of society would think about an action. The criterion is this: Would you carry out the behavior in question if you knew that a description of it would appear in a newspaper headline? If you envision that the headline would be incriminating or cause embarrassment, that's a sign that the contemplated act is morally unsound.

How would you feel if one of the following headlines appeared in the newspaper?

> *Smoker Releases Carbon Monoxide Into Public Restaurant*
>
> *Student Drives Two Blocks Rather Than Walking*
>
> *Strip-Mining Continues due to Lack of Recycling*

Your response could help you decide whether these actions are acceptable. Here are some actual newspaper headlines:

> *Poisonous Legacy: 'Black Village' Testifies to Communism's Toll on the Environment*
>
> *Inco Ltd. Faces Lawsuit Alleging Nickel Refinery Poses a Big Health Risk*
>
> *Expert Says Alabama Plant Should Pay $8.6 Million for PCB Damage*
>
> *States Ask Ford to Remove Mercury Switches*

Some of the associated decision makers might have behaved differently had they subjected themselves to the front-page-of-the-newspaper test as a first step.

How Does This Decision Make You Feel?

The doctrine of intuitionism suggests that, rather than applying an explicit formula to reach moral decisions, people should follow their own intuition. Intuitionists feel that while certain moral principles should be adhered to, corresponding limits on appropriate behavior are self-evident. Thus, as Jiminy Cricket said to

Pinocchio in the classic 1940 Disney movie of the same name, "Just let your conscience be your guide." This is a common approach, and it can work well for those with a strong conscience. Pinocchio, on the other hand, said, "What's a conscience?"

What Would My Role Model Do?

Society is replete with heroes, spiritual leaders, and role models whose behavior is exemplary. When faced with an ethical dilemma, people can imagine what their role model would do if faced with the same situation. When a few respected people in a neighborhood start installing solar panels, that decision can be contagious. When a clergywoman is adamant against the use of toxic pesticides in the chapel, members of the congregation will carry that attitude into their homes. People likewise draw inspiration from admired parents, community leaders, teachers, and friends. Note the importance of the categorical imperative—that people should act as they would want everyone to act—for each of us sets an example for the world.

Conclusions

To seek respect by accumulating wealth and material possessions is to neglect an important lesson. History reveals that admiration and respect follow morality rather than money. Abraham Lincoln, Susan B. Anthony, Mahatma Gandhi, Jesus, Buddha, Rosa Parks, Carry Nation, and so many others made moral decisions for the benefit of others, and for that they will never be forgotten. Insistence on moral high ground is the secret to lasting respect, and it is the not-so-secret ultimate wish of the electorate. The value of morality is more clear than the formula for attaining it. For all of those who see beyond the charade of happiness via profit maximization at all costs, the ethical theories provide alternative criteria for the daily struggle with temptation.

My parents follow their gut instincts.

CHAPTER 10

What Goes Around
Comes Around

A question to contemplate: More of what one thing could benefit virtually everyone in the world?

Money? No. It is clear from economic theory and evidence that a broad influx of money only leads to inflation in prices.

Production? Probably not, for reasons highlighted throughout this book. Production creates winners and losers. With more production comes more pollution, waste, environmental damage, health impairments, and global climate change, all of which make for uncertain trade-offs. Material-based happiness is short-lived due to adjustments in the expectations of recipients of new products, who quickly require even more new products to sustain their happiness. Attempts to find satisfaction through materialism also backfire into greed, envy, crime, debt, and buyer's remorse. After studying cultures in Africa, Asia, Central America, and the Caribbean where people have roughly one-twentieth as much "stuff" as U.S. citizens, I'm unconvinced that we are happier than they are in any general terms. For more jobs, it is better to look to the service sector and employ people to heal, teach, fix, entertain, clean, solve, cook, research, compute, lead, provide care, and so forth.

More food, education, and healthcare would benefit developing nations. However, the story is different in wealthy nations. Universal healthcare is prevalent in developed nations with the exception of the United States. Although the U.S. stands to improve its access to healthcare, the country has less to gain from more food and education: two-thirds of Americans are overweight or obese[1] and the literacy rate is 99 percent.[2] Thus, there are strong needs for food, education, and healthcare in the large sections of the planet that share a small fraction of its resources, but not in the small sections of the planet that consume a large fraction of its resources.

Technology? Maybe, although the jury's still out on that one. I've argued against the contention that robots will put us all out of work,[3] but folks like the Amish, my parents, and author Wendell Berry make valid points about the cons that accompany the productivity pros of our increasingly high-tech lives.[4] Researchers are also finding that technology overload can actually decrease productivity.[5] I'm confident that too many digital slide presentations in my classroom detract from the education of my students—discussions and chalkboard explanations are often more appropriate, engaging, and tailored to the students' needs. The larger technology debate is beyond the scope of this writing, but suffice it to say that the Home Shopping Network, the Mortal Kombat video game, and the omnipresent cell phone might distract us from low-tech activities that are even more important.

Now consider *respect*, that cherished honor too seldom shared across cultures, races, genders, fences, railroad tracks, or religions. It is difficult to overestimate the value of respect. How many purchases of clothing, cars, cosmetics, degrees, and homes are made to gain respect? How many pursuits of athletic, political, community, and career achievements are about respect? How much hatred, violence, misery, and disenfranchisement is the result of apparent disrespect? And how few people act against others who *do* show respect for them?

> How many purchases are made to gain respect?

1 See www.cdc.gov/nchs/fastats/overwt.htm.
2 See www.cia.gov/library/publications/the-world-factbook/geos/us.html.
3 See David A. Anderson, *Economics by Example*, New York: Worth, 2007, Ch. 19.
4 See www.users.dircon.co.uk/~tipiglen/berrynot.html.
5 See, for example, www.ergoweb.com/news/detail.cfm?id=1038.

Respect is Hard to Come By

Humans are not good at respecting lives, privacy, or property lines. If people were respectful enough not to attack each other, in the brief history of the United States, this country would have avoided the premature deaths of 1.2 million citizens in military service and the non-mortal wounding of 1.4 million more.[6] According to one estimate, since 3600 BCE there have been 14,531 wars resulting in 3 billion deaths.[7] There are at least 20 significant, ongoing military conflicts at the time of this writing.[8] In the final tally, Nobel laureate economist Joseph Stiglitz and Harvard lecturer Linda Bilmes estimate that the Iraq war will cost more than $3 trillion.[9]

If people had more respect for the environment, we would have better health, a shorter endangered and threatened species list (currently at 1,927 species),[10] and improved prospects for a stable climate. Do these items matter to people who prioritize wealth over health and don't care about wildlife? Yes. For example, a report by former World Bank chief economist Nicholas Stern indicates that global climate change may hit the nations' economies hard and cause the worst global recession of recent history.[11] Clearly, without a viable environment, there is no economy.

Aside from having the grave consequences of war, crime, and environmental disaster, disrespect is hurtful. The civil rights movement is about the importance of respect for all types of people. The feminist movement is about the importance of respect for women. A United Kingdom organization that works against domestic violence and child abuse has the fitting name of the solution to these tragedies, RESPECT. Advertisers selling everything from lawn grooming services to fake diplomas exploit people's willingness to spend hard-earned money to gain prized respect. What the vociferous commercial messages don't tell us is that respect need not be expensive. The price for respect is seldom more than an initial volley of the same. My children

6   See www.infoplease.com/ipa/A0004615.html.
7   See http://faculty.ncwc.edu/toconnor/areas/worldconflicts.htm.
8   See www.infoplease.com/ipa/A0904550.html.
9   See www.washingtonpost.com/wp-dyn/content/article/2008/03/07/
     AR2008030702846_pf.html.
10 See http://ecos.fws.gov/tess_public/Boxscore.do.
11 See www.hm-treasury.gov.uk/independent_reviews/stern_review_economics_
     climate_change/sternreview_index.cfm.

sometimes wonder why they get no mail. I tell them it is because they send no mail. What goes around comes around.

Respect among Groups

Americans enforce strict immigration policies and then wonder why we don't get a warmer welcome elsewhere. Shoppers wonder why their downtowns are eroding even as they drive to the mall. Retailers wonder why they have too few customers even as they skimp on hours, quality, promotions, or customer service. The circularity of most things good and bad couldn't be more valid than with the human ability to spread happiness. The key ingredient is genuine respect. As it stands, humans tend not to treat each other as they would like to be treated. For instance, the "10/90 gap" describes the controversial 1990 finding that only 10 percent of drug research expenditures were made to seek remedies for the 90 percent of the world's health problems that strike poor and middle-class nations.[12] If the developed world showed more respect for the developing world, the favor would be returned. Ditto for men and women, customers and sales clerks, Christians and Muslims, and blacks and whites.

Beyond neglect of the circularity of respect, misunderstandings abound. I wrote the following for a repertory theatre troupe at the University of Michigan in 1985:

> **White man:** Just the other day,
>
> **Black man:** it was Tuesday, I believe,
>
> **White man:** I was riding the bus
>
> **Black man:** on the way to work,
>
> **White man:** and I was sitting next to a black man
>
> **Black man:** white man.
>
> **White man:** He looked at me as if he was angry, and that made me feel scared.
>
> **Black man:** He looked at me as if he was scared, and that made me feel angry.
>
> **White man:** Actually, I would have liked to have

12 See www.globalforumhealth.org.

spoken with that man.

Black man: I was lonely, and we had a long ride ahead.

White man: I only wish that blacks

Black man: and whites

Both: thought more alike.

As this vignette suggests, the best assumption about other people may be that their way of thinking is a lot like our way of thinking. As another example, for years I watched television programs about native villagers in far-away places and assumed that their exotic-sounding dialog carried conversations quite unlike our own. I then visited a remote Maya village in Belize where English was spoken. Much to my surprise, their conversations were *exactly* like those among friends in U.S. suburbia: "Good afternoon! How was your son's soccer game? May I buy you a Coke? ...."

Like misunderstandings, the ease and entertainment value of criticism also draw people away from respect. Gossip makes for easy conversation. It is relatively simple to bypass efforts to understand other people's seemingly condemnable behavior. Rather than allowing supposed enemies to clarify or defend their positions, it is more convenient to pretend the foes are wrong and evil, and to deny them an impartial hearing. In true circular fashion, that's what we do to others, and that's what others do to us.

Reflections on Respect

Solutions to myriad problems come from real efforts to make respect explicit and to avoid symbols of likely disrespect. A funny thing happened when I wore my bib-overalls into Burger King: the strangers in line around me began talking with me. We discussed food and politics and sports. It was truly a pleasure. Stuffy clothes make people less accessible because the wearers come off as potentially elitist people who might look down on others. No one wants to strike up a conversation with a stranger in a suit who might think too much of himself to respect them. People should wear fancy clothes when they please, and when they have to for work, but I am inspired by Gandhi, whose simple, homemade clothing made him comfortable and approachable. I suspect the humble attire also earned him more respect than would any number of Polo brand horse logos galloping across his chest.

At Christmas time my parents' Christian neighbors place luminaries—those candles in a bag with sand at the bottom—along the sidewalks in front of their homes. My parents are Christians as well, but they resist this practice. They believe that lighting candles in front of Christian homes creates an artificial, unintended distinction between Christians and non-Christians. These candles effectively mark non-Christian homes with darkness, and create an uncomfortable and unnecessary divide between "us" and "them," when in fact no real distinction can be made between what is in the hearts and minds of neighbors near or far. My parents believe that every person is inherently good. They recognize that their own set of beliefs, though strongly held, are based on a particular history of traditions and perspectives, and in no broader terms are they better than anyone else's beliefs. That intentional, respectful, inclusive stance is something people appreciate about my parents. Once again, the respect that goes around comes around.

> My parents go to
> ethnic festivals
> to understand
> and celebrate
> differences.

CHAPTER 11

Money, Success, and Happiness

People ponder the meaning of life; general motives and goals are more transparent. The process of evolution favors humans who crave excitement: minds that pine for stimulation motivate bodies to be more likely to pass on genes. That is, content couch potatoes are less likely to make the effort to get out, pursue others, and seek carnal knowledge. Because sexual pleasures are shallow, elusive, and involve physical and emotional risks, and because artificial stimulants such as methamphetamine ("speed") are deadly dangerous, people pursue a full complement of other sources of excitement. Witness the burgeoning travel and entertainment industries, the perpetual popularity of sports, music, and literature, and the growing interest in flashy computer games and extreme sports such as base jumping, ultra-marathoning, whitewater rafting, and rock climbing.

The thrill seeker in each of us is vulnerable to marketing professionals who seize on the quest for entertainment with claims that material possessions will placate our needs. The message is often that products will provide excitement, popularity, and happiness. Could that message be misleading?

A summary of the research comes later. Let's begin with a

quiz to help guide personal conclusions about the value of salvation via the accumulation of material goods:

- Do you remember what you received for your last birthday?

- When was the last time you used your bread machine or your George Foreman Grill?

- How many articles of clothing in your closet have gone unworn for over a year?

- How many times have you agreed to go on a date with someone because they owned a sexy car?

- Do you spend more time cherishing your material goods or wishing you had more of them?

Sure, it can be fun to shop and purchase things (although perhaps not as much fun as, say, a walk in the woods), but then the burdens of ownership set in. U.S. Census statistics indicate that more than $3.6 billion was spent on self-storage units and mini warehouses in 2002.[1] As that stuff sits in the lock-up, is it giving the owners $3.6 billion worth of benefits each year?

Often less is more. My family cleared the stuff out of our attic and turned it into an open space with an eco-friendly bamboo floor. What had been a useless monument to materialism is now a wonderful place for play, dance, meditation, exercise, and art.

Lessons from the Learned

Respected religious writings adamantly oppose materialism. The second of Buddhism's Four Noble Truths is that suffering comes from the desire for material goods. Buddhists argue that because the ownership of goods is strictly temporary, acquisition is the precursor to inevitable loss and suffering.

The Jewish Torah warns that greed is a hunger that feeds upon itself, and the Midrash, an interpretation of the Hebrew Scriptures, states, "Most people never leave this world with even half their cravings satisfied. If they have a hundred, they want

1   More recent reports are not yet available. See www.census.gov/prod/ec02/ec0253i10t.pdf.

Less is more: the stuff-free attic with a bamboo floor. In our con-sumption-oriented culture, space becomes a precious commodity.

two hundred, and if they have two hundred, they want four hundred" (Eccl. 4.312).

Mahatma Gandhi, the prominent 20th century Hindu spiritual and political leader, lived simply, wore plain clothing, and fol-lowed a vegetarian diet.

The Christian Bible says, "Do not lay up for yourselves trea-sures upon earth, where moth and rust destroy, and where thieves break in and steal. But lay up for yourselves treasures in heaven … for where your treasure is, there will your heart be also" (Matthew 6:19-21).

Muslims are taught that material goods are the property of God and that people are merely God's trustees. The Qur'an states that "those saved from the selfishness of their own souls, they are the ones that achieve prosperity" (64:16).

These great religious books, and the brilliant writings of Aldo Leopold, Henry David Thoreau, Ralph Waldo Emerson, and John Muir, contradict the spirit of marketers and their ideal of rampant consumption. It would be a different world if the ex-plicit anti-materialist messages in these books were taken to heart the way other religious messages are. Imagine crusades against materialism on par with those against pornography. Imagine if fundamentalists stigmatized Hummer ownership the way they stigmatize homosexuality.

Shifts toward sustainable living gain strength from inspirational role models, be they simple-living community heroes, outspoken environmental activists, or spiritual leaders. Personally, I draw courage and guidance from all of the above. I'm not ready to relinquish every material possession as Buddha would have liked, but I respect his ideal, and I feel the predicted release from burden whenever I drop off a load of belongings at the Salvation Army. Try it and see how it makes you feel. Relief is belief: without going to an extreme, less is more!

The Celebrity Test

Those who insist that large quantities of material goods bring happiness should consider the richest of rich celebrities who have access to every imaginable toy. Expensive toys are apparently not infallible keys to contentment. Rather, desperate thrill seeking via alcoholism and drug use is common among the Hollywood elite. Even before Britney Spears shaved her head, bought new tattoos, and entered rehab in 2007, Doug Thorburn listed 120 top celebrities who he claims have particular problems with drugs or alcohol.[2] Those who get stuck on drugs frequently seek rehabilitation—a sure sign that drugs, like material goods, offer only false hopes of satisfaction.

There are other things celebrities get stuck on that cause no such remorse. Entertainers tend to remain immersed in the performing arts long after they stop needing the money. Celebrities are famous for appreciating a good social gathering. And many who could buy every toy imaginable instead find a place in nature to protect and enjoy. Examples include Robert Redford's 6,000 acre Sundance ranch, Ted Turner's 1.1 million acres, Val Kilmer's 1,800 acres, Harrison Ford's 800 acres, Madonna's 1,200 acres, and George W. Bush's 1,600 acres.

The best news is that the true joys of celebrity lives don't require seven-figure salaries. Everyone can practice the arts, enjoy our wilderness lands (the public owns 28.8 percent of all land in the U.S.), and socialize to our hearts' content. I submit that those of us with relatively modest incomes can be even happier

2   See www.preventragedy.com/PAGES/celebs.html.

than the celebrities. The rich have tremendous investments to worry about, their wealth tempts them to indulge in more and more toys whose ephemeral joys distract them from true pleasures, and they can't so much as go out in public without being hounded by paparazzi.

And the Survey Says ...

Consider a thought experiment: Suppose you wake up tomorrow and find yourself with absolutely nothing and no one. A genie appears and announces he will grant you an undisclosed number of wishes that cannot include supernatural powers, money, or more wishes. You must identify one wished-for thing at a time until the uncertain moment when the genie says, "That's it." Because you might be granted only a small number of wishes, it is important to list items in the order of their priority to you. What are the first several distinct things you would ask for? If you're playing along at home, don't look at the next paragraph until you've chosen your wishes. A list might look something like this:

> sunshine, air, water, food, shelter, healthcare, clothing, family, friends, spirituality, affection, wildlife, education, music, sports, ...

This list resembles that of the hundreds of seminar participants I have surveyed about their sources of happiness. Notice that if your list resembles this one, aside from essential shelter, food, and clothing, the things that give you happiness have little to do with money or tangible possessions. Eventually, the genie is likely to get a call for a car, but that's well down the list, and the loss from not having a car simply wouldn't stack up to the loss of any of the items toward the top of the list.

The findings of more formal research confirm that once an individual has enough money to pay for basic necessities, additional income has little to do with happiness. As David Futrelle puts it in his summary of the literature for *Money Magazine*, "Much of the research suggests that seeking the good life at a store is an expensive exercise in futility."[3] For instance, psychology professors Leaf Van Boven and Thomas Gilovich conducted

3   See http://money.cnn.com/magazines/moneymag/moneymag_
archive/2006/08/01/8382225/index.htm.

surveys and ran experiments to determine how the happiness gained from experiences compares with the happiness gained from possessions.[4] The results indicated that in the pursuit of lasting happiness and the enjoyment of life, the creation of experiences such as concerts, ski trips, and dining in restaurants was a better use of time and money than purchases such as jewelry, clothing, and audio equipment.

On the basis of annual survey data on 1500 adults, economist Richard Easterlin reports that having more money and more goods does not lead to more happiness.[5] One problem Easterlin reports is that people quickly adapt their expectations to include new wealth or possessions, and then need more and more of the same to be satisfied. Adaptations and interpersonal comparisons do less to erode happiness received from intangibles such as health, recreation, and the companionship of friends and family.

A 2005 study of happiness based on the GfK NOP Roper Reports worldwide survey of 30,000 people provides further evidence that the path to pleasure does not lead to a factory.[6] The study found that people derive more happiness from good health, a home, children, an interesting job, leisure time, or a yard or garden than from manufactured goods such as a luxury car, a second car, or the latest electronic gadgets. The people with the highest self-reported levels of happiness found satisfaction in their personal appearance, faith, vacations, personal hygiene, and attainment of adequate amounts of sleep. Unhappy respondents reported high levels of alcohol and fast food consumption, both of which are symptomatic of people and cultures bent on finding happiness via money.

Richard Layard of the London School of Economics reports that as real (inflation-adjusted) incomes more than doubled since the 1950s, the percentage of Americans reporting that they are "very happy" remained flat at about 30 percent.[7] The findings were similar in Japan and most of Europe. And in 2008 researchers at Harvard and the University of British Columbia reported

---

4   See L. Van Boven and T. Gilovich, "To Do or To Have? That is the Question," *Journal of Personality and Social Psychology*, 85 (2003): 1193–1202.

5   See www.pubmedcentral.gov/articlerender.fcgi?tool=pmcentrez&artid=196947.

6   See http://sev.prnewswire.com/publishing-information-services/20060208/NYTU19507022006-1.html.

7   See www.iew.unizh.ch/study/courses/downloads/happy.pdf, Table 3, p. 14.

that having more money doesn't make people happier unless they spend it on *others* by giving gifts or donating to charity.[8]

Fancy Clothes Create Barriers, Not Friendships

Don't look for a reminder of the impotence of money and material goods at the entrance to the mall. The wool is pulled well over our eyes, and despite aforementioned warnings that "moth and rust destroy" tangible treasures, we pull the wool over our shoulders and hips with verve—Americans collectively indulge in $18 billion worth of new clothing in a typical *month*.[9] You are what you eat, not what you wear, but one wouldn't know that from clothing ads for the likes of Abercrombie and Fitch, Calvin Klein, Old Navy, and Victoria's Secret that associate happiness, friendship, and passion with expensive underwear. An army of marketing professionals works against general acceptance of the reality that happiness, friendship, and passion come free of charge.

In the past I have bought into the concept of expensive clothes. I thought I would feel more secure in "respectable" clothing, particularly among those who did not know me. A display of affluence made me feel better about myself. I then grew to understand that superficial means yield superficial ends. People with fancy clothes might inspire envy, but that's different from genuine fondness or respect. At best, observers look at people wearing $100 ties or $300 dresses and wish they could have their clothes. More likely, the opulently dressed are charged higher prices, made fun of, pitied for the insecurity that caused them to waste so much money on clothing, or suspected of trying to compensate for weaknesses with showy attire. Some people like to elicit jealousy and envy from others, but this does not make them popular. Despite any appeal of the clothing modeled in *Gentlemen's Quarterly*, I've never heard anyone say they'd like to have a conversation with the models.

> **Superficial means yield superficial ends.**

Easy Street is One Way in the Wrong Direction

Whether success is measured by material goods, acres of wild-

---

8   See www.sciencemag.org/cgi/content/abstract/319/5870/1687.
9   See www.census.gov/mtis/www/mtis_current.html, Table 3.

life preserved, or hours of free time, it is tempting to seek easy paths to get there and to take failure too hard. Indeed, nothing great ever comes easily.

As I stood in line to watch a taping of the *Tonight Show* in Burbank, the NBC staff asked me to read a scripted question for the "Fruitcake Lady," 93-year-old Marie Rudisill, who conveyed wisdom on the show after viewing tapes of inquirers like me. They had me ask, "How can I make a lot of money without working too hard?"

To my knowledge, the Fruitcake Lady did not have the opportunity to reply before she passed away in late 2006, but the question lurks in many a mind. Millions of people have sought easy money and failed. Kentucky Lottery players realized a net loss of $288 million in 2007.[10] Those who fought to have low taxes accompany high levels of government services brought each citizen's share of the national debt above $31,000.[11] Myriad pyramid-scheme participants and work shirkers share the question I posed. What do you suppose she would have said? She might have pointed out that it took her 89 years to first grace the *Tonight Show* stage and that the best fruitcake doesn't come from Easy-Bake ovens.

> The best fruitcake doesn't come from Easy-Bake ovens.

We seldom see the honest work from which success stories are born. Actors John Travolta and Lee Majors began their careers in the Pioneer Playhouse in my rural town of Danville, Kentucky and worked their way up. Bill Gates spent day and night in the computer room from the day in 1968 when his prep school created one. Michelangelo agonized over drawings and discarded countless imperfect pieces while working for years to create each treasured sculpture and painting. The 2004 presidential candidates made 66 campaign trips to the pivotal state of Ohio. Also in 2004 the Boston Red Sox made their World Series win look easy, only after slugging away since their last such win in 1918.

Failure can be invigorating; just ask Bill Clinton, Lance Armstrong, Paul McCartney, Stephen King, and any number of other politicians, athletes, entertainers, and authors, among other

---

10 See www.kylottery.com/apps/export/system/modules/com.kyl.site/galleries/
documents/KYLottery_annual_report/Abridged_Annual_Report_2007.pdf
11 See www.brillig.com/debt_clock/.

successful figures. In seeking success, we must expect and endure failure in part because everything is relative. A day of sunshine is celebrated only because sometimes there are clouds. Ms. Rudisill's nephew, novelist Truman Capote, wrote that "Failure is the condiment that gives success its flavor."

My experience in Burbank is another small example. When I failed to get *Tonight Show* tickets with a written request, I stood in line at 6:00 a.m. for remainders. When I failed to get a remaining seat, I requested a standby ticket. When my standby ticket number was too high for entry, I swallowed my pride and went through the line of ticket holders in search of an extra ticket. Perseverance and legwork paid off. As I entered the studio with someone's extra ticket I was ushered to a spare seat in the section normally reserved for Jay Leno's friends. The guy sitting next to me said I was "lucky" to get in. Lucky? Perhaps, but luck is hard-earned.

In the words of Thomas Jefferson, "I'm a great believer in luck, and I find the harder I work, the more I have of it." This insight is echoed by McDonalds entrepreneur Ray Kroc: "Luck is a dividend of sweat. The more you sweat, the luckier you get"; Billionaire Armand Hammer: "When I work fourteen hours a day, seven days a week, I get lucky"; Brooklyn Dodgers manager Branch Rickey: "Luck is the residue of design"; and author Brian Tracy: "I've found that luck is quite predictable. If you want more luck, take more chances. Be more active. Show up more often."

Ultimately, a successful, happy life rests on the practice of patience, learning, giving, working, and savoring what we have. In John Steinbeck's story *The Pearl*, a struggling seaside family finds the pearl of their dreams, but with that "success" comes such stifling greed and corruption that they finally throw the pearl back into the sea. It might not be so bad to struggle. Perhaps it is in the challenge and intrigue of our daily lives that we succeed in delighting our minds and exciting our souls, and we can thank our lucky stars that we sometimes fail. As L. Frank Baum suggests in *The Wizard of Oz*, maybe we're already closer to the best of all worlds than it appears—"There's no place like home."

A 1960 *Twilight Zone* episode called "A Nice Place to Visit" introduces a man who calls himself Rocky because, as Rod Sterling narrates, "that's the way his life has been—rocky and perilous and uphill at a dead run all the way. He's tired now, tired of running or wanting, of waiting for the breaks that come to others but never to him."

Rocky dies and finds himself in a white place surrounded by wealth, women, and unfailing luck. It is heavenly at first, but then he tires of always winning. He realizes that it is hell when things come too easily and begs to be sent to "the other place." Sterling concludes, "Now he has everything he's ever wanted— and he's going to have to live with it for eternity …."

> My parents
> do not buy
> lottery tickets.

CHAPTER 12

Better Sources
of Excitement

Some businesspeople are driven by financial greed, but there must be more to the story, for theirs is not the most highly paid profession. Medical professions account for 11 of the 12 top-paying occupations in the United States, with chief executive officers (the highest-paying business job) coming in 9th.[1] The many highly intelligent executives who don't apply to medical school may indicate an overarching interest in the excitement of the business world which, for them, trumps the money and quite differerent types of excitement of the medical world. Likewise, people in myriad other careers could earn more, if not as doctors, perhaps as miners or actuaries. As an economist, I could earn more on Wall Street than as a professor, and I have turned down higher-paying positions. These facts reveal a goal beyond simple income maximization. There must be something else that influences decisions about what we do with our lives. In his hierarchy of needs, Abraham Maslow lists survival, security, social acceptance, self esteem, and self actualization.[2] Omitted from this list is an undeniable need at the heart of many re-

---

1   The next-highest-paying business-related occupation is that of marketing manager, which ranked 22nd. See www.acinet.org/occ_intro.asp?id=1&nodeid=1.
2   See, for example, www.ship.edu/~cgboeree/maslow.html.

source depletion problems. It is behind the consumer's visit to the Disney Store and the businessperson's desire for the thrill of market dominance. It is the need to entertain the mind.

When children bicker endlessly about who crossed an imaginary dividing line in the back seat of the car, one has to think there's a human instinct to fight boredom at all costs. Adults share this instinct but take boredom-avoidance to higher heights. Tourism is the biggest industry in the world. Television, movies, spectator sports, parties, games of all types, books, and our own bickering at all levels entertains our minds while accomplishing little else. Materialism is often a byproduct of human desires to be amused. Why else would people collect cars, crystal, or stuffed animals? Trips to the department store are seldom for survival. A material-goods spending spree isn't the worst source of excitement—drugs and wars are far worse—but "shop therapy" does contribute to resource loss, environmental degradation, and personal debt. Given the severity of each of these problems, it behooves us to brainstorm alternatives.

Finding Amusement Outside of the Retail Box

Below are 100 ways to have fun without shopping. In light of the fleeting benefits of material goods, the items in this list could aptly be called 100 activities that are *more fun* than shopping. Some of the activities are seasonal, some of them provide enjoyment for a lot longer than a shopping trip, some of them aren't for everyone, but all are reminders that there is more to do than fill our arms with shopping bags and suffer buyer's remorse.

1. Learn to juggle
2. Plant a garden
3. Watch a movie from the public library
4. Take a cooking class
5. Paint a masterpiece
6. Play a non-competitive or trust game[3]

---

3 *The New Games Book* (New Games Foundation, New York: Main Street Books, 1976) is a great source. Although no longer new, this book and others like it are readily available from online booksellers.

7. Make a snowman or a sand castle

8. Ride your bike

9. Take an aerobics class

10. Write a poem and read it to someone

11. Knit a scarf to give as a holiday gift

12. Research and buy stock in a company that has high moral standards

13. Go jogging

14. Go swimming

15. Go sledding

16. Enter and train for a triathlon or fun run

17. Take a class on massage at the local community college

18. Bake bread

19. Take a hike

20. Surf the Information Superhighway

21. Surf the ocean

22. Go ice skating

23. Take a ballroom dancing class

24. Call a far-away family member

25. Take a luxurious bath

26. Plan your next home-made holiday card

27. Take an art class

28. Write a social-action message with chalk on the sidewalk

29. Write a letter to the editor of the local newspaper

30. Listen to your oldest album and sing along

31. Learn to sew

32. Write a short story or novel

33. Make cookies from scratch

34. Re-read your favorite book, or delve into a new one

35. Visit your best friend

36. Snuggle with a significant other

37. Call the local auto dealers and ask them if they carry electric vehicles

38. Study a foreign language

39. Plan or attend a neighborhood pot-luck

40. Learn to play the piano or guitar

41. Patch your favorite pair of jeans

42. Challenge someone to a tennis match

43. Learn to wind-surf or roller skate

44. Exchange backrubs with a friend

45. Make birdfeeders by putting peanut butter on pine cones and rolling them in seeds

46. Improve your golf game

47. Play Frisbee

48. Learn a new software program

49. Invite a neighbor to sit on your porch with you and share deep thoughts

50. Organize a community volleyball game

51. Make a lanyard necklace or key chain

52. Perfect a chai tea recipe

53. Look into making your own biodiesel fuel

54. Take unneeded clothing to a thrift store

55. Have your favorite old shoes re-soled

56. Read about a religion you've always wondered about

57. Write down your dreams and try to interpret them
58. Gaze at the stars and learn new constellations
59. Visit a museum
60. Volunteer at the local food bank
61. Look into solar energy for your home
62. Visit an elderly friend in a nursing home
63. Tie-dye an otherwise boring T-shirt
64. Watch a stimulating talk show
65. Meditate
66. Go to the gym and work out
67. Make a digital collage with your digital photographs
68. Perform a random act of kindness
69. Go to a karaoke bar
70. Pamper yourself with a spa treatment
71. Learn to identify wild flowers or trees
72. Rake a pile of leaves and jump in it
73. Become more involved in your church or civic organization
74. Make a meal out of wild plants
75. Play Scrabble
76. Take a nap in your hammock
77. Cut your own hair
78. Bike or walk to work
79. Dye your hair
80. Join the choir
81. Practice yoga
82. Run for local political office
83. Frequent the local café

84. Plant a tree

85. Organize your old family photos

86. Paint your bathroom a radical new color

87. Make a decorative wreath with clippings from your yard

88. Vegetate in front of the TV with a cup of hot cocoa

89. Wash and wax your car

90. Dance to rock-and-roll music

91. Make amends with a former enemy

92. Read an online newspaper

93. Mow the lawn with a non-motorized push mower

94. Make a list of the true joys of life and then seek them out

95. Take your dog to the neighborhood park where other dog owners hang out

96. Work on that invention you've been knocking around in your head

97. Collect shells from the beach

98. Make a compost bin or set up a rain barrel

99. Perform a blind taste test of competing fair-trade coffee or tea brands with some friends

100. Try a new food. Oysters? Insects? Sushi? Indian?

The purchase of material goods can be fun, but when we recognize that many shoppers are just out to entertain their minds, the implication is that less damaging activities such as those listed here can satisfy the same needs. Like my parents and so many others raised in the wake of resource shortages, we can replace the challenge of acquisition with the challenge of frugality and the quest to do the most with the fewest resources. As discussed further in the next chapter, those who choose to play the game of life with due respect for natural resources can have at least as much fun as those stuck on the challenge of dying with the most possessions.

In the midst of writing this book I moved my office to accommodate building renovation. My new space had previously been shared by a former president of Centre College and a distinguished member of its board of trustees. Even an amateur anthropologist could learn much from what these two highly successful men left behind. Their desks held relics of frugality. Their trophies were tucked away and left behind. Their office equipment—staplers, telephones, chairs, filing cabinets—were modest and worn. These men accomplished much by exercising their diligence, and by avoiding the distracting quest for newfangled dictation devices and chrome-plated tape dispensers. They understood the unequaled satisfaction from a job well done and built their self esteem on pride. The fact that they maintained working offices long after their formal retirement indicates the vigor of their work ethic

> **They understood the unequaled satisfaction from a job well done.**

and the great joy they gained from their pursuits and contributions. Their perspective on retirement as a time for expanded intellectual curiosity, and not for expanded use of credit cards, led them to remarkable contentment.

A Tongue-In-Cheek Look at the Future of Entertainment

We have much to learn from wise elders, beginning with an appreciation for their favorite non-materialistic pursuits. Before the days of climate-controlled shopping centers and big-box retailers, Americans took to ball fields and sports arenas for entertainment and invigoration. Crowds are now thinning at sporting events from baseball to hockey to horse racing. As professional sports strike out, the question remains: What will be the favorite non-shopping pastime of tomorrow if we do not heed our elders' advice about simple pleasures? We can only hope the population will not retreat to cyberspace, satisfying their social cravings in Internet chat rooms. Perhaps with global warming will come mushrooming interest in water parks, where we can drown our sorrows in artificial waves. Food consumption is a popular enough secondary event at any ballpark or horse track to warrant a spin-off event—just standing around eating—but for those who cannot emulate John Belushi's buffet-line performance in *Animal House*, eating does not satisfy the need for public expression the way spectator sports do. Exposing your bloated midriff to the interior of your refrigerator muttering "where's the beef" just isn't the same as yelling it (with similar exposure) from the stands at some errant linebacker who could bench-press your refrigerator.

Looking back, a variety of past fads could re-emerge to quench our thirst for entertainment. Hoola hoops, yo-yos, pogo sticks, and marbles are all waiting in the wings; pet rocks are unlikely to make a curtain call for an audience seduced by MTV. Public nudity took off in the late sixties when the popularity of sports was waning and the Vietnam War warranted escape. Perhaps streaking and love-ins will replace winning streaks and bat-ins, yet conservative victories at the polls seem to reflect a population that won't show its tan lines. Rather than a revival of the old days, perhaps a new, 21st-century pastime will come along and capture our interests. The evolution of virtual reality may allow us to spend a few hours in an upper-crust restaurant or on Mars without making true contact with rude or probing life forms. We may step into electrode-filled chambers that leave us so happy that we don't care why.

Maybe we'll spend our leisure time complaining. We have long been rehearsing this and we're darn good at it. It is environmentally friendly, social, exciting, and anyone can do it. We can have publications filled with things to complain about. We can have complaint bars, complaint conventions, and team complaining. Solitary types can revert to the complaint channel or telephone complaint lines open 24 hours a day. What will we complain about? To begin with, the lack of professional sports. And imagine the mileage we'll get out of complaining about the volume of complaints. "Have you ever heard such complaining? It makes me sick!" Whatever we occupy ourselves with, those who anticipate it and invest early will be the Henry Fords and Bill Gateses of tomorrow. Take my advice: get out of plastics and into anger. The future is upon us, darn it!

167

Conclusions

Shopping is always something to do. The ubiquitous advertising and marketing industries advance the assertion that nothing could be more fun. That assertion is wrong. Too often it is not the ownership of a new product that makes us happy; it is the brief period of search and acquisition that entertains the mind. Then the purchaser adjusts expectations to include that product, and continued consumption-based happiness requires endless rounds of search and acquisition. On the other hand, the entertainment value of learning to juggle, watching a baseball game, or completing a marathon lingers without the problems associated with making, storing, securing, and maintaining material goods. As the citizens of a small planet that cannot endure consumption-based pleasure seeking from a population of seven billion people, a paradigm shift to finding fulfillment in friendships, services, communities, and activities would be a win-win-win-win- ... solution seven billion times over.

My parents run 5K races.

CHAPTER 13

A Player's Manual
for the Game of Life

My young children are always eager to engage in a new game, even when they are unclear on the rules. They watch me carefully to pick up on my purpose. If I run away, they see that they should chase. If I chase them, they know to run away. If I embrace them, they embrace me. The instincts to succeed, win, and fit in are stronger than any preconceived notions about the rules of games. It may thus be possible to improve the civility, the respect for ecosystems, and the overall number of winners in the game of life by conveying a better set of rules.

Children are by no means the only ones studying the rules for the game of life. As adults, we continue to watch those around us carefully to pick up on norms, standards, and expectations. Most party guests are content to wear formal or casual clothing, but very concerned about which is right for a particular event. Salary negotiations can become standoffs or joint efforts to discover what is fair, depending on how the game is framed and what initial signals are sent. Selfishness is contagious as a game strategy, but so is generosity. If, after a restaurant meal with a group of friends, you say, "I'm going to pay," you've established that the game is to try to pay, and others are likely to say, "No, I'm going to pay."

Sometimes we look to magazines for guidance in conforming to life's rule book. *GQ* and *Cosmo* show us what to wear as we play the game of life. Home magazines show us what our playhouses should look like, and car magazines show us what to drive when we play. We look to neighbors to determine the rules of the yard game—how to manicure our lawns, what sort of mailbox is appropriate, and how to decorate for the holidays. We look to adversaries to see what types of games our disputes will become, and we form different relationships with different people depending on their preferred types of games, be they easy, hard, pleasant, gruff, stingy, generous, green, or greedy.

The Rules of the Game

The objective of the game depends on the players:

- The objective for many businesses is to win market share and profits, even if the associated products or manufacturing processes might be harmful to customers or others.

- The objective for parents is typically to nurture healthy children and maintain personal sanity.

- The objective for plaintiffs is often to win large settlements from defendants.

- The objective for many religions is to encourage generosity, peace, and nonjudgment.

Notice that we are all players, but the games we play vary widely depending on the context. Sometimes we give; sometimes we take. Some games involve cooperation, in others we take no prisoners. Winning can involve adversity or benevolence. All of this tells us that people and their games are malleable.

Sometimes different players have different objectives within the same game. For example, as a professor I have some students who feel they win when they learn and get good grades, while others feel they win when they are able to skip class or party on a school night.

Players in different places can have different rules for the same game. National healthcare coverage and the abolishment of the death penalty, for example, are seen as "wins" in virtually every industrialized nation, but losses in the United States.

The rules of some games change over time in the same places. For instance, during the energy crisis of the 1970s, the game for most Americans was to conserve oil. Today, many Americans feel they win by having more and bigger cars.

Players are open to adaptations in the rules, and they are pleased if they are still playing "correctly," even as the definition of "correct" behavior changes. Think of fashion. When players get dressed in the morning, they very much want to play by the rules, but over time they have literally and figuratively taken off their hats to new trends. Since the 1970s, American consumers have collectively shed their bell-bottoms and jumped into khakis, cut their hair, lengthened their skirts, narrowed their ties, trimmed their collars and sideburns, and put on sweats and running shoes even when not working out. It's not as if all players wear the same uniform, but relative to what people wore in different times or places, Americans dress remarkably alike. When was the last time you saw someone on Main Street wearing a toga, a kimono, or a top hat?

Games with Unfortunate Rules

Looking toward the big picture now: we like to play, we care about and conform to the rules, and we can help set the rules as role models. This is important information because there are non-trivial games people play that need new rules.

- Our use of natural resources is a game with the current rule that whoever dies with the most toys wins.

- Our treatment of foreign countries is a game with the current rules that we are to be suspicious of people who are different from us and we may compete violently with those we do not understand.

- Our treatment of the environment is a game with the current rule that is it is acceptable to destroy old-growth forests, vulnerable animals, and other wildlife if it makes us a buck.

- Our treatment of each other is a game with many complex rules. For example, if we are in an accident with another person, we can try to sue them for everything they've got. It is acceptable to disparage groups on the basis of isolated experiences with individuals. And it is acceptable to explain the behavior of others on the basis of conjecture.

In so many ways, school is a game, dating is a game, work is a game, and life is a game. In economics there is a sub-field called game theory. The classic game is the *prisoners' dilemma*, which involves two crooks apprehended after a bank robbery. There is limited evidence connecting them with the crime. They are taken into separate rooms for interrogation and cannot coordinate their responses. If they both deny involvement, they will get off with a light, two-year sentence because there isn't much evidence against them. If they both confess, they will get a five-year sentence because they did it, but at least they were honest. If one confesses involvement and the other denies it, the honest confessor will get a one-year sentence for her honesty and for her help nailing the other crook, and the lying denier will go to jail for ten years because she did it and she lied about it. Even though they'd be better off if they could trust each other to deny the crime, they end up confessing to avoid the large downside risk of being the lone denier.

There are many real-world applications of the prisoners' dilemma game. In business, the dilemma involves setting high or low prices. Higher prices would be better for profits if everyone followed that strategy, but when it's difficult for Kmart and Wal-Mart to trust each other and coordinate their moves, they end up submitting low prices to the newspaper for the Sunday advertising circular for fear of being the lone store with high prices. (As explained in Chapter 8, low prices cause overconsumption and are not good for the environment.)

An international prisoners' dilemma involves armaments. Every country would be better off if no one spent money on bombs and war machines, for the money spent on arms races could be put toward progress on health, education, and other quality-of-life enhancements. Instead, the lack of trust and cooperation leads countries to spend billions on weapons for fear of being the lone country without them.

Prisoners' dilemmas apply to personal consumption as well. Consider the purchase of big gifts at holiday time, chemical lawn treatments, or uncomfortable dress clothes. If nobody bought these things, the playing field would be level and the players would be wealthier, healthier, and more comfortable. Nonetheless, a lack of coordination presents the risk that a resistor will stand alone, without a gift, on an imperfect lawn, wearing blue jeans.

Since you're reading this book, you probably have the nerve to resist excessive conformity, but the analysis of prisoners' dilemmas helps to explain behavior in society at large. The solution is to change games of ignorance and arrogance into games of cooperation and trust, and to embrace an informal rule against judging others, so as to lower the risk of being the only one to do the right thing.

> **The solution is to change games of ignorance and arrogance into games of cooperation and trust.**

Establishing New Rules

The power of role models to change the rules has been recognized for thousands of years. The Hindu *Bhagavad-Gita* says, "Whatsoever a great man does, the same is done by others as well. Whatever standard he sets, the world follows." Buddha said, "Let each man first direct himself to what is proper, then let him teach others."[1]

As rule makers and role models we must first establish our goals. We can choose to target immediate gratification or long-run success. We can strive for any combination of profit maximization and social-welfare maximization. We can win by giving or taking. And our selection of goals influences those around us. Parents, friends, siblings, spouses, neighbors, teachers, business leaders, clergy, sports heroes, and politicians all help form the rules of the game.

When President John Kennedy advised, "Ask not what your country can do for you, ask what you can do for your country,"[2] he and others like him set the tone for an entire generation, one that established the Peace Corps and achieved progress on civil rights and education among other noble causes. The momentum lasted until another set of role models changed the objective of the game and created the "Me Generation" in the 1980s.

In the 1990s, President Bill Clinton was an exemplary role model in many ways, though not in marital fidelity. Interestingly, Kenneth Star's $50 million probe into Clinton's activities showed that unlike so many other world leaders, members of the clergy, politicians, and presidents, those with a modicum of self discipline can satisfy their sexual appetite without going "all the way." After Clinton's well-publicized episodes of oral sex, teen pregnancies hit a record low,[3] while the incidence of oral sex more than doubled and the number of associated herpes cases increased.[4] Maybe the timing was a coincidence, or maybe the *Bhagavad-Gita* had it right: "Whatsoever a great man does, the same is done by others as well."

Public figures aren't the only ones who influence the rules. We look up to our heroes for inspiration, but we look to each other to see how to succeed in the eyes of our peers. In many ways, then, we all set the rules. If you say to your friends, "I just gave $100 to help build a park, na na na na na!" they will see the objective of the game clearly and their competitive spirit may bring them to play. For a related example, watch documentary filmmaker Michael Moore shame Nike CEO Phil Knight into

1 See www.identitytheory.com/etexts/buddha12.html.
2 See www.speakersforum.fi/john_kennedy/ask_not/35/36/.
3 See www.teenpregnancy.org/resources/data/prates.asp.
4 See www.medicalnewstoday.com/medicalnews.php?newsid=21945.

giving $10,000 to the Flint, Michigan, school system in Moore's 1997 film, *The Big One*.

If as a community leader you eschew conspicuous consumption and embrace charitable giving, the game will be played in society's favor. If as a spouse you compete to see who can do the *most* for your children, your mate will follow your lead. If as a role model you work to understand and appreciate those who are different in gender, race, or sexual preference, and make the game one of peace, love, and understanding rather than judgment and criticism, so will your protégés. You can brag about homogeneity or diversity in your neighborhood or workplace. You can boast about numerous toys or recycling joys. You can brandish bigotry or reverence. You can boast of how little you work or how much.

When your neighbor parades around on her chemically enhanced monoculture of a lawn, mowed by her shining steed of a super power mower, you can counter her game playing and norm setting. Strut out onto your organic, biologically diverse lawn and say, "Isn't nature wonderful! I love to be able to breathe deeply and smell nothing but clover and flowers. Pity those who can't make dandelion wine due to toxic lawn applications!"

Dandelions adorn an organic lawn where children play. Dandelion wine recipes are available at http://winemaking.jackkeller.net/dandelion.asp.

People tend to rise to expectations in the game of trust as well. In Japan, for example, it is considered an insult to count money upon receipt. In that environment of mutual trust, violations are almost unheard-of. The rules are different elsewhere. In places where trust is not the norm, those who don't count their change stand to lose many a game.

Sometimes winning ways in the game of life are analogous to winning strategies in games of sport. In the classic 1978 movie *Heaven Can Wait*, Warren Beatty plays a football player who is taken up to heaven prematurely by an inexperienced angel and must be returned to Earth in the body of someone else whose time would otherwise be up. He returns in the body of a corporate leader. As a ballplayer in business clothes, he makes a compelling speech to his board members about using moral strategies to get ahead in the game:

> Let the other team build the power plants in all the wrong places. Let the other quarterback throw a girdle out so the newspapers get ahold of it .... Let's be the team that makes the rules. Let us be the team that plays fair ... the popular team .... We're not in here for just one game ... Let's get to the Superbowl guys, and when we get there, let's already have won!

With this speech, writers Warren Beatty and Elaine May make a salient point about the ability of business firms and sports teams, like individuals, to set high moral standards and influence society with winning ways in the game of life.

In a game closer to home, my little neighbor, let's call him Dennis, once came over and told me about his father's truck. He said,

> My dad's truck is better than your truck. It's bigger, newer, faster, it has six cylinders and four-wheel drive. It's a much better truck.

I said,

> I'm sure your dad has a very nice truck, but to me, the best truck is the one with the highest gas mileage, the lowest price, and the smallest burden on the Earth's resources. You see Dennis, every time I

drive 200 miles, for the difference between what I pay for gasoline and what it costs to drive the same distance in your dad's truck, I can buy a large pizza and two ice cream cones. And for the difference between what your dad's truck cost and what my truck cost, you could attend a baseball game complete with peanuts and Cracker Jacks every week for the rest of your life. My truck is made with about a ton less steel, which means less dirty air for all of us to breath and more resources that are available to build cars for you and your children. I'm also proud to say that I've achieved over 100,000 miles on my truck. With enough luck and effort, someday maybe *you* can own a small truck with high mileage.

I don't know whether I changed the game for Dennis or not, but I do believe that boasts of efficiency plant healthy seeds in people's minds.

Conclusions

Some people think that environmentalists are overly optimistic because we think that, with effort, the world can become a better place. With our current environmental and social predicaments, I think that non-environmentalists are overly optimistic to think that we'll be just fine without such efforts.

Rather than submitting to materialistic games,

- brag about reducing and reusing;

- show off your secondhand clothing;

- eschew conspicuous consumption;

- rave about your low-flush, dual-flush, or composting toilet;

- display affection for your family and friends;

- work to understand and appreciate those who are different from you;

- share your knowledge that the benefits of material wealth are ephemeral, and that the joy of conservation, moderation, and simple living is eternally satisfying; and

- place your game piece on the high road.

In so doing, you will help to define the game that is your life.

Team apathy has the ball and our goal is to guard the environmental tipping point. Let us be the role models. Let us be the sparks of social and environmental action. Let us be the makers of rules. And when there is a loose ball—when we have the next opportunity to advance policy or society—let's already have won!

My parents won a neighborhood beautifi-cation award with their organic lawn and land-scaping that has never met a power tool.

CHAPTER 14

Actions Speak Louder

When a flash mob hit the Harvard Bookstore, hundreds of people showed up out of nowhere, crammed themselves into the aisles for a few minutes, and then left. On the surface, the point was that there was no point. At a deeper level the feat was a celebration of humanity, a reminder of the power of cooperation, and a blend of collective action, rebellion, performance art, and fun. Similar flash mobs have hit New York's Grand Hyatt Hotel, a Washington D.C. Books-A-Million store, and the streets of San Francisco, not to mention sites in Beirut, England, Scotland, and Japan.[1]

Professor Clay Shirky of New York University says that if they catch on, flash mobs will be adopted by political activists, and they are already being considered by social action groups from the Sierra Club to the Moral Majority.[2] In 2008 a flash mob gathered in a California shopping mall while fake money thrown by a co-conspirator rained down from the mezzanine. Some of the funny money carried the slogan "A dollar for your

---

1   See videos of many of these by typing "flash mob" into the search field at www. youtube.com.

2   See www.csmonitor.com/2003/0804/p01s02-ussc.html.

conscience" as a statement against consumerism.[3] According to Howard Rheingold, author of *Smart Mobs: The Next Social Revolution*, relatively new communications networks that include cell phones and the Internet have already brought people together to sway elections in Korea and the Philippines and to needle such bodies as the World Trade Organization.

The concept of non-violent social action is nothing new. In Aristophanes' anti-war comedy *Lysistrata*, written in 411 B.C.E., the women of Sparta, Boeotia, and Corinth refuse to have sex with their husbands until the Peloponnesian War is ended. Fast-forward to 2006 and the wives of gangsters in Pereira, one of Columbia's most violent cities, refused to have sex with their husbands until they stopped their murderous fighting. After 10 days the sex strike ended with claims of success.[4]

In 1930, Mahatma Gandhi and his followers walked 240 miles to the sea in Gajurat, India, to collect salt in a symbolic protest against the British salt tax. The event became a turning point in India's successful independence movement. In 1955, Rosa Parks, an African American, violated a segregated seating ordinance on a public bus in Montgomery, Alabama. She was arrested and jailed after refusing to give up her seat to white people. Her brave actions sparked a successful boycott of segregated city buses, after which the U.S. Supreme Court affirmed that the bus segregation laws were unconstitutional.

The "sit-in" movement started in 1960 when African American students in Greensboro, North Carolina, protested segregation at lunch counters by taking seats and refusing to leave. The movement spread quickly throughout the South. The sit-ins succeeded in ending segregation at lunch counters in 27 southern cities. Sit-ins were later used to fight segregation in waiting rooms, schools, and various forms of public transportation, and to protest the Vietnam War, during which 5,000,000 Vietnamese and 58,226 Americans died.

Inspired by Gandhi's adherence to nonviolent protest, Martin Luther King, Jr., led a series of successful marches and gatherings for civil rights. King led 125,000 people in a "Freedom Walk" in Detroit in 1963. In the same year more than 250,000 people assembled in Washington, D.C., for the civil rights rally where King delivered his unforgettable "I Have A Dream" speech. In

3   For photos and a video, see www.deconstructionworkers.com.
4   See http://news.bbc.co.uk/2/hi/americas/5372718.stm.

1965 a group of 3,200 people left Selma, Alabama, and swelled to 25,000 before arriving at the state capital in Montgomery to present a voting rights petition to Governor George Wallace.

At the brink of the Iraq war, protesters around the world marched, prayed, and spoke out about the virtues of peace. In the United States, England, Canada, South Africa, and Australia, peace advocates punctuated their message by forming peace signs and spelling out anti-war slogans with their naked bodies.[5] In Pamplona, Spain, one of several cities in which bulls are chased through the streets and into a fighting ring to be slowly killed by matadors, the animal-rights organization People for the Ethical Treatment of Animals holds an annual "running of the nudes" to protest and attract attention to animal cruelty associated with the running of the bulls.[6]

As is evident from the 17-year time span between Gandhi's famous march and Indian independence, the seeds of social justice seldom germinate quickly, but the cumulative effect of long-term efforts is growth in a healthy direction. By 2006, anti-war sentiment brought a change of power in both houses of Congress and new lows in the approval levels for President Bush and the Iraq war. As for progress in the war against animal cruelty, since 2004, 22 Spanish towns including Barcelona, Torello, Calldetenes, and Olot have declared themselves anti-bullfight cities.[7] With the support of 250,000 signatures on a petition,[8] the parliament of Catalonia—an area in northeast Spain that includes Barcelona—is considering a bill that would ban bullfights throughout the region.[9]

Like petitions, marches, flash mobs, and sit-ins, the age-old techniques of demonstrations and boycotts remain in the social-justice toolbox. Each November since 1990, several thousand people have demonstrated at Fort Benning, where the former School of the Americas (renamed in 2000 as the Western Hemisphere Institute for Security Cooperation) allegedly trains dictators and assassins. Graduates include ex-Panamanian dictator Manuel Noriega and convicted terrorist Gonzalo Guevara

---

5   See, for example, www.barewitness.com and
    www.sfheart.com/naked_for_peace.html.
6   See www.runningofthenudes.com/.
7   See www.actionagainstpoisoning.com/page13/page254/page254.html.
8   See http://news.bbc.co.uk/cbbcnews/hi/animals/newsid_3605000/3605949.stm.
9   See www.timesonline.co.uk/article/0,,13509-2239827,00.html.

Cerritos.[10] Boycotts of Wal-Mart helped pressure the discounter to revamp its stance toward the environment in 2006.

The collective-action arm of activism is strengthened by what Thomas Friedman describes as the world-flattening technology of the 21st century.[11] Technology spreads information about injustices like wildfire, and connects coordinators and participants in social action at the speed of a text message. As with the strength of the sword and the still-mightier pen, activists must wield their high-tech powers wisely. Thoughtfully, non-violently, those who are aware of social and environmental wrongs must summon the personal strength to boot-up their computers and transmit their podcasts in the name of justice.

> **Activists must wield their high-tech powers wisely.**

Taking Action

If you could erect a billboard to display a single social-justice message in the middle of a large city, what would it say? Perhaps mine would say, "Peace: It's a better idea. Much better." War is a compelling target for social action because unlike cancer, AIDS, and so many other tragedies that destroy lives and tear families apart, there are wars that could be avoided from the start, or shut off like a water spigot, if the right people were influenced to do so. That being said, there is no short list of problems that deserve action. It would be a good start to address the predicaments of bigotry, environmental collapse, inadequate funding for education, homophobia, exorbitant healthcare costs, disease, torture, poverty, famine, corruption, discrimination, physical abuse, drug abuse, excessive litigation, obesity, and animal cruelty, to name a few.

Social action can be applied to these problems, but the method matters. Most applications of the popular brute-force solution are doomed by human instincts. Millennia of warfare foretell that brute force does not trigger submission. It is not human nature to back down, as is evident in daily life. Scream at people in the car next to yours and they will scream back, or worse. Push someone in front of you in a line and push will come to shove, or worse. Start an unnecessary war and you will invigorate the "enemy,"

---

10 See www.thirdworldtraveler.com/Terrorism/SOA.html.
11 See *The World Is Flat,* (New York: Farrar, Straus, and Giroux, 2006).

stir up broader opposition, handicap more valiant pursuits, or worse. Likewise, when members of the Earth Liberation Front and the Animal Liberation Front caused $23 million in damage to lumber companies, meatpacking plants, a ski resort, federal ranger stations, and an electricity tower, no one backed down as a result. The attacks only hardened the opposition and led to the 2006 indictment of 11 conspirators. And worse, a co-conspirator killed himself shortly after his arrest.[12]

More urbane than force, but still dangerous, nonviolent resistance is a common tactic among those seeking change. The international environmental organization Greenpeace dishes it out and takes it. On March 17, 2003, three days before the U.S. invasion of Iraq, the Greenpeace ship Rainbow Warrior II blocked the entrance to the Rato Naval Base on Spain's southern coast to prevent a U.S. military supply ship from leaving with armaments.[13] In 2006, French fishing boats surrounded the Rainbow Warrior II as it tried to enter the port of Marseille to promote a moratorium on tuna fishing. Among other colorful examples, Julia Butterfly Hill perched herself 180 feet up a centuries-old California redwood tree named Luna for 738 days ending in 1999 to prevent the Pacific Lumber Company from harvesting the surrounding old-growth forest.[14] And in 2001 and 2006, anti-nuclear protesters in Germany chained themselves across railroad tracks to halt trains carrying spent nuclear fuel.[15]

As with force, one cannot be too cautious when stirring the pot of human emotions via resistance. I wrote *Sometimes I Get So Angry! Anger Management for Everyone*[16] after hundreds of interviews with violent criminals in prisons convinced me that, during a fit of rage, all rules of civilized conduct fly out the window. There are many sad stories of nonviolent resistance that provoked violent responses. Dutch photographer Fernando Pereira, father of two young children, died in 1985 when the original Greenpeace Rainbow Warrior was bombed by agents of the French secret service. In 2004, as he sat chained to the railroad tracks, 23-year-old Sebastien Briat was killed by a train

12 See www.washingtonpost.com/wp-dyn/content/article/2006/01/20/
    AR2006012001823.html.
13 See www.planetark.org/dailynewsstory.cfm/newsid/20176/story.htm.
14 See www.circleoflifefoundation.org/inspiration/luna/.
15 See http://news.bbc.co.uk/1/hi/world/europe/1247676.stm and http://www3.whdh.
    com/news/articles/world/BO33876/.
16 Pensive Press, 2007.

carrying radioactive waste from France to Germany.[17] American Rachel Corrie lost her life to a bulldozer as she tried to prevent Israelis from demolishing Palestinian homes.[18] Luna the redwood tree was attacked by criminals bearing chainsaws, although with some braces and patchwork, she lives on.

A third approach to social action is to raise awareness and educate the public about an area of injustice in order to stir up the ambivalent, inform the ignorant, summon the like-minded, and sway the open-minded. Such campaigns are what produced the momentum of the civil rights, environmental, and peace movements of the 1960s. Like Luna, the legislative legacies of these movements live on, however tenuously.

Informational campaigns may not be as cathartic as more aggressive forms of resistance, but they don't provoke the same level of opposition either. It may seem unlikely that relatively mild rallies, marches, letters to newspaper editors, and teach-ins will save the world, but remember that it is not necessary to convert everyone. It is sufficient to reach a tipping point at which enough sentiment is behind the cause to bring about the needed change. For many good causes, the proportion of people in favor of change is already near the tipping point. The majority of sentiment turned against the Iraq war in 2005.[19] Growing consensus on global climate change pushes society closer and closer to a tipping point on environmental policy, fueled by visionary organizations such as the Sierra Club and the World Wildlife Federation, activists such as Al Gore and Laurie David,[20] and documentaries such as *Who Killed the Electric Car*,[21] *Kilowatt Ours*,[22] and *Taken for a Ride*.[23]

Chapter 6 of this book discusses the problem of fiction serving as the basis for common beliefs and actions. The reliance on fiction means two things in the context of social action: First, it means there is a real need to disseminate facts, and that education can be a meaningful part of social action. Second, it means that a good deal of current behavior is not grounded in truth, which

17 See http://news.bbc.co.uk/1/hi/world/europe/3990641.stm.
18 See www.ccmep.org/2003_articles/Palestine/032003_the_moments_before.htm.
19 See www.washingtonpost.com/wp-dyn/content/article/2005/06/07/ AR2005060700296.html.
20 See www.lauriedavid.com.
21 See www.sonyclassics.com/whokilledtheelectriccar/.
22 See www.kilowattours.org.
23 See www.newday.com/films/Taken_for_a_Ride.html.

provides optimism that certain attitudes and belief structures can change as information comes to light. For instance:

- Xenophobic individuals who think that people who are different are for that reason bad, are wrong, and evidence of that can be brought out. Let's enlighten others about, for example, the fact that the murder rate per 100,000 in *our* nation's capital is 69, while in Central America it is 57, in Moscow it is 18, in Paris it is 3, and in all of Japan it is 1.

- War advocates who think violence solves problems can be shown a vast history of world powers that became arrogant and belligerent, only to see their empires crumble.

- Those who do not recognize the throes of environmental problems can be taught, for example, that at current rates of overfishing, scientists warn that the world's seafood industries may collapse by the year 2050.[24]

People can be stubborn about changing their views, but remember that many people—including those "median voters" who determine the fate of elections—are on the fence and are more easily swayed by facts. And don't forget the ability of social action to engage, inspire, and inform. Everyone has pent-up potential for change, it's just a matter of *stirring it up*. There are many things that anyone can do to move people and make them think.

Protests make people think. I remember protesting the Vietnam War with my older sister. We and thousands of other people helped block the main thoroughfare of East Lansing, Michigan for several days. That made more than a few people literally stop and think, and such actions helped end the war.

Speeches make people think. Martin Luther King, Jr., did this with his elegant arguments articulated with his amazing baritone voice. I recently listened to 12 of his speeches on the audio book *A Call to Conscience*. King would start plainly and softly

24 See www.discover.com/web-exclusives/no-fishing-2050-stocks/ or Boris Worm et al., "Impacts of Biodiversity Loss on Ocean Ecosystem Services," *Science* 314, no. 5800, 3 November 2006: 787-790.

and build the intensity of his tone gradually so that, by the end of his speech, the drama and veracity of his words would have people not only moved but transformed.

Letters make people think. When I wrote a letter to the editor of the *Christian Science Monitor* I received comments back from the other side of the world.

Books make people think. Consider the power of Upton Sinclair's *The Jungle*, John Steinbeck's *The Grapes of Wrath*, Kurt Vonnegut's *Slaughterhouse Five*, and Rachel Carson's *Silent Spring*. If you have read them, you remember their messages. If you haven't read them, you must.

Images make people think. Don't neglect the influence of images like that of Kim Phuc in Vietnam, running in agony from the napalm that burned her clothing and much of her skin, or the photo of the boy in China who stood defiantly before a row of tanks, preventing their progress into Tiananmen Square where students were protesting. People who saw these images developed a new outlook on war and a new conception of the power of one individual.

Artwork makes people think. To see examples of thought-provoking environmental art, visit http://greenmuseum.org.

Music becomes woven into our permanent fibers. The fabric of everyone's lives should include such songs as John Lennon's *Imagine*: "Imagine no possessions ... imagine all the people, sharing all the world ...." Let's play it for friends and family and then discuss its meaning.

Overcoming Inertia

We can write those letters. We can sing those songs. We can create that artwork. We can stage those protests and make those speeches. We can, and we must. Without them, the natural tendency of too many people is to ignore the future, to ignore the lessons of history, to ignore environmental and human losses, to ignore the reality that taking the easy path in the short run makes life hard before long, and to fail to think enough. No one's vote, or voice, or pen, matters more than yours can.

We can boycott. I am one of those people who don't buy Nike products because I don't like their labor practices. On May 1, 2006, U.S. immigrant groups and their supporters organized a boycott of stores, schools, and workplaces to call attention to the important contributions of immigrant populations. As with other

social-action efforts, that boycott planted seeds of information and inspiration, and to be sure, it made people think.

There is no shortage of people with conviction, understanding of solvable societal problems, and interest in their resolution, but the power of inertia has a way of sidelining even the strong willed. The real rewards come from fighting that inertia. In the end, it is far more satisfying to go beyond the recognition of a problem, to take initiative, and to make progress. Whether by writing to a member of congress, running for office, hosting neighbors for a viewing of an eye-opening documentary, contributing money to environmental efforts, or volunteering our time to a cause, each of us knows *what* we can do. The biggest hurdle between us and a better world is often that of lethargy, so let us consider the challenge of getting off our back ends and reaching our desired ends.

Humans go through cycles of energy and inspiration. We have periods when we're filled with everything it takes to accomplish our goals, and periods when we're ambivalent and tired and distracted. We make great plans when we're revved up. Do you remember the last day of high school, when you said with admirable intent that you'd stay in touch with all of your friends? Did you? I didn't. We meant what we said at the time, but we were in that energized and inspired mode. Then we got into the ambivalent and distracted mode and plans fell apart. Health clubs profit from all of us who say, in our energized mode, "This year I'm going to get into shape!" We similarly say that we're going to eat better, be better citizens, give more, buy less, and so on. And then we fall into that other mode. Lethargy slips in and plays tricks on us. We know we'll be happier when we do those things, but we'll do them tomorrow.

To overcome lows in the energy cycle, try to capture the virtue of your moments of inspiration by locking them in. When you're primed for action at the peak of that cycle, make a pact and be specific. Write it down or make an absolute mental promise. You might even do that right now. Think about your next move. Think about what action you can take to further a favorite cause and make a commitment that cannot be broken in times of weakness. Perhaps, at least for some period, you will

- go vegetarian,

- buy any needed clothes at a thrift shop,

- write a letter to the editor once a month,

- boycott a major source of pollution,

- carry out a random act of kindness,

- plant an organic garden,

- bypass fast food restaurants,

- recycle everything possible,

- give second-hand or non-material gifts, or

- organize a rally once a year.

Certainly you will feel good about yourself for doing any of these things. Your actions will make a valued contribution to a larger effort by like-minded people. It is only as the result of courageous social action by our predecessors that women and minorities can vote and schools are desegregated. It is now time to create your own legacy. As Gandhi said, "Be the change you want to see in the world."

My parents speak out at city council meetings.

CHAPTER 15

Utopia Isn't So Bad

D isney World is billed as "the happiest place on Earth," but Walt Disney's image of the ideal community had little to do with Mickey Mouse. Disney intended for the city of Epcot to be a utopian community near Disney World in Orlando, Florida. He envisioned a place with no unemployment or homelessness, underground roads, wind tunnels to transport solid waste, and the best of technology and education. Disney died of cancer before the project was completed, although a cutting-edge waste management system is among several of his plans that were implemented in what became the Epcot theme park.[1]

It is fascinating to imagine what an ideal community would look like. I picture a large circle of cozy homes with wide, covered porches to invite neighbors and friends together for deep conversations. Every area of importance would be within walking distance, and motor vehicles would be relegated to the perimeter if not placed in an underground parking garage. There would have to be a community garden, a large pond, a health food restaurant, a bakery, and a bookstore-café. Naturally, every structure would be environmentally friendly. Every rooftop

1   See www.waltopia.com/vision.html.

would have solar panels, every home would have a geothermal heat pump, and every type of waste would be composted, reused, recycled, or fed to the livestock.

Many communities come closer to realizing such ideals than the final incarnation of Disney's Epcot. A global network of thousands of ecovillages allows millions of people to enjoy an alternative lifestyle.[2] I gave one a try. Never having lived in an ecovillage, I didn't know what to expect when I committed myself to teaching a month-long course on sustainability at the Australian "permaculture" (sustainable living) community of Crystal Waters.

My family and I voyaged north of Brisbane into the rural habitat of kangaroos and wallabies. A colleague predicted I would also encounter drug-toting hippies at the ecovillage. However, I never saw any evidence of drug use or subversive behavior on that trip. What I found were people who could not be pigeonholed into any particular classification, except perhaps that of being satisfied with life. Crystal Waters is home to people of all ages and widely varied occupations. Among them are builders, bakers, farmers, teachers, musical instrument makers, scholars, artists, environmental consultants, retirees, and several who commute to assorted jobs in nearby towns.

The village consists of dozens of homes scattered across hillsides, a café, a small grocery store, a shared playground, a lodge with meeting rooms, a classroom facility, several popular swimming holes along ponds and a stream, hiking trails, and more recycling bins than one can shake a stick at.

The giant tree frog living in my toilet was just the beginning of the discoveries I made on that trip. What follows are three of the important lessons I learned.

Lesson 1
Eco-friendly Doesn't Mean Primitive

You can forget about grass skirts, mud huts, and Flintstones-style pedal cars. Crystal Waters residents drive Mercedes and SUVs in sizes appropriate for their needs, but they tend to drive the

---

2 See http://gen.ecovillage.org/.

same car for decades and they don't go on joyrides. Residents take long showers in rainwater collected from their roofs and heated by the sun. The people wear stylish clothing made from fine cotton and wool, they just don't stockpile hundreds of shirts like I do.[3] Some residents enjoy a glass of wine with dinner, not from a strip mall liquor store, but homemade with pride from organic fruit grown in the yard.

Comfortable homes with cross ventilation and cathedral ceilings keep subtropical heat away from living spaces without noisy air conditioning units. The buildings have graceful wood floors and verandas, but they are made from woods such as cedar that are easily reforested and require no pesticides or preservatives beyond vegetable oil. Hand craftsmanship and stained glass adorn windows and doors, not purchased at Lowes, but recycled from old homes, ships, and scrap yards.

The home interiors are elegant in their simplicity. Absent are the predictable, redundant rooms of mass-produced suburbs. In

3   My cramped closets result, in part, from the T-shirts that come with registration for the running races that entertain me on Saturday mornings. I've found a good way to thin the pile: Before I return home from a trip, I leave a set of shirts behind for the hotel staff or others who would appreciate them. It's great to come home with a light suitcase to a closet with a bit more space.

their place are charming, practical living spaces with character and appeal. Some are adorned with bamboo, which is strong, fast-growing, and farmed within the village. Others exhibit the creative use of glass and oiled wood. There is little use of plastic, vinyl, or paint. Fixtures are made of durable metals. Kitchen shelves are lined with recycled glass bottles filled with teas, herbs, and spices. These practices come together to create warm, vibrant, comfortable, welcoming, and relatively care-free homes.

Lesson 2
Many Paths to Conservation Require No Sacrifice

The idea that environmental protection involves trade-offs in terms of money, time, or inconvenience rests on the assumption that everyone is already aware of any costless opportunities for conservation and has thus exhausted them. That is not the case. Existing room for painless gains begins on the water front. Our cities ration it, we fight over who should control it, and the water in our lakes and rivers is embarrassingly dirty. The trouble-free strategy for saving trillions of gallons of clean water in America each year begins with two words: dual flush. The dual flush toilets that are common throughout Australia have two buttons on the top; one triggers a small flush to wash away liquids, the other carries solids away with a large flush.

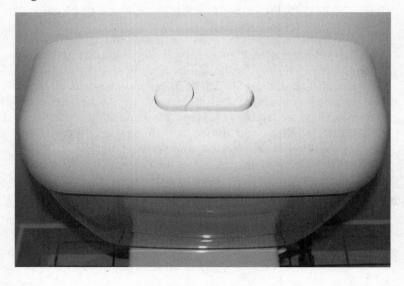

Traditional American toilets offer only a large flush and dispense with about 3.5 gallons of water per flush. Dual-flush toilets use 0.6 gallons per small flush. The difference, 2.9 gallons, would be saved each of the five-plus times a typical person urinates every day if we adopted the dual flush system. That would amount to more than 5,000 gallons of water per person per year that would no longer need to be withdrawn from a water source, treated with chemicals, and treated again after use. Even more water could be saved by converting to advanced toilets with smaller tanks and water-free urinals. If you're interested, a web search for "dual flush toilets" will turn up ample information and suppliers.

Speaking of toilets, I'm environmentally savvy enough to know that one doesn't plug in a hybrid-electric vehicle and that solar cells collect energy even on cloudy days, but I had no idea that composting toilets could flush. A composting toilet turns waste into soil with the help of micro-organisms or worms that eat the waste and turn out nutrient-rich compost. Unlike the "dry" composting toilets that resemble in-home outhouses, the "wet" composting toilets at Crystal Waters look and work like the thrones at home; they just send their waste towards worms and ultimately the garden, rather than towards the treatment plant and ultimately the water supply.

Another water-saving trick can be learned from the Japanese. Many toilets in Japan have a sink attached to the water tank above the toilet. After the toilet is flushed, clean water enters the tank through a spout above the sink. Users can thus wash their hands in clean water on its way to the tank, where it awaits its second purpose of washing away waste.

Opportunities for painless gains don't end in the lavatory. Much of our food is grown with chemical pesticides and fertilizers and transported from around the world at great monetary and environmental expense. At Crystal Waters we ate fresh, local, organic vegetables that made every alternative a culinary sacrifice. Salads were made from dandelions and other greens direct from the yard, and lettuce from the garden, which was fertilized with kitchen compost. Non-vegetarians ate chicken, beef, kangaroo, and eggs from organic, free-range animals. Bread and cheese were made on-site. Healthy eating couldn't be better.

Waste disposal issues at Crystal Waters are easily handled by placing recycling and composting buckets alongside trash containers in homes and businesses. Toss cans to the left, food and paper to the right. Resource conservation is all in the wrist!

Lesson 3
Self Sufficiency is a Practical, Long-Term Solution

The solution to water shortages in the United States has been to place limits on use. Sustainable practices provide a long-term solution and a higher quality of life. Rather than being told that we cannot wash cars or water lawns on certain days, we could collect rainwater in cisterns as is the standard in Australia and other parts of the world. Pollution makes our rainwater unsafe to drink, but it's great for cleaning and watering purposes. Chapter 4 mentions the related option of collecting water in rain barrels.

Solar energy would provide long-term energy independence and solve ongoing problems with blackouts and fossil fuels. You knew that already; let me just report that at Crystal Waters, where alternative energy is commonplace, the Earth-friendly systems work beautifully and the residents adore them. The community actually receives checks from the power company paying them for the solar energy they feed *into* the electricity grid. The same opportunity to receive money for power fed into the grid is widely available in the United States.

Is it Easy Being Green?

I can think of a few reasons why Kermit the frog, the keeper of my commode in Crystal Waters, sings "it's not easy being green." However, he obviously isn't referring to the meaning of "green" that is synonymous with environmentalism, which is neither primitive, painful, nor difficult to apply. The people of Crystal Waters, and two smaller ecovillages I have visited since, clearly exhibit the ease and joy of conservation, moderation, and simple living.

I'm not saying that people leading sustainable lives seem as happy as those of us consuming resources with abandon. I'm saying they seem happier. I attribute that to their ability to focus on the genuine pleasures of life.

My parents
grow their
own organic
peaches.

CHAPTER 16

About Energy

Oil-based polymers are in everything from fertilizers to underwear, and fossil fuels power the production and transportation of virtually all goods. It takes roughly a quart of crude oil to produce one pound of coffee,[1] seven gallons to make one car tire,[2] and 284 gallons to fertilize the corn eaten by one cow before slaughter.[3] Beyond that it takes 1,851 gallons of water to refine each barrel of crude oil.[4] As Americans fill homes with chilled air all summer and drive to shopping centers, the neighbor's house, school, and the gym, we use fossil fuels like consumers in no other country, clinging to the notion that alternative fuels will save the day before energy problems become serious.

Regretfully, the problems are already serious. Oil production in the United States peaked in 1971.[5] The shutter speed on my camera is 1/640 of a second; oil will be an economically viable fuel for an even smaller fraction of the human era. It is only

1 See www.sfgate.com/cgi-bin/article.cgi?f=/c/a/2006/03/26/ING3PHRU681.DTL.
2 See www.grist.org/news/counter/2000/10/13/rubber/.
3 See http://earthsave.org/environment/foodchoices.htm or www.abc.net.au/catalyst/stories/s1515141.htm.
4 See www.nypirg.org/enviro/water/facts.html.
5 See www.energybulletin.net/2544.html.

natural that the cleanest and most accessible reserves of oil and coal went first. To extract what remains we must degrade the same seas and forests that sustain us with food and oxygen. Energy, too, is essential to life. The trouble is that, even though non-polluting energy sources are available, most people in developed nations rely on fuels central to the air pollution that kills an estimated 500,000 to 1 million people worldwide each year.[6] This chapter sheds light on energy and its derivation from ancient dirt and daily sunshine, among other aspects of energy that are worth knowing.

Understanding Energy and Power

As consumers we are helpless in the face of corporate and political energy agendas if we do not understand the realities of alternative energy sources, the inherent trade-offs, and the possibilities for innovation. Spiking fossil fuel prices already force us to grapple with renewable sources. It is valuable for a society wedded to energy-intensive products and services to study the inner workings of energy as the indispensable input into everything we do.

The word *energy* refers to the amount of work a physical system is capable of performing. Strictly speaking, energy cannot be created, consumed, or destroyed. The catch is that entropy—the amount of energy not available to perform useful work—increases with every movement of a body or machine as energy is dissipated into the universe in the form of heat. Energy can be converted or transferred into many different forms. Kinetic energy is the energy of motion. The kinetic energy of air molecules in motion can be converted into rotational energy by the rotor of a wind turbine, and then converted into electrical energy by a wind-turbine generator. With each conversion, some of the energy is lost as heat. The thermal efficiency of an energy source indicates the percentage of its energy that can be used directly in the next link of the energy-conversion chain rather than being converted into heat. A coal-fired power plant is about 33 percent efficient, meaning that 3,000 megawatts (mW) of energy stored in coal can generate 1,000 mW of electricity. The other 2,000 mW are lost as heat. The thermal efficiency of a typical car is about 26 percent. A racing engine can have a

6   See http://www1.worldbank.org/devoutreach/nov03/textonly.asp?id=218.

thermal efficiency of 34 percent.[7] The photovoltaic cells in a solar panel are around 7 to 17 percent efficient.

Power is the rate of energy transfer per unit of time. Power is measured in watts or horsepower. Energy is measured in joules or kilowatt-hours (kWh). A watt is one joule per second, so a 100-watt light bulb uses 100 joules of energy per second in the process of converting electric energy into light energy and heat energy. One horsepower equals 746 watts. One calorie equals 4.18 joules—the energy needed to raise the temperature of one gram of water by one degree Celsius. A British thermal unit equals 1,055 joules—the energy needed to raise one pound of water one degree Fahrenheit. One kilowatt equals 1,000 watts and one megawatt equals one million watts.

Mentions of energy "production" or "generation" refer to the conversion of energy into a more usable form. Energy "loss" means that energy escapes as heat or becomes unavailable for use for some other reason. Most commercial electricity production involves making turbines spin and thereby creating an electrical current. Both nuclear fission and coal combustion create steam that turns turbines. The kinetic energy from wind and falling water can turn turbines directly. You can generate electricity yourself by peddling a properly rigged bicycle or turning the crank on some emergency radios. A photovoltaic cell, in contrast, converts light energy into direct-current (DC) electricity with no moving parts and no emissions.

The United States obtains most of its energy from petroleum (40%), followed by coal (23%), natural gas (22%), nuclear power (8%), and renewable resources (7%). The following sections offer a primer on the information necessary to sort out the energy debacle.

---

7   For more about what efficiency means in engine science, see www.auto-ware.com/combust_bytes/eng_sci.htm.

Fossil Fuels

Oil

Long ago labeled "black gold," oil is still the font of envy and international conflict. When a product is scarce or costly to produce, high prices can moderate the quantity demanded, but this pricing mechanism fails for oil and other fossil fuels. The price paid at the pump does not reflect the costs of road congestion, ill health, or global climate change. The pump price also omits the costly environmental damage from extraction, processing, vehicle emissions, and around 7,500 annual oil spills.[8] Even having reached record levels, the price per gallon of gasoline in the United States remains low relative to the prices in many parts of Europe and Asia, due in-part to relatively low taxes. Critics also attribute lower prices to the heavy government subsidization of rail, water, and road transportation systems that serve the energy industry.[9] As prices escalate, the silver lining may be that they more closely reflect the full cost of oil to society, and high prices trigger conservation. On the other hand, high prices may lead to retreat on the protection of environmentally vulnerable areas from oil drilling.

With not quite 5 percent of the world population, U.S. residents use more than 26 percent of the oil consumed in the world today. Crude oil, or petroleum, is made of the hydrocarbon remains of pre-dinosaur plant and animal life from the Carboniferous Period of the Paleozoic Era.[10] The relevant chemistry lesson is about how hydrogen and carbon atoms link together to form molecular chains of all lengths. Shorter chains are liquid at room temperature; longer chains form solids. In the refinery, distillation separates the hydrocarbon chains into "fractions" that can be blended to produce fuels with desired characteristics. For example, hydrocarbons with between 7 and 11 carbon atoms per molecule form gasoline. Alternative blends form kerosene, diesel fuel, fuel oil, lubricating oil, and asphalt.[11]

Less than half of the oil consumed in the United States is

8   See www.uscg.mil/hq/g-m/nmc/response/stats/chpt2001.pdf.
9   For example, see the Union of Concerned Scientists site at www.ucsusa.org/publication.cfm?publicationID=149
10 See www.energyquest.ca.gov/story/chapter08.html.
11 For more on oil processing, see the U.S. Department of Energy Web site at www.fossil.energy.gov/programs_oilgas.html.

produced domestically; major producers of the rest include Canada, Saudi Arabia, Venezuela, Mexico, Nigeria, and Iraq. As a remedy for this reliance on foreign oil, a 2006 report published by the University of California at Berkeley's Renewable and Appropriate Energy Lab outlined policies and practices that could reduce oil consumption by 22 percent and completely offset imports from the Persian Gulf by 2021.[12] The authors of the report recommended improved corporate average fuel economy (CAFÉ) standards, expanded use of biofuels and hybrid-electric vehicles, and a shift toward ultra-efficient plug-in hybrid vehicles such as the Toyota Prius+.[13] Europe is a showcase for the feasibility of fuel economy advances. Not only are their cars smaller and their fuel taxes higher, but one-third of all new cars and two-thirds of luxury cars are powered by "clean diesel" engines that burn 30-60 percent less fuel than gasoline engines with comparable power. Less than one percent of new U.S. cars make use of clean diesel technology.[14]

Beyond the political and financial ramifications of oil dependency, the extraction, transportation, refinement, and combustion of petroleum products are major sources of pollution and environmental losses. Chapter 7 explained that oil use causes toxic releases of particulate matter, volatile organic compounds, sulfur dioxide, carbon monoxide, nitrogen oxides, and ozone. Interests in energy security and environmental health support efforts to switch to blends of gasoline and ethanol, among other renewable, domestically produced, and cleaner-burning fuels, as discussed further in the section on alternative fuels.

Coal

Coal is the compressed remains of tropical and subtropical plants, predominantly from the Carboniferous and Permian periods 225 million to 345 million years ago. Coal includes varying levels of carbon, hydrogen, sulfur, and nitrogen. Coals are classified according to their carbon content, from the lowest to the highest,

---

12 See http://rael.berkeley.edu/old-site/ei2025-report.pdf and www.renewableenergyaccess.com/rea/news/story?id=44613.

13 See www.evworld.com/electrichybrid.cfm. In 2007 the Google Corporation launched an initiative to promote plug-in hybrids. See www.technewsworld.com/rsstory/57926.html.

14 See www.dieselforum.org/news-center/news-releases/012402-statement-before-the-united-states-senate-committee-on-commerce-science-transportation-hearing-on-corporate-average-fuel-economy-standards/.

as lignite, subbituminous, bituminous, and anthracite. Coals with higher concentrations of carbon are harder and hold more energy. Lignite, with the least energy available to burn, is the most abundant in the United States. High-energy anthracite is relatively rare. In general, coals from the eastern and midwestern United States are bituminous, with high heat values but high levels of acid-rain-causing sulfur as well. Coals from the western states are largely subbituminous or lignite, with low heat value and low sulfur content. Pennsylvania holds most of the country's anthracite supply.

The first commercial coal mine in the United States opened in Richmond, Virginia, in 1745. The United States is now a major producer and consumer of coal, with almost 2,000 mines producing over 1 billion tons of coal each year.[15] Coal is burned to produce heat and electricity, and is a component in electric stoves, refrigerators, and water heaters.

15 For more on the U.S. coal industry, see www.eia.doe.gov/cneaf/coal/special/ coalfeat.htm.

The Union of Concerned Scientists describes coal as "cheap, plentiful, and dirty—as cheap as dirt, as plentiful as dirt, and as dirty as dirt—since after all, coal is little more than dirt that burns."[16] The March of Dimes organization reports that mercury, a byproduct of coal combustion, can cause mental retardation, blindness, deafness, and chronic seizure disorders.[17] In 2004 the EPA estimated that 630,000 babies born in the United States each year are at risk for lowered intelligence and learning problems due to in-utero exposure to unsafe levels of mercury.[18] Thirty-five million American children live within 30 miles of mercury-emitting power plants.[19] According to a study by Abt Associates commissioned by the Clean Air Task Force, each year 24,000 Americans die an average of 14 years prematurely due to pollution from power plants.[20] Beyond that, black lung disease caused by coal-dust inhalation claims the lives of around 1,500 miners each year.[21]

Mercury is not the only damaging release from coal-fired power plants; another is carbon dioxide, a primary source of global climate change. In 2007, coal consumption in the United States resulted in 1.9 billion tons of carbon dioxide emissions,[22] but it gets worse. In China, where $321 billion worth of goods were made for the U.S. market in 2007,[23] about 70 percent of the energy comes from coal and Chinese carbon dioxide emissions exceed those in the U.S.[24] Coal combustion also releases sulfur and nitrous oxides, the sources of acid deposition, which affects one-third of China's cropland.[25] According to the World Bank, almost 400,000 people in China die prematurely due to air pollution each year.[26]

While land reclamation programs and new "clean-coal technologies" (CCTs) make it possible to reduce some of the

16 See www.ucsusa.org/clean_energy/fossil_fuels/offmen-how-coal-works.html.
17 See www.marchofdimes.com/aboutus/10651_11551.asp.
18 See www.pbs.org/now/science/mercuryinfish.html.
19 See www.cleartheair.org/fact/children/emissions.vtml.
20 See www.cleartheair.org/dirtypower/docs/dirtyAir.pdf.
21 See www.umwa.org/blacklung/blacklung.shtml or http://www.courier-journal.
    com/dust/.
22 See www.ens-newswire.com/ens/mar2008/2008-03-18-04.asp.
23 See www.census.gov/foreign-trade/balance/c5700.html#2008.
24 See www.guardian.co.uk/environment/2007/jun/19/china.usnews.
25 WorldWatch Institute, *State of the World 2006: Special Focus: China and India*, Washington D.C., January, 2006.
26 *Clear Water, Blue Skies: China's Environment in the New Century*, Washington, D.C.: World Bank, 1997.

environmental impact of coal mining and combustion, as with solar cells and electric cars, the widespread implementation of new technology can be a long time coming. Legislative stall tactics such as the cleverly named Clear Skies Initiative (S. 485, H.R. 999) threaten to weaken and delay Clean Air Act pollution limits that would press coal plants to adopt safer practices.[27] CCT critics argue that greater benefits would come from expenditures on emission-free, renewable energy sources.[28]

Natural Gas

Like coal and oil, natural gas has its origins in the swamps of past geologic periods. Natural gas is primarily methane with a mixture of other hydrocarbons. It is obtained from gas wells and as a byproduct of oil extraction. Although it is a fossil fuel, it can also be considered an alternative fuel because of its clean-burning qualities and domestic abundance. Unlike most alternative fuels, natural gas has a broad infrastructure available to transport it, making it relatively accessible and affordable. The industrial, residential, electricity-generation, and commercial sectors represent 39, 24, 21, and 16 percent of the natural gas market respectively.[29] Experimental natural-gas vehicles are currently in operation, although they require a $2,000 to $4,000 compressor station for overnight refueling.[30]

Natural gas is produced in most regions of North America and transported through pipelines in liquid or gaseous form to every mainland state. The primary ingredient, methane, is a highly flammable, odorless gas. Leaks of unburned gas have the potential to ignite and explode, although problems are uncommon. Gas companies have inserted foul-smelling additives into natural gas to make leaks detectable ever since a natural gas explosion killed 293 people in a New London, Texas, school in 1937.

Nuclear Energy

Fission is the splitting of atoms to release energy. Fusion is the combination of atoms, again with the release of energy. Nuclear power can come from the fission of uranium, plutonium, or tho-

27 See www.nrdc.org/air/pollution/tdh0403.asp.
28 For example, see http://copirg.org/CO.asp?id2=4996&id3=CO&.
29 See www.eia.doe.gov/oil_gas/natural_gas/info_glance/consumption.html.
30 For more on natural gas vehicles, see the Natural Gas Vehicle Coalition site: www. ngvc.org/ngv/ngvc.nsf.

rium, or from the fusion of hydrogen into helium. Convenience and accessibility make uranium the fuel of choice in today's reactors. The real draw of nuclear power is that the fission of a uranium atom produces 10 million times the energy produced by the combustion of a carbon atom in coal. Excluding naval power reactors, there are 103 active nuclear reactors in the United States and about 400 in the world. These reactors satisfy 20 percent of electricity consumption and 8 percent of total energy consumption in the United States.

The greatest environmental threats from nuclear power involve the storage of spent radioactive fuel from reactors and the possibility of accidents. The worst accident in a commercial reactor occurred on April 26, 1986, when a reactor in Chernobyl, Ukraine, melted down and released at least 3 percent of its core radiation. The incident killed 32 local workers immediately and thousands more in the following years. The plume of radiation reached Asia, Europe, and parts of the United States. Radioiodine and radiocaesium contaminated food supplies, increasing the incidence of thyroid cancer, mutations, and related health effects. In the United States there are currently more than 40,000 metric tons of depleted uranium fuel stored in 34 states. The Department of Energy plans to open a nuclear waste repository under Yucca Mountain, Nevada, by 2010. Both the storage of radiated waste and its transportation across the country have met with opposition. Proponents of nuclear energy point out that nuclear power plants are responsible for less than 1 percent of all radiation exposure.[31] Of course, since most radiation exposure comes naturally from the ground or from outer space, nuclear power is responsible for a much larger share of *avoidable* radiation exposure.

Alternative Fuels

Humans are selfish creatures. Without other attractive choices, our oil orgy might go on until prices become prohibitive. It is fortunate that the clean energy paths have their own appeal. The bicycle is the most efficient mode of transportation in the world, and perhaps the most fun. Guys like "Veggie Van" creator Josh Tickell impress people by driving around in hot rods fueled with

---

31 See the U.S. Department of Energy's Nuclear Q and A: www.nuc.umr.edu/nuclear_facts/answers/answers.html/.

biodiesel.[32] People who live off the electricity grid beam with pride. And owners of gas-sipping cars sleep well thanks to their service to humanity and wildlife.

The alternative fuels discussed here are generally renewable, available domestically, and less toxic than their mainstream counterparts. The U.S. Department of Energy promotes alternative fuels not only for their environmental benefits, but because they provide "energy security" by reducing reliance on foreign sources of fossil fuels.[33] One trade-off is that many alternative fuels are not cheap. The direct costs of ethanol and liquefied natural gas are higher than those of gasoline, although improved technology and economies of scale via mass production could make any of the alternative fuels economically viable.

Biodiesel

Biodiesel is a cleaner-burning diesel fuel made from renewable plant oils or animal fats. It can run in current diesel engines, either blended with petroleum diesel fuel or straight. B20 is a common biodiesel blend of 20 percent biodiesel and 80 percent petroleum diesel. Biodiesel emissions are sulfur dioxide free and contain 75 to 90 percent lower levels of unburned hydrocarbons, aromatic hydrocarbons, and carbon dioxide than diesel emissions. Biodiesel is also less flammable than petroleum diesel, thus reducing the risk of vehicular fires. On the downside, unless you obtain your oil by siphoning out fast-food restaurant fryers as Josh Tickell did, biodiesel is relatively costly to produce. Soy-based biodiesel currently costs about three times as much as petroleum diesel. As one way to lower the overall cost of biodiesel, researchers hope to increase the oil content of soybeans so that fewer beans are required to make a given amount of fuel.

Electric Fuel

Electric vehicles (EVs), a type of zero-emission vehicle (ZEV), require no tailpipe and provide no opportunity for fuel evaporation. Their electric power can come from solar cells on one's home or from the traditional power grid that feeds electricity to most homes. Unless the power source itself uses an

---

32 See www.veggievan.org.
33 The U.S. Department of Energy provides an "Alternative Fuels Data Center" at www.afdc.doe.gov/.

alternative fuel, the problem of pollution from the power plants remains. Some EVs are expensive, although high start-up costs are balanced by low fuel costs if electricity is cheap or free, as it is from private solar, wind, and hydroelectric power sources. Tax incentives and manufacturers' promotions also serve to ameliorate up-front pricing concerns. With the current state of technology, rechargeable battery packs for EVs cost between $3,000 and $8,000 each, last 80 to 220 miles per charge,[34] and must be replaced and disposed of every 3 to 4 years.[35] The 2006 documentary film *Who Killed The Electric Car?* claimed that oil companies have purchased crucial patents on battery technology to prevent improved batteries from appearing in U.S. electric vehicles.[36] Similar claims have been made about solar power patents,[37] although the true intentions of those purchasing the rights to this technology are unclear.

Ethanol

Ethanol, also called ethyl alcohol or grain alcohol, is a clear, colorless liquid with an agreeable odor. Ethanol is distilled from a mash of renewable sources that can include corn, barley, wheat, and waste accumulated from wood and paper processing. When considering ethanol sources it is important to measure the energy required to obtain a possible source against the energy received from the resulting ethanol. Several studies suggest that the production of ethanol from corn and other crops actually takes more energy than it makes, due to the energy required to grow and process the crops.[38] Ethanol combustion releases lower levels of greenhouse gases than gasoline combustion, and the growth of corn and other ethanol feedstocks draws carbon dioxide out of the atmosphere. Ethanol is already popular as a fuel in Brazil and serves as a common octane-enhancing additive to gasoline in the United States, Canada, and Europe. One common mixture containing 10 percent ethanol and 90 percent gasoline is known as gasohol. Gasoline-ethanol blends that contain 85 percent and 95 percent ethanol, called E85 and E95 respectively, are avail-

---

34 See www.teslamotors.com/.
35 See www.epa.gov/oms/consumer/fuels/altfuels/420f00034.htm.
36 See http://en.wikipedia.org/wiki/Who_Killed_the_Electric_Car%3F and www.ev1.
    org/chevron.htm.
37 See www.motherjones.com/news/feature/2000/03/solar.html.
38 See www.ens-newswire.com/ens/jul2005/2005-07-13-01.asp, www.physorg.com/
    news4942.html, and www.news.cornell.edu/stories/july05/ethanol.toocostly.ssl.html.

able in parts of North America, Europe, and Asia. However, their use is limited to flexible-fuel vehicles now available from the major automakers,[39] and only 1,261 of the roughly 170,000 service stations in the United States sold E85 in 2007.[40]

Hydrogen

Hydrogen gas can power combustion engines and fuel-cell electric vehicles such as the Honda FCX Clarity.[41] Electricity generated from the reaction of hydrogen fuel and oxygen from the air provides fuel cells with clean, quiet power. The only emissions are pure water and heat. Electrolysis or extreme heat can split hydrogen atoms from the oxygen atoms in water. The bad news is that it takes energy from another source to fuel these processes, so hydrogen production is only as clean as the energy used to split the atoms. Scientists are working on improved photoelectrical, photobiological, and thermal dissociation methods of hydrogen production that may someday make hydrogen easier to obtain.

The distribution and storage of hydrogen present additional challenges. Because hydrogen is bulky, energy-intensive compression is required to facilitate storage and transportation. Hydrogen is also an explosive gas at room temperature, and there are ongoing investigations into more manageable forms, including compressed hydrogen, liquid hydrogen, and chemical bonding between hydrogen and, for example, metal hydrides. At present there is little infrastructure in place to transport hydrogen, although Shell Oil has launched a joint venture with fuel-cell maker Xcellsis to develop such an infrastructure.

Fuel cells and hydrogen-fueled internal combustion engines already power cars and buses; trains and submarines are in the works. The military is interested in fuel-cell vehicles because their relatively cool and quiet engines are more difficult to detect. For travel in space, where the bulk of hydrogen is less of an issue, hydrogen is the primary propellant. Hydrogen fuel cells on board the space shuttle power life-support systems and computers, returning drinkable water as a by-product. In a display of optimism that the difficulties of obtaining, storing, and transporting hydrogen are surmountable back on Earth, almost

39 See www.cleanairchoice.org/outdoor/FlexibleFuelVehicles.asp.
40 See www.americanprogress.org/issues/2007/12/e85/e85.html.
41 See http://world.honda.com/FuelCell/.

every major automaker has introduced a prototype for a fuel-cell vehicle.

Methanol

Methanol, also known as methyl alcohol, wood alcohol, or wood spirits, is a light, poisonous liquid that can serve as a gasoline additive, a replacement for gasoline and diesel fuels, and a source of hydrogen for fuel cells.[42] Methanol sources include natural gas and almost any renewable resource containing carbon, including seaweed, waste wood, and garbage. Relative to gasoline, methanol offers low emissions of hydrocarbons, nitrogen oxides, and particulate matter. Methanol's fuel efficiency is currently half that of gasoline, a statistic that may improve with ongoing research on enhancements. Methanol's high-octane performance and low flammability make it the only fuel used in Indianapolis 500 race cars.

Liquefied Petroleum Gas

Commonly known as LPG, liquefied petroleum gas is either propane or butane, typically in a mixture that includes butylenes and propylene. LPG is a by-product of petroleum refinement and natural-gas processing. Though gaseous at room temperature, LPG can be transported as a liquid 270 times more compact than propane gas. LPG fuels cause less carbon buildup than gasoline or diesel fuel and extend the lives of spark plugs and engines. LPG has been in use worldwide for over 60 years. More than 350,000 LPG-powered vehicles are driven today,[43] including many police cars, school buses in Kansas and Oregon, and the Las Vegas taxi fleet. The Ford Motor Company offers a LPG-powered F-Series truck that is eligible for the Alternative Fuel Vehicle tax incentive in California. LPG vehicles are popular for corporate fleets thanks to lower emissions and fuel prices that are 5 to 30 percent below the price of gasoline.

P-Series and D-Series

Stephen Paul of Princeton University developed P-series, a combination of ethanol, natural gas liquids, and biomass-derived

42 See www.iforest.com/docs/FactSheetHfuelcell_Final.pdf.
43 For more information, see the Department of Energy's propane site: www.afdc.doe.
    gov/altfuel/propane.html/.

methyltetrahydrofurans (MTHF). The ethanol and MTHF are obtained from renewable resources such as agricultural and wood waste. Relative to gasoline, the virtues of P-series include fewer toxins and faster biodegradability. P-series is designed for use in flexible-fuel vehicles (FFVs), which can burn various mixtures of ethanol or methanol and gasoline. Chrysler, Ford, GM and Mazda are among the makers of America's four million FFVs. For more information about P-series fuels see www.iags.org/pseries.htm. D-Series, a product of the Pure Energy Corporation, is another mixture of renewable and fossil fuels designed to protect the environment and bolster energy independence. The makers hope that it will ultimately be a cost-competitive alternative to gasoline.[44]

Solar Fuel

Each year the Earth receives about 1.56×10^{18} kWh of energy from the sun.[45] The world energy market provides about 1.47×10^{14} kWh of energy per year.[46] Thus, energy consumers require less than 0.01 percent of the energy provided by the sun. Capturing solar energy is the hard part, but it's not that hard. Solar thermal applications use the sun's energy directly to heat air or liquid, primarily for residential use. Photoelectric methods use semiconductors and photovoltaic cells to convert solar energy into electricity. A photovoltaic cell can convert between 7 and 17 percent of sunlight's energy into electrical energy. Once the thermal or photoelectric applications are in place, the use of solar energy creates no emissions and no noise. Worthwhile amounts of solar energy can be collected even under cloudy conditions, although energy is not produced at night, and sunny places generate larger amounts of energy than cloudy places.[47] Batteries fed by solar panels permit the use of solar energy even when and where there is no sunshine.

A chicken-and-egg problem exists for solar energy among other alternative fuels: Solar energy probably won't gain wide-

---

44 For more on D-Series and a new diesel-ethanol fuel mixture called E-Diesel, see the Pure Energy Corporation Web site: www.pure-energy.com/products/D-series.html.

45 The Earth receives 5.6×10^{18} megajoules (MJ) of energy per year (see www.science.org.au/nova/005/005key.htm). One kWh equals 3.6 MJ, so the Earth receives 1.56×10^{18} kWh per year.

46 World "marketed" energy consumption in 2007 was around 500 quadrillion BTU (see www.eia.doe.gov/oiaf/ieo/world.html). One quadrillion BTU equals 2.93×10^{11} kWh, so energy consumers purchase energy at a rate of around 1.47×10^{14} kWh per year.

47 For more, see the Department of Energy's photovoltaic site: www.eren.doe.gov/pv/.

spread popularity until the start-up costs come down, and it will be difficult to bring down the start-up costs before popularity allows for economies of scale. Fortunately, the operating and maintenance costs are remarkably low, and solar energy is already flourishing in states such as Colorado and Florida. Sacramento, California, hosts a photovoltaic power plant that supplies energy to 660 homes.[48] New solar power plants planned for Arizona[49] and California[50] will be among the world's largest. Despite the subsequent removal of the solar panels Jimmy Carter placed on the White House roof, the government is getting into the act as well. With its Million Solar Roofs initiative, the U.S. Department of Energy has the goal of one million public and private solar rooftops by 2010. The Energy Policy Act of 2005 provides a 30-percent business investment tax credit for expenditures on solar electricity, solar heating, and lighting via fiber-optic sunlight distribution.[51] These incentives will help solar energy gain traction and advance the march toward mass production and associated cost savings. The increased use of solar power is likely to boost employment levels too: The National Energy Laboratory estimates that solar power plants create 2.5 times as many skilled jobs as fossil fuel plants.[52]

Wind

Wind whips some regions of the Earth at speeds exceeding 200 mph. Average wind speeds in the United States range from 4 to 20 mph. Small wind turbines can create energy using a minimum of 8 mph winds; large turbines require 13 mph winds to achieve efficiency. Wind turbines use long blades called "rotors" that spin by the force of the wind and create electricity. Wind energy is an attractive supplement to other power sources due to its lack of emissions and its infinite kinetic energy source. A disadvantage is that the turbines are currently expensive, and "wind farms" with large fields of turbines are needed to power a town of significant size. On the upside, between 1981 and 2000, the equipment cost per kilowatt of wind energy fell from around

48 See http://yosemite.epa.gov/oar/globalwarming.nsf/UniqueKeyLookup/
    SHSU5BVR3A/$File/solarenergy.pdf.
49 See www.inhabitat.com/2008/02/25/world%E2%80%99s-largest-solar-power-plant-
    coming-to-arizona-in-2011/.
50 See www.inhabitat.com/2008/04/10/mojave-desert-solar-power-fields/.
51 See www.sunlight-direct.com/products.html.
52 See www.nrel.gov/lab/pao/concentrating.html.

$2,600 to around $790.[53] Further price decreases are expected to make wind energy competitive with traditional fuels soon.[54]

Wind turbines offer a sustainable source of clean energy. Sizable wind farms operate in 17 states, the majority being in California. The 14-turbine Pakini Nui Wind Farm in Hawaii, pictured above, supplies enough energy for 10,000 homes. In order to expand the use of wind energy and supplant the health and environmental costs of fossil fuels, the Energy Policy Act of 1992 provided a 1.5 cent per kWh tax credit for new wind-energy facilities. As of 2008 the federal tax credit was still in effect, as were assorted state-level tax credits.[55] On the downside, there are concerns about birds being swept into the rotors. However, collisions are uncommon, and the Danish Ministry of the Environment reports that power lines from any source are a far greater threat to birds than wind turbines.[56]

> **Power lines from any source are a far greater threat to birds than wind turbines.**

Geothermal

Geothermal energy comes in the form of heat held beneath the surface of the Earth. This energy can be brought up to heat buildings or icy sidewalks, or converted into electricity for broader applications. Geothermal power plants in the western United

53 See www.awea.org/pubs/factsheets/EconomicsOfWind-Feb2005.pdf or www.repp. org/repp_pubs/articles/chapman/chapman1.html.
54 See www.energy.ca.gov/wind/overview.html.
55 See www.ucsusa.org/clean_energy/clean_energy_policies/production-tax-credit-for-renewable-energy.html.
56 For more on the compatibility of birds and windmills, see www.windpower.dk/tour/env/birds.htm.

States, Hawaii, and Alaska pipe steam and hot water up from deep wells.[57] Put together, U.S. geothermal power plants have a generating capacity of 2,700 mW, enough electricity to satisfy the needs of more than 3.5 million people.[58] Even in areas not blessed with hydrothermal reservoirs, liquid antifreeze can be cycled underground to pick up the Earth's relatively constant ground temperature. In the winter, geothermal heat pumps (GHPs) transfer heat from the ground into homes and buildings. In the summer, GHPs transfer indoor heat into the ground and draw up the relatively cool temperatures from below. More than 200,000 GHPs are operating in the United States, including one in the home of this author. The Galt House East Hotel and waterfront office buildings in Louisville, Kentucky, share the world's largest GHP. The owners estimate they will save $2,250,000 relative to the cost of normal heating and cooling systems.[59]

Direct-use geothermal systems located in the western United States pump hot water from underground directly into buildings and greenhouses for heating, and below city streets for effortless snow removal. Drivers and pedestrians in Klamath, Oregon, for example, cherish the safety of their snow-free streets and sidewalks, all cleared by underground hot water pipes.

Conclusion

Whether due to the influence of oil companies or our own stubbornness, most Americans are steadfast users of fossil fuels. Citing consumer inflexibility, U.S. automakers have literally destroyed electric vehicles such as the GM EV1[60] and continue to focus on gas guzzlers. Meanwhile, energy producers stoop to increasingly egregious assaults on the Earth to replenish supplies of oil and coal. As one of their last acts in 2006, Congress opened 8.3 million previously protected acres within the Gulf of Mexico to oil drilling, and in 2008, President George Bush urged Congress to lift a ban on offshore drilling. The onus is on voters and consumers to demand a shift away from dirty fuels. Buyers

57 See the Department of Energy's geothermal site: www.eren.doe.gov/geothermal/
   geobasics.html/.
58 For more on this, see the National Renewable Energy Lab's geothermal site: www.
   nrel.gov/lab/pao/geothermal_energy.html/.
59 See the International Ground Source Heat Pump Association's Galt House site:
   www.igshpa.okstate.edu/Publications/CaseStudy/Galt_House/Galt.html/.
60 See www.sonyclassics.com/whokilledtheelectriccar/.

of GHP systems, hybrid cars, wind turbines, and solar cells won't recoup their expenditures immediately, but immediate gratification is overrated. Tomorrow will come, and, as always, we will reap what we sow. Many clean-energy investments pay for themselves over a few years, which is more than can be said for sports cars, jewelry, and fancy clothing. Clean energy sources provide the double bonus of long-term savings and immediate pride for people who feel good about reducing cancer rates, protecting the wilderness, leaving a beneficial legacy, being good role models, or achieving energy independence.

Everyone should experience the joy of consuming clean energy, and soon. Physicist Amory Lovins describes a "hard energy path" of a few large, centralized sources of nonrenewable energy—as with regional coal-fired power plants—and a "soft energy path" of many small, decentralized sources of renewable energy—as with solar panels on rooftops. The further we travel down the hard path, the harder it is to turn back, because the design of infrastructure is source-specific and users become reliant on existing sources. A new push to develop alternative energy would be a boon to our health, economy, and foreign policy. Cancer is the second leading cause of death in the United States, and cancer rates are expected to double within 50 years if we continue on the current path.[61] A serious initiative to put solar panels on rooftops would employ thousands of workers. And new energy technology could relieve third-world dependence on loans to purchase Middle East oil, not to mention U.S. dependence on fossil fuels from any source. The sun, wind, and water will provide boundless energy if we embrace these sources from above rather than those from below. Given the toxic heritage of fossil fuel combustion that includes global climate change, mercury exposure, and cancer, it is truly a choice between heaven and hell.

> My parents
> drive a
> compact car,
> if anything.

---

61 See www.findarticles.com/p/articles/mi_m0843/is_4_28/ai_90317124.

CHAPTER 17

Dealing with Uncertainty

How safe are our foods, plastics, bug repellents, fertilizers, pesticides, cleaning fluids, lotions, fabrics, dyes, paints, flu shots, X-rays, and grilled meats? Society is awash in uncertainty about daily health risks, in part because of the difficulty of testing potential carcinogens on humans. Small animals are routinely subjected to large enough doses of toxic substances to cause malignancies within an observable time frame. There are infamous cases in which groups of humans were similarly exposed,[1] but such episodes are rare, as are natural experiments in which an identifiable group of people is exposed as the result of their occupation or location.[2] Thus, although substances including saccharin, aspartame,[3] and sassafras[4] have been reported to cause cancer in laboratory animals, the studies that could possibly confirm them as human carcinogens are prohibitively dangerous.

1 For example, in the 1960s, C. Alvin Paulsen used X-rays on the testicles of 64 prisoners at the Washington State Penitentiary to determine the threshold for sterility. See www.hcn.org/servlets/hcn.Article?article_id=250.
2 An example of such an experiment is explained at www.pubmedcentral.nih.gov/articlerender.fcgi?artid=1185548.
3 See www.cancer.gov/cancertopics/factsheet/Risk/artificial-sweeteners.
4 See www.drugdigest.org/DD/PrintablePages/herbMonograph/0,11475,552413,00.html.

It is hoped that some substances harm rodents but not humans, which would mean that we need not fear all of the rodent carcinogens. On the other hand, substances that cause cancer in humans but not in rodents might elude the scientific community, for tests on rodents are typically the first indication of danger and the precursor to further testing. What we do know is that cancer killed 559,650 people in the United States and roughly 7.6 million worldwide in 2007.[5] Alas, ambiguous links between rodent carcinogens and human carcinogens provide wiggle room to those selling products that contain potentially hazardous chemicals.

Some cancer sources are well known to scientists, although they are often neglected. In 2005 the Department of Health and Human Services listed 54 known human carcinogens[6] and 188 agents that are "reasonably anticipated" to be human carcinogens.[7] The known carcinogens include alcoholic beverages, environmental tobacco smoke, sunlamps/sunbeds, wood dust, and vinyl chloride (used to make PVC plastic). Reasonably anticipated human carcinogens include diesel exhaust particulates, the common herbicide amitrol, and chloroform (a byproduct of chlorine disinfection in drinking water and swimming pools). Kenneth Olden, director of the National Institute of Environmental Health Sciences and the National Toxicology Program, warns that half of all men and one-third of all women will get cancer in their lifetimes.[8]

The myriad possible health and environmental risks create overwhelming uncertainty. Denial is a convenient coping mechanism for consumers, and a lucrative one for risky businesses to promote. In 1994, seven top cigarette-company executives denied that tobacco is addictive and expressed uncertainty about

---

5   See www.cancer.org/downloads/stt/CFF2007EstDthSelSiteByState.pdf and http://www.webmd.com/cancer/news/20071217/2007-world-cancer-deaths-top-7-million.
6   See http://ntp-server.niehs.nih.gov/ntp/roc/eleventh/known.pdf.
7   See http://ntp-server.niehs.nih.gov/ntp/roc/eleventh/reason.pdf.
8   See www.niehs.nih.gov/oc/news/canceragents.htm.

it causing disease or death.[9] In the mid-1990s the coal industry allegedly paid global-warming skeptics Patrick Michaels, Robert Balling, S. Fred Singer, and other scientists close to $1 million to spread their perspectives across the country.[10] With the help of such pretend-it-isn't-so road shows, the proportion of people who said they "worried a great deal" about global warming dropped from 35 percent in 1991[11] to 24 percent in 1997.[12]

Ignorance may start out as bliss, but reality always comes knocking with a vengeance. The "inconvenient truth" of global warming arose amid so many claims of alarmism. Now there is consensus among all but the most extreme fringe of the scientific community.[13] In fact, a *Science Magazine* review of 928 climate-change-related abstracts published in refereed journals between 1993 and 2003 found that none of them disagreed with the consensus on global climate change.[14] Melting glaciers,[15] rising sea levels,[16] dying coral reefs,[17] stronger storms,[18] and yes, rising temperatures[19] are constant reminders of climate-change realities. There are many similar stories. The asbestos industry brushed aside cancer concerns for more than 60 years before the EPA banned the product in 1989.[20] Manufacturers and fishers downplayed the risk of losing the white dolphin, native to China's over-fished and industry-laden Yangtze River, until a large-scale search in 2006 turned up no sign of the large mammal.[21] A 2006 search for the ivory-billed woodpecker in the swamps of Arkansas ended the same way.[22] In our culture of denial, we can expect many more inconvenient truths.

9   See, for example, www-tech.mit.edu/V114/N21/tobacco.21w.html or http://archives.cnn.com/2000/LAW/06/16/florida.smokers/.
10 See www.motherjones.com/news/feature/2005/05/snowed.html.
11 See www.physics.rutgers.edu/~karin/140/articles/galluppoll2006.pdf
12 See www.cnn.com/SPECIALS/1997/global.warming/hot.air/.
13 See, for example, www.rsc.ca/files/media/other/G8_climatestatement2005-en.pdf, www.grida.no/climate/ipcc_tar/wg1/index.htm, www.royalsoc.ac.uk/downloaddoc.asp?id=1630, http://gristmill.grist.org/story/2006/11/13/221250/49.
14 See www.sciencemag.org/cgi/content/full/306/5702/1686.
15 See www.worldviewofglobalwarming.org/pages/glaciers.html.
16 See http://news.nationalgeographic.com/news/2004/04/0420_040420_earthday.html.
17 See www.sciencedaily.com/releases/2001/07/010726101653.htm, www.csmonitor.com/2005/0310/p14s01-sten.html, www.stopglobalwarming.org/sgw_read.asp?id=1153075232006.
18 See http://news.bbc.co.uk/2/hi/science/nature/5335362.stm.
19 See www.grida.no/climate/ipcc_tar/wg1/figspm-1.htm.
20 See www.atla.org/pressroom/FACTS/asbestos/whynot2.aspx.
21 See www.cnn.com/2006/TECH/science/12/13/china.dolphin.ap/index.html.
22 See www.cbsnews.com/stories/2006/05/19/tech/main1635143.shtml.

Approaches to Risk and Uncertainty

*Education is going forward
from cocksure ignorance to
thoughtful uncertainty.*

—Docendo Discimus

At the collision of greed and the environment is a mountain of uncertainty. There are good and bad approaches to the puzzles that result. Consider the stance of Craig Manson, Assistant Interior Secretary for Fish, Wildlife, and Parks under President George W. Bush. Manson recast enforcement of the Endangered Species Act, which, for three decades, protected the critical habitat of endangered species.[23] In Manson's words, the new policy involves an "era of cooperation" with developers and a common response of, "Let's see how we can make this work."[24] Manson justifies inaction with uncertainty that development is a cause of extinction. He stated:

> The most that one could say on that evidence [that extinction rates correlate to the rate of industrial development and population growth] is that there may be some connection. And it is a logical fallacy to suggest that because two things happen concurrently that they are necessarily related, without further evidence.[25]

President George W. Bush took a similar uncertainty-means-inaction tact to precautions against global warming. He explained it this way during the 2000 Presidential Debates:

> I don't think we know the solution to global warming yet. And I don't think we've got all the facts before we make decisions. ... And before we react, I think it's best to have the full accounting, full understanding of what's taking place.[26]

Speaking of logical fallacies, another is to conclude that nothing should be done because a danger is uncertain. Such mistakes are regrettably common. Uncertainty fuels optimism

---

23 See www.fws.gov/endangered/esa.html.
24 See www.grist.org/news/maindish/2004/04/15/griscom-manson/.
25 See www.grist.org/news/maindish/2004/04/15/griscom-manson/.
26 See www.debates.org/pages/trans2000b.html.

that only other people will be victims. More than 44 million Americans smoke and 127 million adults are overweight or obese. Never mind the fact that smoking kills almost one in five Americans[27] and, by increasing the risks of high blood pressure, type-two diabetes, heart disease, stroke, gallbladder disease, and breast, prostate, and colon cancer, obesity is the second-leading preventable cause of death in this country.[28] The notion that uncertain *environmental* problems will only victimize other people is similarly ill-founded. For instance, 150 million Americans live in areas where they are exposed to unhealthy levels of ozone or fine-particle pollution,[29] despite repeated findings that such pollution shortens human lives, contributes to heart disease, asthma attacks, and lung cancer, and interferes with lung growth and function.

Note that virtually everyone does relatively easy things as precautions against uncertain risks. We wash our hands to avoid uncertain disease. We look both ways at intersections to avoid uncertain accidents. These activities are rational, and they are evidence that we know better than to do nothing in the name of uncertainty. Therefore, to use uncertainty as an excuse for inaction when precautions are not so easy, as when addressing wildlife conservation and global warming, is disingenuous.

Rather than slipping from uncertainty into indifference, it is appropriate to consider precautionary efforts in proportion to the likelihood and enormity of the potential calamity. Attention to problems with a small probability of occurring is justified when the associated losses would be large. It is very unlikely that our homes will burn down, but due to the tremendous loss that would result from a fire, almost everyone takes out fire insurance. The same reasoning drives the purchase of car and health insurance and the use of seat belts, rubber gloves, guard rails, and airport metal detectors. The Federal Deposit Insurance Corporation insures our bank deposits. Insurance policies have even been written for the legs of supermodel Heidi Klum and *Lord of the Dance* creator Michael Flatley.[30] Klum's legs were insured for $52 million, Flatley's for a mere $40 million. People take precautions against losing many things, none of which are

---

27 See www.cancer.org/docroot/PED/content/PED_10_2X_Cigarette_Smoking.asp.
28 See www.obesity.org/subs/fastfacts/obesity_what2.shtml.
29 See http://lungaction.org/reports/sota06_full.html.
30 See www.answers.com/topic/michael-flatley and http://goliath.ecnext.com/coms2/
    gi_0199-4317483/Body-guards-a-growing-number.html.

more important than the air, water, and soil needed to sustain life. More and better-informed environmental precautions are warranted.

Learn the Risks

The chemicals we use in agriculture, lawn care, manufacturing, pest deterrence, transportation, food service, and household cleaning pose uncertain risks to humans and wildlife. Uncertainty does not convey to us the right to whatever belief is convenient. Uncertainty does not give us a license to throw up our hands and say we'll expose our families, our neighbors, and ourselves to these products with the rationalization that maybe the repercussions won't be so bad. Rather, uncertainty about potentially dangerous substances gives us the responsibility to find out as much as we reasonably can about the dangers, and about alternative products and procedures that would reduce those dangers. Only then can decisions be made as they should be—by weighing costs against benefits—with a strong caveat that *all* costs and benefits must be considered, and by no means is it sufficient to compare only financial costs and benefits.

A good first step is for everyone to develop realistic perceptions of risk. Studies find that people overestimate risks that are small, publicized, visible, or dramatic, such as the risks of death from tornados, floods, and pregnancy in the United States. Conversely, people underestimate risks that are large, less visible, or relatively mundane, such as the risks of death from heart disease, diabetes, and cancer.[31] The environmental and health risks from air and water pollution are also large, invisible, mundane, and as the research findings predict, largely dismissed. The solution hinges on expanded educational and research efforts. It's not a bad idea to teach students the 50 state capitals, but might it be even more useful to teach them about the 54 or so known human carcinogens?[32] Estimates of the risks associated with global warming,[33] acid rain,[34] coal power,[35] and combus-

---

31 See, for example, http://fds.oup.com/www.oup.co.uk/pdf/0-19-829363-1.pdf.
32 For a list with links to more information, see http://ntp.niehs.nih.gov/ntp/roc/eleventh/known.pdf.
33 See www.nrdc.org/globalWarming/fcons.asp.
34 See www.pubmedcentral.nih.gov/articlerender.fcgi?artid=1568495.
35 See www.ucsusa.org/clean_energy/fossil_fuels/carbon_risk.html.

tion engines[36] are readily available, but seldom conveyed. More research dollars should be directed to deserving categories of potential risks, including household and agricultural chemicals, indoor air pollution, and the heavy metals, hormones, and additives found in some fish,[37] dairy products,[38] and processed foods, respectively.[39]

What is Tomorrow Worth?

Cost-benefit analyses are confounded by the need to discount the future. Each dollar we might ask a power plant to spend today on new smokestack scrubbers will provide benefits in the future, and likewise for most spending on the environment, regardless of the degree of uncertainty involved. If future benefits were valued as highly as benefits today, people would be willing to spend *without limit* to preserve, for example, any environmental asset that would provide even a very small benefit for the rest of time. In reality, there is a preference for benefits that come sooner rather than later. Borrowers are willing to pay back more than a dollar in the future in exchange for a dollar today because of a preference to have money and the benefits it provides now. Lenders demand to receive more than a dollar in the future in exchange for each dollar today for the same reason. The diminished value people place on future benefits can be expressed in terms of an annual discount rate. If your discount rate is five percent, that means that you would be indifferent between a dollar today and $1.05 in a year, and that you would approve of spending $1.00 on an environmental policy that would yield $1.05 or more in benefits in a year.

I asked members of the President's Council of Economic Advisors under Jimmy Carter, Ronald Reagan, Bill Clinton, and George H.W. Bush what rates their administrations used when making environmental policy decisions. Under Carter the discount rate was as low as zero. Under Reagan it was 10 percent. Under Clinton is ranged from 2 to 8 percent. Under Bush it ranged from 3 to 10 percent. The rates are subjective, but I think you will agree that there is room for improvement, in that

---

36 See, for example, www.vpirg.org/campaigns/environmentalHealth/dieselExhaust.php.
37 See, for example, www.ewg.org/reports/brainfood/foreword.html.
38 See www.preventcancer.com/consumers/general/milk.htm.
39 See http://chge.med.harvard.edu/education/food/index.html, John Robbins, *Diet for a New America: How Your Food Choices Affect Your Health, Happiness and the Future of Life on Earth*, Tiburon, California: H.J. Kramer, 1998.

future benefits are often discounted too heavily. For instance, with a chosen discount rate of 8 percent, and placing the value of unidentified human lives at $6 million dollars each, as economists find that people do on average,[40] society would be willing to spend a total of 56 cents now to save 1,000 lives 300 years from now. If you think society should spend more—say $100 or $1,000,000—to save those lives, the implication is that you favor a lower discount rate. The general consensus among the General Accounting Office, the Environmental Protection Agency, the Congressional Budget Office, and the New York University Program on Environmental Regulation, among other prominent agencies and economists, is that appropriate discount rates fall in the 2 to 3 percent range, which would have society spend between $845,247 and $15.8 million today to save those 1,000 lives in 300 years. Whenever decisions on precautionary expenditures are made on the basis of excessive discount rates, efforts to serve future generations are inappropriately compromised.

Take the Easy Steps

Even with expanded efforts to shed light on environmental uncertainties, many mysteries will remain. It is impossible to know when researchers will develop a new source of clean energy, what environmental misdeed will break the back of the critically endangered Bactrian camel, or what dangers lurk within new-fangled industrial processes. One simple approach to inestimable risks is to take at least those precautionary steps that are easy. If the cost of a precaution is close to nil, it is of little issue whether it creates a great benefit or not, and the benefit of avoiding worry is likely to be enough to justify a small measure of avoidance. Consumers can reduce worldwide freighter travel by choosing bottled water from the grocery store shelf of domestic waters ten inches below the shelf of imported waters. The use of plastic bottles can be avoided by grabbing a glass bottle a few inches to the left or right. The need to manufacture both types of bottles and transport them anywhere can be avoided by refilling the bottles you already have at the tap. If these steps

---

40 See Jahn K. Hakes and W. Kip Viscusi, "Automobile Seatbelt Usage and the Value of Statistical Life," *Southern Economic Journal* 73, no. 3 (2007): 659-676; W. Kip Viscusi and Joseph Aldy, "The Value of Statistical Life: A Critical Review of Market Estimates Thoughout the World," *Journal of Risk and Uncertainty* 27, no. 1 (2003): 5-76.

are heartbreaking to you, they may not be worth the trouble. If they're easy, why not avoid the associated problems, uncertain as they may be?

I'm uncertain about when the local landfill might leak, but I find it easy to divert toxic heavy metals toward more proper disposal by collecting spent nickel-cadmium rechargeable batteries and taking them to Radio Shack or a cell phone service provider for recycling when I'm going there anyway. One can enjoy comfort in temperatures between roughly 60° F and 90° F by donning appropriate clothing—perhaps a sweater or a tank top—rather than by artificially heating or cooling air and blowing it throughout a building. My parents reduce toxic emissions by setting the temperature in their house down to 60° F in the wintertime; they have no air conditioning. As a nice alternative to pesticide use, my mother removes insects from the plants in her garden with a spray of used dishwater. For decades she has set out bowls of beer as an easy way to attract and kill slugs in the garden. Now I read that the chemical in once-popular commercial slug killers, metaldehyde, is toxic and a potential groundwater contaminant.[41] Chalk one up for easy alternatives that turn out to evade real risks.

> **Chalk one up for easy alternatives that turn out to evade real risks.**

Many risks can be avoided by opting for alternatives that require little or no sacrifice. I haven't heard anyone lamenting the removal of lead from paints and gasoline, DDT from pesticides, arsenic from treated lumber, or chlorofluorocarbons from spray cans and cooling systems. Many an automobile ride could be replaced with a walk or a bike ride, especially if bike lanes and paths became more prevalent. Hybrid-electric engines now provide gas-sipping alternatives to gasoline engines. The technology is also available for affordable automobiles that travel 80 miles or more on a gallon of gasoline.[42] Too much progress on the environmental front is held back merely by a lack of implementation. For those who take advantage of alternatives to harsh chemicals, avoid unneeded material goods, recycle, bypass motorized transportation, and circumvent pollution *when it is easy to do so*, these small steps make a worthwhile difference.

---

41 See www.pesticideinfo.org/Detail_Chemical.jsp?Rec_Id=PC32878#Toxicity.
42 See, for example, http://news.windingroad.com/category/auto-news/mini/page/2/.

Public Policy Options

Like individual choices, policy decisions are made in the milieu of uncertainty. In the context of unpredictable outcomes there are underused-but-intelligent approaches that prepare for the worst but allow for the best. One is the precautionary polluter pays principal (4P), which has those who take risks with the environment post a large enough bond to cover the best estimate of the worst-case scenario. For example, those building a new nuclear power plant would post a bond sufficient for the healthcare and cleanup costs if it were to melt down, and those building a new landfill would post an assurance bond for recovery costs in the event of groundwater contamination. If the feared damages were not forthcoming or it was demonstrated that the worst-case scenario would not be as bad as originally thought, the bond and all accumulated interest would be returned to the developers. Such policies require developers to take risks with their own money rather than with public money or environmental assets. The result is an incentive to stick to risks that make sense after weighing the benefits against the potential costs.

The 4P concept and more general precautionary principals may be overlooked in U.S. policy making, but variations are common among international environmental agreements. Examples appear in

- Principle 15 of the Rio Declaration on the Environment and Development,

- the Convention for the Protection of the Marine Environment of the North-East Atlantic (OSPAR) treaty,

- the Convention on International Trade of Endangered Species of Wild Fauna and Flora (CITES) treaty,

- the revised Treaty of Rome,

- Article 3.3 of the UN Framework Convention on Climate Change,

- Amendments to the Montreal Protocol on Substances that Deplete the Ozone Layer, and

- the UN Convention of Biological Diversity.

The version of the precautionary principle adopted in the Australian Intergovernmental Agreement on the Environment (IGAE) is explained this way:[43]

> Where there are threats of serious or irreversible environmental damage, lack of full scientific certainty should not be used as a reason for postponing measures to prevent environmental degradation. In the application of the precautionary principle, public and private decisions should be guided by
>
> (i)   careful evaluation to avoid, wherever practicable, serious or irreversible damage to the environment; and
>
> (ii) an assessment of the risk-weighted consequences of various options.

There are fine examples of precautionary measures throughout the world. Countries across Europe have mandatory recycling programs, sustainability education programs, and strict controls on toxic substances to help ward off uncertain risks. The United States has yet to take a leadership role in precautionary policy.

The Politics of Uncertainty

During prosperous times such as these, when 90 percent of the population is above the poverty line and the unemployment rate is five percent, most Americans have the opportunity to go beyond providing for their families and achieve higher goals. Society can choose to invest in security against environmental uncertainties and take steps to preserve resources for coming generations. This could be a pivotal time to stem environmental losses, bolster research on possible carcinogens, broaden school curricula on sustainability and global diplomacy, and shift toward energy-efficient transportation, but little progress has been made. Instead, the most recent Bush administration has targeted cuts in the U.S. Forest Service, the Environmental Protection Agency, the National Oceanic and Atmospheric Administration Fisheries, the National Ocean Service, the Clean Water State Revolving Loan Fund, the National Park Service, the U.S. Fish

---

43 See www.netspace.net.au/~jnevill/igae.htm.

and Wildlife Service, the Transportation Department, and the Energy Department, among other agencies that address environmental problems.[44] The United States is alone among wealthy nations in its failure to ratify the Kyoto Protocol and other initiatives that embrace the precautionary principal. And the cost of unpopular military offensives has prevented alternative advances on eco-friendly fronts.

What are the constraints on sensible environmental policy? This is where politics rears its ugly head. If you stand in the voting booth during the next election thinking, "I don't really like these choices," remember that the choice is not among the smartest Americans or the most capable Americans or the most accomplished; it is a choice among a few of the very richest Americans. Federal Election Committee chairman Michael E. Toner estimated that spending on the 2008 presidential election would reach $1 billion, and that at least $100 million is required to launch a serious candidacy.[45] The financial requirement precludes many potential candidates who take stock in environmental concerns and quality-of-life issues rather than wealth maximization. In the great political spending race, even the rich candidates have little choice but to submit to manipulation by corporations and special interests that provide funding.

The wealth criterion for a viable candidacy effectively limits the pool of applicants for national leadership positions to a fraction of one-percent of the country's population. The wealthy candidates have a natural affinity to serve their own kind, and at a personal level, those setting the policies for our nation are relatively insulated against uncertain environmental outcomes. If global climate change brings the predicted storms, floods, droughts, and disease,[46] members of Congress will assuredly live in relative comfort and safety. Pollution is already affecting food crops,[47] but the rich will have abundant food for as long as food can be grown. The uncertain effects of placing coal and nuclear power facilities in close proximity to homes are relatively unimportant to the rich, who seldom live in the shadow

---

44 See http://us.oneworld.net/article/view/102922/1/7263, www.commondreams. org/headlines05/0208-04.htm, www.ucsusa.org/news/positions/president-bushs-fy-2006-budget.html.

45 See www.washingtontimes.com/national/20061220-121843-2600r.htm.

46 See www.ClimateCrisis.net.

47 See www.omafra.gov.on.ca/english/crops/facts/01-015.htm, www.equalearth.org/ agriculturepollution.htm.

of a power plant. When health problems do reach the rich, they can afford treatments that the average citizen cannot. Thus, it is individually rational for those who make the decisions for this country to downplay the need for precautions.

There are exceptions. Former Vice President Al Gore is a tireless crusader for the environment. Gore and President Bill Clinton advocated the Kyoto Protocol[48] and an energy tax that would encourage conservation and reduce the downside risks of rampant energy consumption. As senators, John McCain and Barack Obama voted to include oil and gas smokestacks in mercury regulations.[49] Senator Hillary Clinton stated interest in ratifying the Kyoto Protocol and offering energy conservation tax credits.[50] These anecdotes indicate the will of some leaders to address environmental concerns. The threat is that politicians, who are unlikely to bear the brunt of environmental disasters, will not feel an appropriate sense of urgency or place environmental protection ahead of short-term political goals.

The ascent of short-sighted policymakers is aided by the limited set of candidates and by well-financed special interest groups that pull the strings of politicians and voters alike. Marketing campaigns backed by the might of corporate coffers persuade consumers to ignore the risks and consequences of seeking more and more ma-

Vigorous promotions for designer clothing overtake entire buildings in New York.

48 Bill Clinton signed the Kyoto Protocol but it was not ratified by Congress and it was later abandoned by President George W. Bush. See http://edition.cnn.com/2001/WORLD/europe/italy/03/29/environment.kyoto/.
49 See www.ontheissues.org/Senate/John_McCain.htm and www.ontheissues.org/2008/Barack_Obama_Environment.htm.
50 See www.ontheissues.org/Senate/Hillary_Clinton_Environment.htm.

terial possessions. The idea that products should trump preservation is reinforced by the roughly 3,000 commercial messages a typical individual is exposed to daily.[51] Indoctrination into consumerism begins at an early age with advertisements beamed via satellite into 12,000 schools across the country on Channel One.[52] In what should be the last bastion of independent thought—our colleges and universities—think about who is on the boards of trustees—corporate CEOs; think about who funds research grants—large corporations. Influence toward consumerism permeates radio and television programming. It is on placards at the ballpark, billboards along the road, and blimps in the sky. Ending a 112-year tradition of noncommercialism, runners in the 2008 Boston Marathon were subjected to corporate advertising placed directly on the start and finish lines. Is nothing sacred?

The political, community, and organization leaders who receive corporate sponsorship on top of the usual influences to dismiss uncertain risks are unlikely to orchestrate a sea change toward sustainability. It will take passionate role models, an educated populace, and activism on the part of the informed in order to move society into a more proactive stance. As mentioned in the discussion of good and bad activism in Chapter 14, the most influential activists of all time, including Martin Luther King, Jr., Mahatma Gandhi, Buddha, and Jesus, made their marks peacefully. The most successful activists don't cause trouble in a violent way. Rather, they cause thought. We can all go out and cause some thought.

- Ask your neighbor where those chemicals go after they are sprayed on her lawn and garden.

- Ask your roommate whether the people who made her shoes will ever be able to afford such a pair of shoes.

- Ask a businessperson whether maximizing profit is really the same as maximizing happiness.

- Ask Dick Cheney why we would drill for oil in the Arctic National Wildlife Refuge when

---

51 See http://money.cnn.com/2006/03/21/technology/business2_thirdscreen_
   mobileads0321/index.htm.

52 See www.ChannelOne.com.

we have a virtually unlimited source of clean energy shining down from the sky.

- Ask someone who has seen the effects of war whether a military solution is an oxymoron.

- Ask a politician whether his or her actions are ever inconsistent with doing what is best for the wealthy.

- Ask your child what her hamburger used to be.

- Ask your parents what the gas mileage is on their SUV.

- Ask the local college president how many of the campus buildings are LEED certified (an indication of relatively sustainable design and construction or renovation practices).

- Ask a person who wants smaller government which three administrations overstepped the government's financial boundaries by the greatest margins ever. (The Answer: those of Ronald Reagan, George H.W. Bush, and George W. Bush.)

- Ask the media whether the types of stories they choose to run are causing more thought about hard questions or hard-ons.

In your own way, with your own questions, by all means, cause some thought.

When in Doubt

Unending controversies confound every good citizen's intention to do the right thing. Is it worthwhile to recycle glass or to up-grade to a higher efficiency heat pump? How important is it to car pool, bike to work, or use public transportation? Should you drive a hybrid-electric car? It is not necessary to punt on solutions when uncertainties make consensus elusive. Judgmental heuristics, instincts, and rules of thumb provide guidance when the facts are unclear.[53] Chapter 9 provides specific criteria for

53 For a rich discussion of snap decision making, read Malcolm Gladwell's *Blink*

solving ethical dilemmas. When in doubt, one's conscience can be a surprisingly good source of direction.

For better or worse, some decisions must be made quickly on the basis of a one-question litmus test determined by the favored cause of the decision maker. That question might be: Does this policy benefit

> business owners?
>
> the working class?
>
> the environment?
>
> me?
>
> my children?
>
> my company?
>
> my pocketbook?

Because such decision rules are so common in practice, it is easy to predict how ardent members of either political party will respond to suggestions of increased funding for education, solar energy initiatives, or stricter emissions standards.

Implicit in common rules of thumb can be beliefs that what is good for business owners (or the working class, or the environment) is good for society at large. Advocates of business growth see economic development as a way to serve rich and poor alike. Ecological economists, and most notably Herman Daly,[54] point out that the economy is a subset of the environment and not vice versa. The natural resources used in production by businesses stem from the environment, and the economy's workers and consumers rely on moderate temperatures and the sustained availability of clean air, water, and food. There would be no economy without a viable environment; the environment did just fine for millions of years without the economy.

When the cost-benefit analysis of an environmental policy could come down on either side due to fuzzy facts, a precautionary environmental strategy would be to err on the safe side and opt for the greener of two policies. The sacrifices of modest environmentalism are so small, and the foreseeable losses from

(New York: Little, Brown, and Co., 2005).

54 See Herman Daly, *Beyond Growth: The Economics of Sustainable Development,* Boston: Beacon Press, 1997.

environmental destruction are so large, that a "better safe than sorry" approach is a no-brainer.

In the battle over environmental protection, some critics write-off both developers and conservationists as being driven by biased agendas. The difference is that conservationists seldom share developers' financial motive for bias. In reality, the debate is between developers compelled by opportunities to make more money and conservationists compelled by the problems caused by unfettered greed. If you're concerned that conservation efforts will prohibit worthwhile developments, see Chapter 3, "Ode to Moderation."

Environmental Uncertainties and the Economy

> *Is that good economics?*
> *Is it sound for the country?*
>
> —The Lorax[55]

People ask me as an economist, "Wouldn't the economy suffer if we started buying less stuff in order to protect the environment?" Let's do the math: To begin with, if we bought half as much stuff, having half as much work wouldn't be a problem because we would only need half as much money. Note also that most jobs—namely those in the already burgeoning service industries—do not hinge on resource exploitation and do not rely heavily on practices with uncertain environmental effects. Manufacturing jobs currently make up only 11 percent of all jobs in the U.S. economy.[56]

The unemployment rate of 5 percent at the time of this writing is low by historical standards, and there are ample opportunities to create new, high-paying jobs without sacrificing environmental quality. For example, according to the Breast Cancer Fund, more than 90 percent of chemicals are untested before they are approved for commerce.[57] To invest in more complete tests of these substances, or to develop alternatives to potentially damaging transportation systems, plastics, and manufacturing processes, would be to create good jobs. Employment is also promoted by expenditures on environmental clean-ups, green

---

55 Dr. Suess, *The Lorax*, New York: Random House, 1971.
56 See www.bls.gov/iag/manufacturing.htm.
57 See www.breastcancerfund.org/site/pp.asp?c=kwKXLdPaE&b=1486213.

energy, reforestation, education, and healthcare. There is no need to destroy lives or the environment in order to create employment or boost the standard of living.

Conclusions

The chances may be small that a particular individual will fall victim to a car crash, a lawsuit, or a major earthquake, but costly precautions are taken against these events because, though uncertain, the results could be devastating. It is similarly uncertain that rampant consumerism will result in more extinctions, cancer deaths, global climate change, illness, and environmental losses, but society should take precautions against those risks for the same reason. Failures to adopt safety precautions stem from ignorance, shortsightedness, selfishness, politics, and the excessive discounting of future environmental and health losses.

The luxuries of time and uncertainty attract rationalization and ambivalence. It is deceptively comforting to read that experts are "pretty sure" that oil supplies will meet demands for at least 25 years.[58] Just ask any senior citizen how quickly 25 years pass. Twenty-five years ago I was 18. It seems like only yesterday. There is no stopping time, and we will regret missed opportunities soon enough.

> My parents avoid the uncertain risks of paints and solvents.

58 See www.reason.com/news/show/117681.html.

CHAPTER 18

Thinking Globally

The global village on this small planet is increasingly close-knit. No land mass on Earth escapes human influence.[1] Consider, for example, the polar bears in the Arctic that are born as hermaphrodites due to northward-drifting flame retardants used on furniture and carpets in the United States and Europe.[2] On the day of this writing I studied environmental issues first-hand on the Caribbean island of Dominica, conducted business in the United States via the Internet, watched television broadcasts from three continents, and visited stores in rundown huts that sell beer from Germany and shoes from Vietnam.

As it barrels along without conscience or foresight, the locomotive of global commerce has far greater momentum than any efforts to pick up after it. Ships cross the oceans to bring metal and plastic beverage containers from all over the world to sensitive environmental hot spots like Dominica, but they don't take them away. Ten sips later, the plastic water bottles (ironi-

---

1 Few bodies of water do either. The depths of the oceans may be the least affected places on Earth, although they are not untouched. For example, the Natural Energy Laboratory of Hawaii Authority is pumping up deep sea water for purposes such as cooling, irrigation, aquaculture, and innovative sources of alternative energy. See www.nelha.org.
2 See www.theregister.co.uk/2006/01/12/arctic_pollution/.

cally, one can drink directly from many rivers in Dominica) and the ice tea cans from New Jersey and New York (with brand names such as *Colorado* and *Arizona*) only add to the carpet of non-biodegradable packaging from wealthy nations that litters the ground.

Whose responsibility is it to think deeply about how business practices touch delicate ecosystems across the planet? The stockholders'? The consumers'? The governments'? Business leaders resist government intervention and say they merely serve the interests of their customers. The customers have the least information about dangers inherent in products and their manufacturing, and place reliance on producers and governments to assure the safety of everything going into food and coming out of smokestacks. Business-related campaign donations and lobbying efforts are too large for government leaders to ignore. And amid finger pointing and blind faith, all three levels of potential accountability are defeated.

As an example, the nonpartisan, nonprofit advocacy group Common Cause looked into the puzzling failure of a Connecticut bill that would have updated the five-cent deposit placed on beverage bottles, adjusting it for inflation and expanding the program to include non-carbonated beverages. Behind the scenes, the researchers found $704,722 in campaign and political action committee contributions by Bottle Bill opponents over the previous four years.[3] That left a government distracted by money, a consumer base poorly informed about the problems, and self-interested businesses with little oversight from above or

---

3   See www.commoncause.org/atf/cf/%7BFB3C17E2-CDD1-4DF6-92BE-
    BD4429893665%7D/CT.BOTTLEBILL.PDF.

below. Ergo, beverage-container manufacturing roars on using exorbitant amounts of raw, non-renewable materials processed in New York factories that belch toxins to produce containers that say things like *Arizona* on the side. And then diesel trucks take the bottled beverages to Connecticut and every other neck of the woods.

> A wonderful alternative to purchasing packaged beverages is to pull mint from the garden and make tea by steeping the mint in boiling tap water.

Modest improvements in government decision making might come from advances in campaign finance reform, but the threat of corruption in government will remain. It is possible that more companies will become environmentally enlightened à la Patagonia and Newman's Own, but the influence of profits will persist. The most promising opportunity may be to inform the consumers and voters of the world, for humans will always be curious and interested in self preservation.

This chapter addresses key debates over where problems truly exist and where the moral high ground lies. Whole books could be written about these and hundreds of global environmental issues. Hopefully these eight morsels of global surveillance will be enough to start some conversations or cause some thought.

Who's trashing the place?

There are concerns that developing nations have lower environmental standards and thus pose a threat beyond our own.[4] This concern is valid in some contexts. I have seen manufacturing plants in China that ostensibly sullied the countryside with reckless abandon. Countries such as Russia have air quality standards inferior to our own.[5] Most developing nations, however, are predominantly agrarian. For instance, you won't find automobile manufacturing plants in Dominica; only banana plants. So although some poor countries might have weak standards or enforcement policies, the problems aren't so much about smokestacks as they are about deforestation for agriculture, as is the case for the bananas Dominica exports to the United Kingdom. Even the agricultural practices tend to be less chemically depen-

---

4   See, for example, www1.worldbank.org/economicpolicy/globalization/documents/AssessingGlobalizationP4.pdf.
5   See www.eia.doe.gov/emeu/cabs/russenv.html.

dent in developing countries thanks to the limited accessibility and affordability of chemical fertilizers and pesticides.

The worst environmental problems arise when people are rich enough to cause a lot of damage, but not sufficiently financed, focused, or principled to adopt the best practices. Environmental economists often characterize the relationship between pollution and prosperity as an inverted *U* shape. People with very low incomes can do little damage because they have limited means by which to inflict harm. If their intentions are pure, people with very high incomes can afford to protect parks, clean-up rivers, purchase organic and fair trade products, and require the best pollution-abatement systems. Indeed, the world's richest countries—Luxembourg, Norway, Iceland, Switzerland, Ireland, and Denmark—do exhibit some of the highest environmental standards.[6] People in the middle cause a disproportionate amount of environmental destruction because they have enough money to fuel a manufacturing frenzy but not enough to easily afford conservation measures. Couple the middling incomes of most Americans with a lack of environmental focus and you have a

A bus stop in Dominica promotes fair trade products made and priced to address humanitarian and environmental goals.

6   See www.yale.edu/epi/.

population that buys mass quantities of consumer goods, but relatively few solar cells, hybrid-electric cars, composting toilets, products with recycled content, organic coffee beans, or geothermal heating systems. Among all Organization for Economic Cooperation and Development countries, the United States generates the highest per-capita levels of carbon dioxide emissions, nuclear waste, and municipal solid waste.[7]

Americans Out-consume Others Five Fold

Everyone has seen pictures of impoverished areas. We know they exist in pockets around the globe. The surprise is that life as U.S. residents know it is "normal" nowhere else on Earth. Our tremendous capacity to create waste is symptomatic of another divergence between the United States and the rest of the world: the routines of our way of life devour resources at an astonishing rate. If everyone in the world consumed resources at an equal rate, each 5 percent of the world population would consume 5 percent of the world's resources. With under 5 percent of the world population, the United States consumes 26 percent of the oil, 25 percent of the coal, and 27 percent of the natural gas consumed in the world. We also contribute 25 percent of the world's total carbon dioxide emissions, more than China, India, and Japan combined.[8] Indeed, the biggest problems, and the greatest opportunities to make a difference, are here at home.

As a former camp counselor and college trip leader I've accompanied young people on journeys away from their air-conditioned abodes and into conditions typical in other countries. For most of the world's population it is normal to have a small dwelling with a dirt floor and share it with a large extended family, domesticated animals, and wildlife. Even in the wealthy countries of Europe and Asia, homes are a fraction of the size of U.S. homes. My experiences staying in small quarters in Japan, Australia, and Belize were much like those of my campers upon entering their cabins—the change is uncomfortable at first, and then we fall in love with the modest surroundings. Many a camper started the week with phone calls to parents and hopes to return home, and ended with pleas for permission to stay at camp longer. Like those campers, I truly regretted leav-

7   See www.census.gov/prod/www/statistical-abstract-2001_2005.html, table 1332.
8   See www.nrdc.org/international/osuperpower.asp.

ing the cozy, intimate, easy-to-maintain living environments of simple places. It may be disconcerting to consider a lifestyle that treads more lightly on the Earth, but if we turn the corner on our excesses, we might just reach a superior comfort level almost overnight.

Remember (as explained in Chapter 15) that despite common misunderstandings, simple living does not mean primitive living. There is no need for Americans to replicate the dirt floors found elsewhere; bamboo, cork, and recycled-fiber carpet provide elegant simplicity with minimal environmental damage. Between 1970 and 2006 the average size of a single-family house in the United States rose from 1,400 square feet to 2,500 square feet. That additional 1,100 square feet—the equivalent of eight 11.5' by 12' rooms—separates loved ones and must be cleaned, heated, cooled, furnished, decorated, searched for missing items, and updated like the rest. Having lived in houses small and large, I know from personal experience that clutter grows to fill any space provided—I think you'll agree. Despite the contention that bigger is better, there are consequential burdens to bigness, excess is overrated, and a small house may feel more like *home*.

The Best Things in Life are in the Third World

To be certain, people in developing nations need better health-care and education, but if wealth is figured on the true sources of happiness, they are one rich group of people. My wife's parents, Bud and Linda Falkenhain, travel to a different third-world country every year to provide free eye exams and glasses to poor natives. The sites for this good work have included Indonesia, Nepal, Cambodia, Paraguay, Ecuador, Tibet, Kenya, Guatemala, Vietnam, Mongolia, and many more. In post-trip presentations in the United States, my father-in-law shows pictures of peasants who own few clothes and fewer material goods and says, "I want to tell you something: these people are happier than you are." His message is echoed by my own parents on the basis of their global travels, and by my experiences in slums as described in Chapter 2. The food, art, dance, companionship, family ties, intimacy, and mutual support of village culture make it charming and alluring. Yes, the third-world citizens yearn for more money, but so do Donald Trump, Bill Gates, Christy Walton, and most other

> **These people are happier than you are.**

people at all income levels. The universal myth is that bliss would be attained if only our income could double. The reality is that every time income does double, our bliss point moves another doubling away.

Opportunities to earn sizable incomes in developing countries are relatively slim, making the pursuit of material-based happiness less of a distraction. One who earns $2 a day doesn't spend time combing e-bay for sources of pleasure. People in less developed countries enjoy a treasure of a different sort: time. In the rural areas of Africa, Asia, Central America, and the Caribbean, for example, people enjoy more family time, community time, rest time, and play time. More time is spent conversing with friends, cooking good food, eating, making music, expressing creativity, sharing affection, and walking—they do *so* much walking—which turns out to be quite a pleasant way to get to work and to health. Largely absent are the rat race, the traffic jams, the desk jobs, the home maintenance, the deadlines, and most of the bills.

If the third world has so much to offer, why not move there? Actually, there are examples of Americans choosing to live throughout the developing world. My sister has lived in Somalia, Sierra Leone, and India, and I've yet to visit a country where transplanted Americans aren't easy to find. (We do tend to stick out like sore thumbs, but that's another story.) The Dominican lodge in which I write this chapter is owned by a couple from Belgium, and down the road are modest restaurants run by other Westerners. Personally, I would rather pursue an atypical slow life in the United States than a typical slow life away from home. What is clear is that life in America could be made even better with inspiration from smiles on the faces of peasants rich in culture, tradition, wildlife, and time.

Immigration Isn't the Problem It's Made Out to Be

Anti-immigration groups describe immigration as a source of overpopulation, urban sprawl, air pollution, poverty, and water depletion.[9] An honest assessment reveals that we are all immigrants or descendants of immigrants, and the United States has always been a nation of immigrants. Even the Native Americans

---

9   FAIR offers state-level information related to immigration. See, for example, www.fairus.org/site/PageServer?pagename=research_research07f0.

arrived by sea or land bridge from elsewhere, primarily Siberia. Today, foreign-born individuals make up 11 percent of the population and 14 percent of its workforce, including 23.7 percent of all physicians.[10]

Immigration fluctuates with business cycles, increasing when more workers are needed and decreasing when labor is abundant.[11] The influx of working-age immigrants into the country also lowers the average age of the population and assists "pay-as-you-go" entitlement programs such as Social Security and Medicare, which collect from current workers to pay for current retirees. Economists Rachel Friedberg and Jennifer Hunt studied the effects of immigration and found no evidence of economically significant reductions in employment among native-born workers.[12] These researchers concluded that a 10 percent increase in a country's share of immigrants reduces wages for natives by, at most, 1 percent. Factor in the lower prices and higher profits that immigrant labor allows and you'll come up with a bargain. Former Federal Reserve chairman Alan Greenspan sees immigration as beneficial, saying that

> unless immigration is uncapped ... the continuous reduction in the number of available workers willing to take jobs ... would intensify inflationary pressures or squeeze profit margins, with either outcome capable of bringing our growing prosperity to an end.[13]

Pollution and stresses on natural resources do indeed grow with population, but remember that immigration changes the location of people, rather than adding to the number of people. Immigrants who adopt the American lifestyle will have fewer children than do people in the countries from which most immigrants come—Mexico, China, India, the Philippines, and the Dominican Republic.[14] Technology, healthcare, and eldercare

10 See www.ama-assn.org/ama/pub/category/211.html.
11 For example, the Office of Immigration Statistics reports that the number of people caught attempting to cross the southwestern border between the United States and Mexico increased by about 50 percent during the prosperous late 1990s and fell sharply during the recession of the early 2000s.
12 "The Impact of Immigrants on Host Country Wages, Employment, and Growth," *Journal of Economic Perspectives*, Spring 1995, 23–44.
13 See www.bc.edu/bc_org/mvp/fincon/greenspanspeech.html.
14 The exception in terms of birth rates is China, where the birth rate is similar to that in the United States.

systems in developed countries mitigate the need to have inordinate numbers of children to provide labor, assure the survival of a few, or care for aging parents. The most serious environmental problems, including climate change, acid deposition, and resource depletion, are global problems, and it makes little difference where the pollutants are released or where the resources are used.

The Rest of the World Doesn't Dream of Being Us

Mention that the United States should adopt more respectful policies and environmental actions in part to rekindle its image in the world community and you're likely to meet the rebuke that everyone really wishes they were us anyway. The United States is a great nation and should be proud of what it has accomplished over a short period of history, but it is important to qualify the claims of envy. In a newspaper article titled "Americans Think They're Envy of the World," Pat Morrison notes:

> Americans are the world's luckiest teenagers, with the best car, the fattest allowance and the biggest line of brag, yet like all teenagers we're secretly afraid that someone is laughing at us. Here's a news flash. They are.[15]

Despite our placement on many a wall map, the United States is not the center of the world. The broad international criticism of U.S. policies is a well kept secret domestically. For a reality check, visit the London Times site at http://sitesearch.timesonline.co.uk (or any other news site written for a non-American audience) and do a search for "American policy." I have tried this many times and have never failed to be embarrassed by the results. Most recently I pulled up an article by Matthew Parris that characterized the report of the Iraq Study Group, presented to President Bush by James Baker and Lee Hamilton, as "shallow," "dishonest," and a description of how to "weasel a way out of trouble and leave former friends to fall, undefended, by the wayside." Parris is wrong in his criticism, as are many detractors. The point is that most of what *we* hear domestically has gone through strong filters that select for adoration.

We do have our admirers, for the grass is always greener on

15 See www.commondreams.org/views02/0620-01.htm.

the other side of the ocean. The draw of money incites envy for American income levels, but claims of worldwide "U.S. envy" are exaggerated. When talking with people in non-Western countries I typically discover that we are not even on their radar, and that they know and care as little about us as the average American does about them.

The reality has more to do with Western values being foisted upon other nations. Religion, entertainment, and agricultural practices have already been exported aggressively. Don't look now, but Wal-Mart just hit China, not to mention Mexico, Brazil, Argentina, Germany, Puerto Rico, the United Kingdom, Canada, and South Korea.[16] I'm told that KFC has pecked its way into formerly chain-free Dominica. These types of large corporations make it difficult for local competitors to stay afloat unless they match the chains' low standards of service, quality, and ethics. The restaurants in Dominica currently serve their food almost exclusively on reusable ceramic plates. It is more expensive to hire dishwashers than to use Styrofoam plates, but using ceramics is the sustainable thing to do. If KFC comes in and charges a dollar less per meal by serving on Styrofoam and taking other shortcuts, the options for local "snackettes" are to lower service standards or concede to the competition.

Large Corporations Aim to Please

Big and bad are not necessarily synonymous. There are economies of scale that serve society well in terms of both prices and the conservation of resources. One big factory can often produce more output with less waste than two medium-sized factories, which would require more managers, more furnaces, more smokestacks, and more paperwork. It is unlikely that a particularly small company could market affordable photovoltaic cells, ultra-efficient cars,[17] or path breaking heating and cooling systems because the up-front research and development costs would be prohibitive. General Motors spent over $1 billion on its ill-fated electric vehicle, the EV1, and plans to spend a similar amount on fuel cell technology. Only large-scale production would spread the necessary costs across enough units to place the products within the financial reach of the masses. We have

16 See www.wal-martchina.com/english/walmart/wminchina.htm.
17 Tesla motors is a relatively small company that did create an ultra-efficient vehicle, but the price tag on the Tesla Roadster is an unaffordable $109,000.

automotive giants Toyota and Honda to thank for jump-starting the hybrid car market. At the retail level, only after corpora-, tions such as Whole Foods Market grew large did they pressure Kroger and Wal-Mart into the business of selling healthier, Earth-friendly foods.

Big stores certainly can sell organics, pay their employees well, refuse sweatshop products, and tread lightly on the environment. The problem is that too many businesses regard profit as a solitary goal and have little environmental foresight or recognition that being a good company means being a good global citizen. The corporate philosophy of one mega-store chain is that profitability is "a vital yardstick of progress."[18] A broader commitment to societal needs that included genuine concern for communities and the environment would make everyone better off, but don't hold your breath.

The good news is that profits come from serving the perceived needs of the population, and ethical consumers can guide profit-frenzied firms to the high road. Consumers can establish a link between stockholders' short-sighted focus on profits and society's long-term interest in sustainability. This influence is achieved with targeted purchases of goods with recycled content, minimal packaging, opportunities for re-use, and possibilities for repair, among other desirable qualities. The brave can also be proactive by telling store managers that their spending money will beat a path to locally grown organic food, fair-trade coffee, shoes made by well-treated workers, and stores that serve customers with a conscience. Companies from McDonalds to Nike have already responded to such messages with biodegradable packaging and safer working conditions, but they have a long way to go. If we as customers demand fair pay and fair play, corporations can and will respond.

The World Population is On Course to Double by 2068

Individual efforts to protect resources are eroded by population growth. An annual birth rate of 20.05 per 1000 people and a death rate of 8.67 per 1000 give the world a growth rate of 1.14 percent per year.[19] At that rate, the world population of nearly 7 billion will double in 60 years—before today's children retire.

18 See www.meijer.com/pr/.
19 See www.cia.gov/cia/publications/factbook/print/xx.html.

That means that if per-capita levels of resource use and pollution were cut in half over the next six decades, with twice as many people each creating half as much burden on average, there would be absolutely no reduction in the rates of pollution or resource depletion.

Progress on environmental goals will come only with an accelerated rate of conservation, a slower rate of population growth, or some combination of the two. Meanwhile, Eric Keroack, the 2006 appointee as deputy assistant secretary for population affairs at the U.S. Department of Health and Human Services, opposes the distribution of contraceptives and favors the abstinence-only approach. For the 95 percent of global citizens whose consumption levels pale in comparison to those in North America, it will be difficult at best to make drastic cuts in resource use. These realities place particular importance on new purchasing patterns domestically, and on careful family-planning approaches everywhere.

War

Chapter 12 described the instinct to entertain the mind. This can wreak havoc at the global level. If you don't think conflict is exciting, consider not only the 1057 war movies available on Netflix.com, but the standard formula for any story from *Tom and Jerry* to *The Iliad* and *The Odyssey*: protagonist + antagonist = entertainment. As the Vietnam-era slogan held, "War is unhealthy for children and other living things," but the serenity of a world at peace is threatened by human instincts for conquest and thrill-seeking. We are not programmed to swallow our pride.

The process of evolution was the first culprit, weeding out people who were not inclined to fight for their lives in primitive times when primitive problem-solving techniques fit in. The furry antagonists of prehistoric times had no concept of compromise. As a remnant of that evolutionary selection for fighters, people the world over flock to battles between race car drivers, sports teams, professional wrestlers, chickens, dogs, and game show contestants. Could war be the same phenomenon at the reality level? Let's hope not.

It's difficult to imagine a truly necessary offensive in this era, although we could quibble over the definition of "necessary." Compromise and respect are universally applicable in the absence of untamed instincts. In some cases the explanation for conquest may come down to the promised pride and exhilaration of control over more land, people, oil, or other resources. The wars in the Middle East, Korea, Vietnam, Africa, and Iraq, like the world wars, have all been about control, and with a respectful, civilized mindset on both sides they might all have been settled with compromise. But anger is part of the fight-or-flight defense mechanism that allowed our distant ancestors to stand up against wild beasts, and it now lingers in our system to destroy civility among enemies who could be friends.

We cannot deny our instincts, but we can train them to some degree, and we can give them alternative foci. From an unemotional, logical perspective, it must be recognized that wars are negative-sum games, meaning that the overall losses always exceed the overall gains. No new land, people, or resources are created in the battle for control, whereas losses are incurred. There are better ways to seek excitement, such as standing under a waterfall or hiking through a rain forest. There are better things to capture, such as the rays of the sun, which convey unfathomable power. There are better ways to spend the more than $3 trillion allotment for the Iraq war, such as on energy independence. And there are better ways to achieve national security, as by waging peace and respect. Our approach, be it problem solving via violence or via diplomacy, turns out to be overwhelmingly contagious.

Conclusions

I recently went bowling with my family. My wife, son, and daughter toppled pins with admirable success. I did not. I would approach the lane with great desire, optimism, and determination to score the string of strikes that would turn my game around. Alas, great desire, optimism, and determination are worth little on their own, as all those determined to get rich quick or save the world have learned. In every effort, we get out what we put in, and progress is generally hard earned and incremental. I will get nowhere as a desirous bowler who shows up at the lanes only on occasion.

If we could harvest all of the willpower ever exerted by people pressing for a new global revolution of environmentalism, we could surely fly to the moon and back, but to dream of sudden improvements is to set one's self up for disappointment.

Personally, I reserve my optimism, tender my two cents worth, and share the inspiration I gained from my parents.

With writing after writing, speech after speech, and march upon march, the civil rights movement caught on over several decades. The foothold it gained was never taken for granted and progress continues. When the environmental movement gradually gained speed in the 1960s, it was spurred by thousands of acts, from the nature photography of Ansel Adams to the books of Rachel Carson. The collective momentum led to landmark environmental legislation and a broad awareness of the Earth's vulnerability. The momentum did not last. Today we are even closer to dangerous environmental tipping points, but further from a groundswell of grassroots environmentalism, than we were in 1970.

I believe that we could all enjoy better lives by shifting away from the impossible dream of bliss through consumerism. By contrast, bliss through environmentalism is a winning strategy. By embracing the genuine pleasures of simple lifestyles in our own communities, we offer present and future generations of the world community much needed resources, reprieve from pollution, and respect. Let us conserve, buy less, recycle more, ride a bicycle, plant a garden, eat slow food, question consumption, and apply creative solutions to myriad resource problems. Gimmicks and quick fixes will be of little help as we ween ourselves from self-destructive tendencies, but good deeds spread ripple effects across the global village. The best way forward is to be proud role models of the joy of conservation, moderation, and simple living, and to find ways to share the joy—patiently, incrementally, with others.

My parents
are teachers.